On Saint Patrick's Day
an M-1 rifle engraved wi̶t̶h̶ ̶t̶h̶e̶ ̶n̶a̶m̶e̶ ̶o̶f̶ ̶...
in Normandy 72 years after its owner, Martin (Matty) Teahan, Jim's
uncle, had been killed in the June 1944 D-Day invasion of France.
A young private in the 508th Parachute Infantry Regiment, Matty had
been laid to rest beside his fellow heroes in the Normandy American
Cemetery, but now French Army General Patrick Collet was writing
to inform the family that Matty's rifle had been recovered and was safe
in his possession. Luck of the Irish!

Thus began Jim Farrell's adventure of discovery and self-discovery, as
he and his family embarked on the successful quest to bring his uncle
home in spirit by repatriating his historic rifle. A saga spanning four
generations and multiple countries, the rifle's extraordinary journey
and recovery is also the story of Matty Teahan, a humble private made
of the stuff that made so many of his generation great—the strength
of character, courage, and will-power to prevail against great odds, and
the guts, determination, and sheer daring-do to jump out of a perfectly
good airplane over enemy territory.

Martin Teahan's emblematic M-1 rifle cur-
rently hangs in office of the Chief of Staff
of the US Army, awaiting donation to the
new US Army Museum at Fort Belvoir,
Virginia. Similarly, the Farrell family's quest
represents something larger than itself: the
intensifying search by the children of the
Greatest Generation to understand the facts
and meaning of their fathers' and grandfa-
thers' war, and their intense desire to come
to terms with the often tragic, yet seldom
discussed, repercussions of the death and
violence their elders experienced in World
War II.

ABOUT THE AUTHOR

Jim Farrell—Born in New York City in 1956, Jim Farrell grew up on the same rough streets of the Irish South Bronx as his much beloved uncle, Martin ("Matty") Teahan, a paratrooper in the 508th Parachute Infantry Regiment who was killed in Normandy a decade before Jim's birth. Early fascinated with stories of his fabled uncle's exploits as a charismatic entertainer and World War II hero, Jim followed his uncle's example and joined the Army in 1974, serving at Fort Lewis, Washington, and Camp Ames, Korea. Returning to New York in 1977, he graduated from SUNY Binghamton in 1983 with a BS in Accounting, and is the co-founder of Single Throw, Inc., a thriving digital marketing firm in Wall, New Jersey. Jim and the love of his life, his wife Monica, live in East Brunswick, New Jersey, with their golden retriever Piper.

In March 2016, Jim's life took on a new meaning when he received the news that his Uncle Matty's D-Day rifle had been located in Normandy, where his uncle was buried in the American Cemetery. Jim had prayed daily for his uncle since childhood, and strongly felt the news as a call to bring Uncle Matty home in spirit by repatriating his rifle. *Uncle Matty Comes Home* chronicles the accomplishment of this mission and stands as a testament to one family's love and determination to memorialize a loved one, honor a fallen war hero, and heal the wounds of the past.

www.unclemattycomeshome.com
www.facebook.com/unclemattycomeshome

ABOUT THE EDITOR

Gayle Wurst, PhD, runs Princeton International Agency for the Arts, LLC, a full-service literary agency offering consulting, editorial, translation, and agent services. Specializing in memoirs, military history, and oral history, the agency has a particular interest in World War II, Normandy, and airborne-related material. She is the co-author with her uncle, Col. Spencer F. Wurst, of: *Descending from the Clouds: A Memoir of Combat in the 505 Parachute Infantry Regiment, 82d Airborne Division.*

UNCLE MATTY COMES HOME

UNCLE MATTY COMES HOME

THE SAGA OF A D-DAY
PARATROOPER IN NORMANDY,
HIS RIFLE, AND HIS FAMILY'S
QUEST OF DISCOVERY

JIM FARRELL
WITH GAYLE WURST

For information about this title or to order other books and/or electronic media, contact the publisher:

James Farrell
194 Applegate Lane
East Brunswick, NJ 08816
jim@unclemattycomeshome.com
www.unclemattycomeshome.com

ISBNs: 978-0-9991514-0-2 Hardcover
        978-0-9991514-2-6 Softcover
        978-0-9991514-1-9 eBook

Printed in the United States of America

Cover and Interior design: 1106 Design

This book is dedicated to my Uncle Matty (Martin Teahan), born December 3, 1923—Killed in Action, June 1944. Uncle Matty and everyone born in his era are affectionately known as "The Greatest Generation." Thank you, Uncle Matty, for laying down your life for us. Because you made the ultimate sacrifice, today I have the freedom to write this book and honor your memory.

TABLE OF CONTENTS

PART ONE

UNCLE MATTY'S WORLD: THE IRISH SOUTH BRONX NEIGHBORHOOD, FAMILY, AND THE GREATEST GENERATION

PART TWO

UNCLE MATTY'S WAR: D-DAY, NORMANDY—THE 508TH PARACHUTE INFANTRY REGIMENT IN COMBAT

MAPS

PART THREE

SEARCHING FOR UNCLE MATTY: THE FAMILY QUEST IN EUROPE—ADVENTURES IN NORMANDY AND NOTTINGHAM

PART FOUR

UNCLE MATTY COMES HOME: MISSION ACCOMPLISHED

PART FIVE

RECALLING TIMES PAST: FRIENDS AND HEROES AT HOME AND IN COMBAT

PART SIX

TORCH BEARERS: YOUNGER GENERATIONS PRESERVING HISTORY

INTRODUCTION

M e—write a book? Not a chance! Numbers have always been my life. As the Chief Financial Officer of several companies, I never considered putting pen to paper to spill my guts. All this changed in March 2016, when the story of my heritage began to reveal itself. Now, at the age of sixty, I find myself so inspired by what I am learning that the words are coming more easily than I could have ever imagined.

Sharing thoughts and feelings was never natural for me. I grew up in the South Bronx in 1960s and '70s, an introvert among extroverts, a shy Irish American kid finding his way in a neighborhood that was—well, let's just call it rowdy. I was always the quiet one, and with the changing world and struggles dictated by poverty, no one in our family or anyone else I knew had time to sit and reflect about life. We were too busy worrying about the next day, and the day after that.

My maturation took place during a time of great change. This was the era of protest, new music, and the sexual revolution. The streets of New York were flooded with conflict, and my neighborhood was far from safe. In 1974, I enlisted in the Army to serve my country, following the example of my father and my maternal uncle, Martin Teahan, who both served in World War II. But I also wanted to escape from the Bronx.

May 29, 2016 Paris, France. At the home of my host, Colonel Patrick Collet, I hold Uncle Matty's historic M-1 Garand for the first time. That big smile on my face says it all! It gives me great joy to be able to share this once-in-a-lifetime moment with "Uncle Matty" fans. Colonel Collet was promoted to Brigadier General in July 2016. General Collet, Uncle Matty salutes you from Paratrooper Heaven!

I served at Fort Lewis, Washington, and Camp Ames, South Korea. Coming out of the service post-Vietnam was unnerving. The shift in cultural sentiment against the military was palpable. It was a time of peace protests and demonstrations. Veterans were no longer honored, respected, or considered heroes. On the contrary. On my return home in April 1977, I used the G.I. Bill to get an education and finally graduated in 1983 with a BS in Accounting from SUNY Binghamton.

Through the years, I held several successful CFO positions. Then, in 2001, my best friend, Larry Bailin, and I founded the digital marketing agency Single Throw, Inc. We officially opened our first office on September 11, 2001. A tragic time in our nation's history, it was also an exceedingly difficult period to start a new company. The odds were stacked against us, but we pushed on. Together we created a successful, thriving agency, now located in Wall, New Jersey, employing more than thirty very talented people.

So how did I come to write this book? There were many factors, most of which are discussed in the following pages. I will say this: My journey in life has inexorably led me right to this point. I am meant to tell this story of my family. I have always survived by looking forward. But the story of Uncle Matty has made me look deeply into my past, an exercise I formerly never bothered to entertain. I here share many of my consequent thoughts and experiences, which, again, is very new for me. And I have been rewarded with perspective, peace, and growth.

Two events, occurring within five days of each other, awakened my spirit. On March 12, 2016, my brother Jackie and I returned, after many years' absence, to visit our childhood church, Saint Jerome's, on 138th Street in the South Bronx. There we marveled at a bronze plaque listing our uncle, Martin Teahan, as one of the parishioners who had died in World War II. It was a beautiful sight to see, and it made us very nostalgic. Growing up, we had both heard stories of Uncle Matty (as we called him), and how he was much beloved, from the maternal side of our family and especially from our grand-mother and mother, Matty's mother and sister, respectively. But neither Jackie nor I had ever noticed the plaque as kids, and, given the volatile nature of the neighborhood, we hadn't been back since we'd been teenagers.

Incredibly, five days after the reunion, on Saint Patrick's Day (of all days), my sister Liz and I received word from an active-duty French Army Colonel that my Uncle Martin Teahan's rifle had been located. The M-1 rifle that our Uncle Matty had jumped with in Normandy had been found and identified after seventy-two years! The accompanying photographs showed our uncle's name engraved on the butt of the rifle. I don't know how, but I instantly knew I had to write a book about this.

Initially, I thought it would be a small, self-published book, per-fect for family memories. Then things quickly started to happen. Apparently, no rifle of a D-Day trooper killed in action in Normandy had ever before been identified and traced back to his family. Our French contact, Colonel Patrick Collet, graciously invited my wife Monica and me to France to see and hold Uncle Matty's rifle.

Next, we met Chief of Staff of the U.S. Army General Mark A. Milley, who loved the story and invited us to the Pentagon to offi-cially donate our piece of history. Later, on our travels in France, we also met Susan Eisenhower, the granddaughter of the legendary general and president, who listened and agreed that the story must be told. I set up a Facebook page dedicated to my uncle's story. The overwhelming response of more than eighty-five thousand followers to date is that this is a story that indeed must be told.

The process of learning about Uncle Matty's life and times has taken many twists and turns I never could have expected. Researching the history of his unit and tracing his footsteps in England and France, where he trained and participated in the 508th Parachute Regiment's jump into Normandy, have taught me new things about myself. And not only about myself: It has taught me much about my heritage, my family, and the thousands of other families and veterans who have been impacted by the gruesome sorrow of war.

And the upshot of it all? At sixty years old, I have learned to never say "never." I'm just a simple kid from the Bronx born to tell this story.

2016: Army Chief of Staff General Mark A. Milley walks to Uncle Matty's grave at the American Cemetery in Normandy. General Milley ensured that Uncle Matty's rifle would return home to a proper resting place, where it would honorably be displayed for public viewing.

PROLOGUE

SAINT JEROME'S CHURCH: A LANDMARK
AND A TRIGGER

It all started—and, for my Uncle Matty, it all sort of ended—at St. Jerome's Church in the Bronx, where I returned for the first time since 1967, when I'd been eleven years old. As I stood again in the cathedral on 138th Street and Alexander Avenue, I found myself gazing at a large bronze plaque etched with names in two long rows. One name captured my attention: *Teahan, Martin J.* Tales of Matty flooded my mind—Matty, my fabled uncle, who had influenced me so much, even though I had never met him. Strangely, it was the first time I'd ever noticed the plaque, although it must have been there when I was a boy. It was now March 12, 2016, and I was fifty-nine, almost three times the age of Uncle Matty when he died—much older, in fact, than most of the men whose names were borne on that wall in memorial to the dead of World War II. Seeing Matty's name there jolted me and took me back in time. I do not know how long I stood before it, remembering our harsh family circumstances in the Bronx. Matty's generation, mine, and those after us—all we wanted was to find a way out.

Uncle Matty did find his way out of the Bronx by doing what so many young men did in his day. He joined the Army. While many were drafted, Uncle Matty proudly volunteered and died in uniform serving his country overseas. Although he died before I was born, I realize now that sharing the South Bronx streets he knew so well, growing up hearing stories of his life, I identified with my uncle and drew strength from him. I realize, too, how much the core values I hold dear today were born from both his legacy and an unfortunate event that forced our family to flee our home, never to return until that day at Saint Jerome's Church.

Saint Jerome's Church on 138th Street and Alexander Avenue in the Bronx, where Uncle Matty, my siblings, and I grew up. My visit to Saint Jerome's after many years' absence triggered thoughts of Uncle Matty and led to the return his M-1 rifle, which was lost in Normandy in World War II.

Matty was my mother, Ann's, brother. She, her sister Francie, and their mother, my Grandmother Nora, never talked much about him. The few times they did, it was to reminisce about his vibrant personality and extraordinary bravery. My mother's face would light up with a beautiful smile of love, yet her eyes revealed deep sadness. This special, wistful look was reserved for times she spoke of Matty.

On December 23, 1943, Uncle Matty's unit, the 508th Parachute Infantry Regiment, was stationed at Camp Shanks, New York, waiting to ship out to Europe. He received his boots and wings as a fully qualified paratrooper and came home to the Bronx on a two-day pass to see the family for Christmas before he was sent overseas. This would prove to be his last visit home. My mom last saw her brother on Christmas Eve. She watched him from the window as he walked down the block and kept on looking until she saw him no more. "I had to keep watching him as long as possible," she always said. "Something inside me knew I would never see Matty again."

My mother often told us that Uncle Matty was heroic in battle. His regiment was attached to the 82nd Airborne Division and made their first combat jump on D-Day in Normandy. Two of his 508th brothers-in-arms visited Mom after the war and recounted their days with Matty. One was his best friend, Jim McMahon. Only my mother knew the name of Matty's second buddy. For some reason, she never revealed it. He had been captured with Uncle Matty in Normandy, and the two of them had made a pact: if one survived and the other did not, the survivor would visit his buddy's family after the war. All we knew from my Mom's stories is that this hero fulfilled his vow. It obviously meant a great deal to her. Uncle Matty's mom, my grandmother Nora, often recalled Matty as a war hero. *"He was so well liked,"* she would sigh and say. *"He always made everyone laugh. And he was such a wonderful singer and dancer!"* All her listeners agreed we had missed meeting a very special person, and all of us so wished Uncle Matty had survived the war.

Uncle Matty had volunteered for the paratroopers, knowing he would likely die in combat. He faced this grave danger with fervor, my mother said. After listening to her praise his feats of courage so often as I faced my own dangers growing up in the Bronx, it's no wonder Uncle Matty became my boyhood Big-Time Hero.

Contemplating my uncle's name engraved on that plaque in Saint Jerome's Church, I also remembered our family's struggles and the dire event that proved to be the tipping point, abruptly forcing us to flee our home in 1967. My father, like Uncle Matty, was baptized "Martin," but went by the nickname "Mickey." He had served in the 454th Bomb Group, 15th Air Force, 737th Squadron, in what was then called the Army Air Corps, before it became the Air Force. His plane, *The Pissing Moon*, was shot down in October 1944 over Austria. My father spent the rest of the war in Stalag Luft III, a prisoner-of-war camp for airmen that had been the site of the Great Escape months before he arrived. Unlike Matty, whose heroic death was surrounded by poetry, Mickey was a survivor. Liberated in the chaos of war's end, he returned to the Bronx, where he settled down to hard drinking and work in a butcher's shop. By the time I came along, he was a New York City cop.

In February 1967, my father prevented an armed robbery in the Bronx. He drew his service revolver and shot and killed the attacking perpetrator, who belonged to a terrorist group, Fuerzaz Armadas de Liberación (FALN), a violent Puerto Rican nationalist organization that later set off two bombs at Manhattan department stores, Korvette's and Macy's Herald Square. For my sister Liz and me, the day after the shooting was frightening, full of threats at school. "Your father's a killer!" kids yelled, and much worse. The nephew of the man my father had shot was in my class. He cornered me with some of his friends and was prevented from doing me great harm only when a big guy in my class named Teddy Dalton stepped in. He spared me a terrible beating at the least and probably saved my life.

Community chaos ensued. No one was safe. Not only my father, but our entire family received death threats. We had 'round-the-clock police protection—Joe O'Brien, a police officer and brother to my mother's former boyfriend John was stationed with a shotgun outside our apartment building. The situation got so bad so quickly that we abruptly had to leave 138th Street. We packed and left like thieves in the middle of night, scuttling out, warned never to return. My big brother Jackie, sister Liz, and I stuffed what we could fit into a single bag and were immediately sent off to a relative's in the North Bronx. Eventually we moved to 184th and the Grand Concourse, but we never went back to 138th Street—that is, until our family reunion in 2016, when Uncle Matty's story came vividly into focus. Mickey's sister, my aunt Bridie, told me the shooting profoundly affected Mickey for the rest of his life, "He was never the same" she said.

Under the influence of the uncle I'd never met, my own exit from the Bronx also occurred by volunteering for the Army. It was 1974, and I was fresh out of high school. The draft for Vietnam was over, but I volunteered to serve my country and hoped to become a better person for it. During my service in Fort Lewis, Washington, and Camp Ames, Korea, I often thought of Uncle Matty when things were tough. I thought of the hardships he'd endured and the ultimate sacrifice he'd made, and said to myself, *How can I (or most people, for that matter) say anything is hard, compared to what he and so many others of his generation suffered?* I define "a hero" as a brave and special person, someone who performs honorably in the face of danger and uncertainty. Uncle Matty was then, and still remains, my hero. In this, I am not alone: thoughts of him continue to help all four of my brothers and sisters as we each face our own challenges.

Ironic, coincidental, fortuitous, or fateful—call it what you will, but on Saint Patrick's Day, March 17, just a few days after I'd returned to St. Jerome's during a family reunion, Uncle Matty's M-1 rifle was located in Normandy. Luck of the Irish! Matty had inscribed his name on one side of the stock, and the name of his girlfriend, Kitty, on the other. It was discovered by a French Army officer, Colonel Patrick Collet, who traced it back to our family through the Family and Friends of the 508th PIR Association, and notified us. Colonel Collet, now General Collet, is a Farrell family friend for life.

Only after his rifle was discovered did I learn how Uncle Matty died. Unlike some of his buddies, he had no wife or children, so he took the danger upon himself and volunteered as scout on a patrol. The dates remain unclear, but we believe it was on D-Day, or just the day after, that Uncle Matty was wounded and taken prisoner. His friend and fellow 508th paratrooper, Art Jacoby, told me the story this way: *Me, Frank Pesce, Bill Wilkinson, and your uncle, Marty Teahan, used to go everywhere together. Frank and I were hell-raisers, always fighting. Everyone, it did not matter. All the time. How Marty got in with us, I will never know. He was just a fun-loving kid. Subsequently, Marty was killed in Normandy. He was wounded and captured, and had to use his rifle as a crutch. He moved his hand, and the dirty Kraut shot him.*

Rest in peace, Uncle Matty. Your memory lives on. As I stood in Saint Jerome's Church and as I write this now, I recognize your influence on the way I live my life and honor your spirit. I truly feel our family was lucky. We survived, made a good life for ourselves, and albeit a lifetime later, were eventually able to visit the old neighborhood again. You never had that chance: you died on a battlefield in France. Whenever I struggle with what life brings, I think of you, Uncle Matty, as I did at Saint Jerome's, and realize how fortunate I am to be here to tell your story.

PART ONE

UNCLE MATTY'S WORLD: THE IRISH SOUTH BRONX NEIGHBORHOOD, FAMILY, AND THE GREATEST GENERATION

Chapter 1
BORN TO BE AIRBORNE

As family legend has it, Uncle Matty was a happy-go-lucky teenager who thrived on challenge. Challenge him to anything, and you knew he would bring his A-game. He went at everything full blast, so you'd better be careful about what you dared him to do. In the early 1940s, when the first airborne infantry regiments were being formed, Uncle Sam posted many attractive advertisements calling young men to see if they had what it took to join the new, elite, all-volunteer paratroop forces. This dangerous job and adrenalin junkie's dream was perfect for daredevil Matty. No doubt about it, he was born to be airborne.

Growing up, Matty and his friends played many games to get the airborne feeling. One of the safest and most amusing ways was "Johnny on a Pony," a popular New York City street game. To play, a group of friends get together and choose up sides. Players on one side line up, bend from the waist, grab onto the kid in front, and brace to receive fury from the sky. The other side runs one at a time and jumps onto the backs of their opponents. If you can make the kids in the line break ranks or fall to the ground, your side wins.

Uncle Matty at Rockaway Beach, New York City, in 1939. Matty was in rock-solid shape from playing all the street games that defined him as born to be airborne.

The important thing in choosing sides is to get the right balance of firepower. You've got to have some strong kids to hold the line, but you also need some who can fly, and, of course, there are always the weak links. The weakest is usually placed at the end of the line, which requires the longest jump. If you've got people who can jump high and far, your side has a big advantage.

There are many ways to strategize this game. Uncle Matty would try to get one or two guys on his team who could jump on the weakest link. Then Matty himself would come in for the kill. He could jump both high and far, and often won by pouncing on top of his teammates, using his weight and momentum to crush the stability of the opponent beneath who was holding on for dear life. What a rush it was to make that long, high jump to win the game. C'mon now, he was born to be airborne.

When you think about this game, it is perfect: it requires no transportation, just a walk from the apartment; does not cost a penny; encourages social and strategic skills; and regardless of level, everyone participates. And oh, is it fun! I know, because we played, too, as I was growing up, and my friends and I never got tired of it.

"Johnny on a Pony" has been around forever, but Matty and his buddies also made up new games to get that airborne feeling. One of these, the "Umbrella Jump," involved taking an umbrella down to the schoolyard, climbing up the fence a few feet, and jumping off, using the open umbrella as a parachute. From just a few feet up, the boys did not get much of a rush, so (you guessed it) they started climbing higher on each jump. At eight feet up, they started to get some fun and could feel the tension mounting in the umbrella. "Ah, this is good, but we've got to climb higher!" proclaimed their fearless leader, Matty.

Ten feet up produced a good rush and quite a bit of tension in the umbrella. The game was getting better and better. But at what point would the umbrella break? Of course the budding paratroopers had to find out. Higher they went until *boom!* they reached the tipping point. The umbrella flipped inside out, making their landings harder. "OK," they thought, "we've got the point where the jump gets fun, and the point where the umbrella flips. Now, we just have to keep on trying until we find the highest jump-off point where the umbrella still holds out."

People soon learned to attend to their umbrellas. If the umbrella did not survive the fall, our weighty calculations could take hours, as Matty and his band scoured the neighborhood hunting for suitable replacement matériel. "The stronger the umbrella, the higher that we climb, the maximum the rush we can achieve," was the driving thought. Little could Matty know he was learning problem-solving skills that would later be drilled into him on practice jumps for D-Day in Normandy.

For poor Irish American kids, the "Umbrella Jump" was the perfect game, but it was also great training for budding troopers. Seeking the thrill of being airborne, Matty and his band were naturally learning the effects of altitude and how to fall from a jump. Yet, as any adrenalin junkie knows, the search for an even more dangerous thrill starts when the thrill you've got starts to fade. The umbrella game was no different, so Uncle Matty and his boys began to search for better ways to get that airborne feeling.

The new game they found had plenty of risk, like cuts, bruises, and broken bones. It also required some climbing skills, as you needed to navigate from street level up to the bottom of a first-floor fire escape. This meant getting a toehold between the bricks while working your way up to a ledge, or otherwise figuring out how to climb the distance from the street to the folding ladder at the lowest level. The first one to reach the fire escape released the ladder, and everyone else climbed up. Oh, what fun! Now Matty and his buddies could jump from the lowest fire escapes to the ground, completing that airborne rush as often as they wanted, simply by climbing up the ladder again and taking another jump. For an additional rush, they could mount the metal stairs to the second floor, dangle in the air, and jump down to the first-floor fire escape. There was just one little hitch. At any one location, game time was limited—people inevitably began to bitch and yell. So up to the roof ran Matty and his boys, from whence they made their escape.

Thus began a new game, the "Roof Jump," that upped the ante on danger and produced the feel of the real airborne deal. All you needed was two adjacent buildings close enough together to allow you to jump from one roof to the other. Danger was written all over it, and some kids died by miscalculating leaps. But the bigger the danger, the more Uncle Matty was attracted to it. Attraction and fear had the same source: for a second you were literally airborne, five or six stories above the street.

I must admit, out of stupidity, I, too, played this game a few times growing up in the Bronx. It reminds me now of the popular Army cadence, "I want to be an Airborne Ranger, I want to live a life of danger." My own roof jumps were very short and required nothing but a quick leap. But Uncle Matty and his friends would take some mighty risky jumps, and when his mother found out—and she always did—he was in big trouble. But in spite of many good Irish-mom spankings, Matty grew quite a reputation as a rooftop jumper.

Uncle Matty also loved Coney Island Beach and went there often with his band of friends. The rush of the waves, riding them in, getting knocked down by a monster wave—oh, boy, he loved it! He and his friends wrestled and play-fought on the sand as if it were for real. This improved their fitness and fighting skills—important in the Irish South Bronx. Then it was time to laugh, clown around, make fun of things, and sneak some beer to drink. And naturally, he had to flirt with the girls. Matty could always tell a great story, sing like a star, and dance like one, too, even in the sand. He had quite a reputation with the girls of Coney Island, and why not? Good-looking, popular, tremendously fit! Matty had it all. Most of all, he was born to be airborne.

Another of Matty's favorite haunts was Steeplechase Amusement Park, Coney Island, Brooklyn, the home of his favorite ride, the

Parachute Jump. In 1936, the inventor of the ride, retired Naval Commander James H. Strong, erected his first jump platform in (fittingly named) Hightstown, New Jersey. Originally designed for military testing, the platform fascinated so many passers-by, it soon became the talk of the town. When people from all walks of life began asking if they could try it out, Mr. Strong decided to capitalize on his invention.

The first civilian model for the Parachute Jump Ride was unveiled at the 1939 World's Fair in Flushing, New York. Standing two-hundred-fifty feet high and weighing one-hundred, seventy tons, the ride featured twelve parachutes, each with a two-person seat, and produced a sensation described as "flying in a freefall." The fall was completely controlled by parachute, with a landing softened by shock absorbers. After enjoying huge success at the World's Fair, in 1941 the Parachute Jump was moved to Coney Island. It became a huge hit, attracting more than a million and a half riders a year. It was as close as you could get to the feel of an airborne jump outside of the real thing. *Hmmm*.... Had Mr. Strong been watching Uncle Matty and his band practice with their snitched umbrellas? Had he expanded and capitalized on their idea?

The Parachute Jump Ride became Uncle Matty's favorite pastime. How many of the half a million rides he personally enjoyed is a matter of speculation—as many as he could afford, no doubt. Obsessed with everything airborne, passionate about becoming a real paratrooper one day, he was also fascinated that the ride had two seats. Now he and his buddies could get that airborne feeling parachuting down side by side.

The Parachute Jump Ride was eventually closed in 1964. It was scheduled for demolition on at least two occasions. Once, it was granted landmark status, but this was revoked, and only the cost of demolition saved it. Eventually, however, it received permanent landmark status and was renovated. Affectionately called the Eiffel Tower of Brooklyn, it is now the only remaining structure from the

Steeplechase Amusement Park. The funny thing about the Parachute Jump ride is that it survived sure destruction and stuck around, if only as a reminder of an earlier time. It makes me think of Uncle Matty's rifle, too, which lay unbeknownst in France for seventy-two years but resurfaced to remind of us of a bygone time and the ever-present cost of war.

Bringing home Uncle Matty's rifle has led me to read a lot of airborne stories, including those about his great friend and fellow D-Day paratrooper, Art Jacoby, who served in the HQ1, Battalion Intelligence Section (S2) of the 508th Parachute Infantry Regiment from March 1943 to November 1945. I've also had the privilege to talk with Art. It seems the job of being a paratrooper was made specifically for certain people. Art believes the job was created for him. Uncle Matty believed the same thing about himself.

The physical demands, the discipline, the extreme hardships—all were criteria to weed out anyone unfit for the task of jumping into combat out of a perfectly good airplane. But guys like Art and Matty thrived on the clear and present danger of the job. It emboldened them even further until they became the best-trained fighting soldiers the world had ever seen. Paratroopers well knew those silver wings made them special. At a very young age, Matty knew he was born to be airborne, and he made damned sure to experience everything that meant anything in his short and precious life. Now, after all these years, his story can be told. Uncle Matty has come home, and his family has found some closure.

Chapter 2

UNCLE MATTY'S IRISH
SOUTH BRONX

In August 2016, I wrote an article about my uncle and his rifle at the request of Ellen Peters, the Treasurer of the 508th PIR Association, whom I had met that June on our trip to France to view Uncle Matty's rifle and grave. It was published in the September 2016 issue of Diablo, *the 508th Association Newsletter. To my surprise, it was also picked up by* The Bronx Times, The Bronx Chronicle, Irish Central, The Irish Echo, The Asbury Park Press, *and other publications. I had often wondered what life was like for Uncle Matty growing up, and I was now about to find out. The Irish were proud to hear good news about one of their heroes, and an overwhelming number of reactions and comments poured in. Many were about the good old days in the neighborhood. As a kid, I had heard stories from relatives about the poverty, the street games, the church, the bars, and, of course, the fighting, but I was unprepared for the amount of emotion and affection readers expressed about the Irish South Bronx of the 1930s and 1940s.*

Of the many people who responded to Matty's story, William McWeeney stands out. Although he did not know my uncle, Bill grew up in the same South Bronx streets and graduated from St. Jerome's Grammar School

in 1940, just two years after Uncle Matty. Bill looked up my number,
and his phone call was one of the best I've ever received. We had a great
chat, shared funny stories, and promised to stay in touch. Then it dawned
on me—perhaps there was a reason for Bill's call. I'd already begun to
write about Matty with the idea of turning out a book, but I'd been strug-
gling with how to give readers a glimpse into what it was like for Matty
growing up. Historical research failed to capture the real flavor of the
old neighborhood, but Bill McWeeney had lived there, survived it, and
loved it with a passion, and he could tell stories like he still was seventeen
and living in the old neighborhood. Moreover, he would tell them for me.

Uncle Matty in action, smoking and flirting with pretty girls on a street in the Irish South Bronx in 1940. The streets were a playground and social gathering place, and Matty was famous for singing, dancing, and being the life of the party. His best friend, Peter Donahue, is behind Matty's right shoulder.

Bill was very happy that I called him back, and we spoke or e-mailed
each other several times a week while I was writing this piece. His words
proved to be the very best way to paint a picture of Uncle Matty's South
Bronx. A very special relationship grew out of our exchange, and we still

correspond today. Bill no longer travels much, but meeting him in person one day is definitely on my bucket list! The following account is composed of highlights from Bill's letters.

I was born on Manhattan Island in 1927. Our family moved to the South Bronx at the height of the Depression, when I was five years old. For better or worse, that's where my outlook on life was formed.

In order to get a full picture of the South Bronx before World War II, you should imagine the streets teeming with people, young and old alike. The streets were a playground for the young and a social center for the adults. There was no television and very little radio. I was seven years old before we had our first one. We did not have a phone until after the war. I'd guess the area was about eighty-five percent Irish. The rest of the populace was Italian, German, and Polish, with a smattering of other nationalities. There were a lot of small mom-and-pop businesses—grocery stores, hardware stores, cleaners, barber shops, and more bars than in any other place in New York City.

Stickball was played everywhere. In my area, the older guys played a team from Italian Harlem on our streets and theirs. As much as one hundred dollars was bet on the games. We younger guys played the older guys on a quiet street near the Harlem River. We played for a barrel of beer, which was consumed while the game was on. It led to a merry game. There was also street hockey on roller skates, off the point (otherwise known as stoop ball), and punch ball. We were fortunate to live about a mile from Yankee Stadium and the Polo Grounds. When the Yankees were out of town, the Giants were in. I have seen Lou Gehrig, Joe DiMaggio, Phil Rizzuto, and Mickey Mantle, as well as Ted Williams and Willie Mays.

It would be neglectful not to mention swimming and fishing. In a sense, we were lucky to have the Harlem River in our backyard, only two short blocks from our house. At the end of 132nd Street to Lincoln Avenue, there was a dock affectionately known by all as the Horseshit Dock. It got this name because tugboats would pull up with large barges and park them there. The dock had two levels, one at street level and one about fifteen feet high. Big dump trucks would back up to the higher one and unload tons of horse manure into the barges. Some of it would fall to the ground, so you had to watch where you walked. Once a barge was full, a tug would arrive to haul it off to God knows where.

We all learned to swim at Horseshit Dock in our underwear, at times naked. It worked, because I was later recruited to join my high school swim team. Things took a turn for the better when the city opened Jefferson Pool at 114th Street and Pleasant Avenue in Italian Harlem. Admission was free up until noon or five cents after noon. Considering the Harlem River had open sewers, the pool was a major improvement. I believe myself to be immune from cholera and all other diseases associated with polluted water.

My father was a dedicated fisherman who told stories about fishing the clear, clean waters of Ireland for salmon and trout. Naturally, he turned his attention to the Harlem River. He didn't find any salmon or trout, but there was an abundance of eels. They were about the only thing able to survive the polluted waters. We ate eels for breakfast quite often. Breaded, they taste a little like chicken. I spent years with him as a boy on the waters of the Harlem, City Island, the Hudson, and Pelham Bay.

Pigeons were an integral part of life in the South Bronx. Pigeon flying was a favored sport of the Italians in other parts of the city as well. My friends kept a large coop on their roof. They would have "throws," where they would throw their flock up into another flock from the area. The birds would come together and, in time, return to their coops. If you were lucky, you caught some of the other guy's birds, after which he could buy them back or you could keep them. I recall one time when a birder "fell" off his roof and was killed. Rumors in the neighborhood said he had been murdered by a rival birder.

The centerpiece of the neighborhood was St. Jerome's Church and Grammar School. The pastor, Father Campbell, could put fear into the coldest of hearts. He was constantly preaching about not having enough money. I was at Mass on a particular Sunday when he told the poor Irish in attendance that he did not want to hear the clinking of coins. He wanted to hear the rustle of paper bills! Then he took a collection. When the basket came back full of coins, he threw them down the center aisle! There were times when many a poor parishioner would not go to church because they did not have a dime to put into the collection basket.

There was a man in the South Bronx named George who ran a small movie house called the Haven. He did more for the poor than Father Campbell ever did. He charged five cents to get in, and you saw a newsreel, a cartoon, and two pictures. If you did not have the five cents, he would take three cents and a milk or soda bottle, which he later took to the local A&P and cashed in for the two-cent deposit. I saw him more than once struggling to the A&P with a load of bottles to get his very small profit for the day. George was a small, dapper man with a white mustache who took away some of the pain of the times. Father Campbell would preach against the Haven, calling it a den of iniquity. But believe me, George was a true saint.

The Grammar School was manned by La Salle Christian Brothers, Ursuline Nuns, and lay teachers. The teachers, particularly the La Salle Brothers, were great. I had a Brother Joseph in the eighth grade. He was a young man from Rhode Island. More than twenty-five years later, I was at an afternoon movie in Washington, D.C., and when I came out of the show, I ran into Brother Joseph. It was my pleasure to invite him to dinner at a nice French restaurant I knew there. He told me that when they disciplined a boy at St. Jerome's, the Brothers never knew if they were going to get hit back. He brought me current with remarks like, "Remember so and so? He's a judge today. Remember so and so? He went to the electric chair at Sing Sing for murder." When I met up with him, Brother Joseph was in

Washington, studying art at Catholic University and teaching art at a high school in Providence. I found this ironic, since I'd never seen him as an artsy person.

I graduated from St. Jerome's in January 1940. We were very well prepared for high school. My class had thirty boys. In 1990 we had a fifty-year reunion at the Oyster Bay home of one of our graduates. I came up from Houston, Texas, and found about ten of us were there. There were attorneys, an airline executive, a successful author, a retired NYPD captain, and a detective. They all seemed to have done very well in spite of growing up in the worst slum in New York.

To fully understand the South Bronx in the '30s and '40s, we must open the window on the Italians. My best friend was a guy named Ray Rondinone. His mother died when he was three years old. His father raised eight boys and a girl. Ray was the youngest. Four of the boys married Irish girls, including Ray. All of the boys except one served in World War II and Korea. One brother, Mike, was killed in Sicily, a sad day for the family. Ray's father was a small, dapper man who spoke very broken English. He welcomed me into his home and for years fed me great Italian food. A fine man.

Of course, the Italians had shops in the area. I lived a few doors from a one-man barber-shop owned by a man named Lorenzo Ferrari. He charged thirty-five cents for a haircut. He was good at it. In time, he grew too old to run his business, and his family closed his shop. I then went to another shop on the next block. It was run by two Italian men. If one was not busy, he played the guitar while the other cut your hair. The two of them sang opera as well. I had to pay fifty cents there, but what the hell—they threw in a floor show!

Then there was Sam the Radio Man, who ran a radio-repair business out of his ground-floor apartment on 137th Street between Alexander and Willis Avenues. Sam was a World War I veteran, and I recall him participating in the Veterans March on Washington for their bonuses. In 1935, there was a World Series between the Detroit Tigers and the Chicago Cubs. Sam decorated his storefront window with a diagram of a baseball field in white Bon Ami type, showing all the positions and as much information as he could. He had a little red ball, and as he listened to his radio, he had that ball follow every pitch, the windup, where the batter hit the ball, everything. It was just as good as present-day TV. I was eight years old then, and, as small boys do, I chose sides, picking Detroit. They won, and I stayed a Detroit fan for years.

Street fires were common in the South Bronx during the 1930s. They really did not serve any purpose except for us to stand around and keep warm in the winter. A bunch of us kids were standing around such a fire when some idiot threw an empty gasoline can on it. There was a huge explosion, and one of the kids, known as Cookin' Eggs, caught fire and became a human torch running up the street. Sam ran after him, caught up with him, wrapped his heavy World War I Army coat around him, and smothered the flames. The kid was later taken to a hospital. Sam had saved his life.

Adding to the street color during the Great Depression were the street vendors. One of the most prominent was Johnny Line Up. There were no electric dryers at the time, and clothes were hung on lines to dry. My mother used a scrubbing board to wash and then hung our clothes from a line that went from our fire escape to a clothes pole. In time the line would rot, and Johnny's famous call would be heard in the back yard: "Hey, Line Up!" He would climb the pole, often three or four stories tall, replace the line, and only charge one dollar. As we grew older, my brother or I would climb the pole in order to save the dollar. A junkman with a large pushcart also came around regularly. My brother and I would save old rags and newspapers, for which he would give us a nickel or a dime. There was a knife sharpener, too. He had a wheelbarrow-like thing painted green, with a sharpening stone about three feet in diameter. He spun the wheel with a set of pedals and charged very little for his work, as I recall.

Then there was Tony the Hurdy Gurdy Man. You don't know what a hurdy-gurdy is? It was a musical thing that made its sound after you cranked a lever. Tony was helped by a monkey on a leash carrying a tin cup. He passed the cup around, collecting coins. Another guy had a merry-go-round mounted on a truck chassis that held about ten kids. You got a short ride for five cents. Every once in a while, two guys showed up with about ten Shetland ponies. You could get a ride down the block for five cents, too.

Some of the bars in the Irish South Bronx were dumps, and others were places you could take your family to without worry. Some served a free meal of cold cuts and cheese along with the beer. My favorite was a place on 138th Street called McGowan's. One night there, I saw a detective pull his gun on a patron. The patron actually took the gun away from him, thus ending the confrontation. This was a nice bar, and I have some fond memories of it. At the time, my girlfriend had split up with me. I called her from McGowan's and told her I missed her, and it resulted in our getting back together. We later married and are still together after some sixty-three years.

On 139th Street between Alexander and Lincoln Avenues was a little bar called the Old Homestead. The couple who owned it tolerated us sixteen- and seventeen-year-olds, even though we were too young to drink. An older guy who hung out there said he used to play sax in the famous Jimmy Dorsey Band. He took a couple of us on tours of the Manhattan nightclubs like the Copacabana and the Latin Quarter. The Copa at that time was run by the Mafia and was world-famous. The Latin Quarter was run by Lou Walters, the father of Barbara Walters. I preferred the Copa. Our sax player seemed to know every bartender in Manhattan as we bounced from club to club.

There was another bar with a dance floor called the Leitrim House on 138th Street, next to the 3rd Avenue El Station. On weekends there was live Irish music and traditional Irish dancing. It could get rough there, and I saw quite a few fights. One man I know of was killed in a brawl. The best beer in the area was to be had at a place called Rudy's, run by an old German man on Willis Avenue between 133rd and 134th Streets.

The Morgue was a bar on 134th Street and Lincoln Avenue. It was a quiet, out-of-the-way bar. Some of the New York Yankees would hang out there. Spec Shea, the pitcher, parked his white Cadillac outside. It had a personalized license plate, SPEC.

I recall another bar that some local wags called Ding Dong Denny's Dirty Dive. The owner was a man named Denny. He was very tight-fisted. It was customary in some bars to buy you a third drink free after you bought two. Not Denny. He kept a sharp Irish eye on the cash register and made sure his bartender rang up all sales and was not stealing. The "Dirty" part of the name of the bar came from a huge, mangy dog he kept that was always lying on the floor.

Ed Daly, a friend of mine, built a wooden bench near Ding Dong Denny's on Alexander Avenue. It was only fifty feet from the bar, which made it convenient as the need arose. My friends and I used to call it "hanging out on the bench." If you take another look at the bench, you might see the ghost of a guy named J.B. He was the embodiment of all that was the South Bronx. He was very intelligent, had a weird sense of humor, and the girls all loved him. He joined the Navy in World War II. How we won that war is beyond me.

I have three stories about J.B. We were once sitting on that bench when there was a car accident in front of us. The occupants were black. J.B. ran over, identified himself as an attorney, and began taking statements until the cops arrived, and then he ran off. Another time, J.B. and I were sipping a beer in Feeleys on Willis and 137th Street. Out of nowhere, he let out a scream and fell to the floor, grabbing his chest. This was a very old-time Irish bar frequented by old Irishmen who felt that whiskey was a cure for whatever ails you. Somebody administered a whiskey to him, and he recovered in no time. When he left, I chewed him out, knowing he was faking. He told me he was broke and wanted a whiskey and that was why he put on the act.

Another night, J.B. came close to getting me killed. He lived on 138th Street across from the 40th Police Precinct. He was drunk, and I was taking him home. I entered the vestibule of the house, rang the bell of his apartment, and his mother stuck her head out the door. I had just told her I had Justin with me when the door of the vestibule was smashed open. Two detectives with drawn guns came in, one of whom persisted in ramming his .38 into my navel. They wanted to know what was going on. I found out later that a guy I knew had been badly mugged in the same area a few days before that. The cops thought I was mugging J.B. Then came the moment: J.B. told them he did not know me and had never seen me before! The .38 was pressed even more firmly into my tender gut. I finally was able to explain it all to one of the cops because I knew of a bar he hung out in.*

After the war, a placed named White's opened up on Willis Avenue and 140th Street. If there was an upscale bar in the area, this was it. You could take a girlfriend there and not worry. Guys using the G.I. Bill for college hung out there. I was there one night with three or four gang members I knew. They said they were going to another bar called the Paradise, on Brook Avenue, and asked if I wanted to come along. I said "No, thanks," because I was waiting to meet a buddy at White's. On the way to the other bar, they ran into a gang of Puerto Ricans, and a fight ensued. One of the gang had his stomach slashed open; another got several knife punctures on his face. When word got out, other members of the gang went home and got their guns out. That night, two Puerto Rican men were shot. I do not remember if they were killed. This sort of thing was common after World War II, as Puerto Ricans and blacks moved into the neighborhood.

Before the war, there were two pretty rough gangs in the South Bronx, too. Word reached them of an abortion mill operating in New Jersey in an apartment house. The doctor had a safe that was supposed to be stuffed with cash. It would be an easy target since he was operating illegally and was not likely to call the cops. Two guys from each gang went to New Jersey and crashed into the apartment with guns. Having some sense of dignity (after all, they were Irish), they escorted the women into a back room while forcing the doctor to open and empty the safe. This was a mistake, because one of the women slipped out a back door and somehow called the police. When the men left the apartment house, it was surrounded by police. There was a shootout, and three of them were captured. The one who got away made it to Greenwich Village and hid out. But he could not stay away from the comfortable South Bronx. The next week he was picked up by our local cop and was not seen for some time thereafter.

No, it was not all peaches and cream as I was growing up in the South Bronx. One day, two seventeen-year-old Irish kids decided to go up to the Fordham Road area and stick up liquor stores. The first one they hit was a success, so they figured to try another one in the same area. Another winner! Why not three in a row? By that time, police were swarming the Fordham area. There was a shootout with two detectives, and one of the kids caught a bullet in the forehead and died. He was such a good-looking guy that he could have starred in a Hollywood film. Sometime later, an altar boy from St. Jerome's tried the liquor-store bit in the Rockaways and was caught.

Most people in the area were concentrating on how to survive. Evictions for nonpayment of rent were common in the 1930s. They were carried out, literally, by New York City Marshalls, who would remove all of the renter's possessions and dump them on the sidewalk. I recall one poor Irish woman standing on the sidewalk screaming and crying as her sticks of furniture were being removed. Two or three small kids were hiding behind her skirts, peeking out. This was on 137th Street off Willis Avenue. Some landlords at the time were offering the first month free to new tenants. Some of the poor would move in for the first month, move out in thirty days, and repeat the process the next month.

As for politics, it was a Democratic area, and Roosevelt was popular, having been elected in 1932, 1936, 1940, and 1944. I do not recall any sermons at church or comments by teachers at school. The center of political action prior to World War II was more or less 138th Street and Willis Avenue. Speakers for the Nazi Bund, the Communist Party, and the America First Party would set up speaker platforms on the different corners. They drew good-sized crowds. Since there was no TV, the speakers were a form of entertainment. I was there one night when the Nazis were passionately railing against the Jewish businesses in the area. They led a crowd of protestors all the way to 149th Street. We kids tagged along, expecting some action. Nothing happened.

Another night, we kids threw paper bags full of water from a nearby rooftop onto the Communist speaker. We then went down to the street and mingled with the crowd. The cops had been called, but we innocent fighters of the Red Menace were not suspected. The Nazi and the Communist speakers often argued with one another from across the street. The speakers were loud and entertaining, using Nazi and Russian flags as backdrops. The America First people were a conservative group dedicated to preventing the United States from entering the war to help Britain. They were led by Charles Lindbergh. They found a ready audience among some of the old Irish, who were against anything English. World War II changed all that.

World War II cast a pall on the South Bronx. You could walk the area and see windows with blue- or gold-star banners, gold signifying that a boy had died. Today, the Church of St. Jerome has a wall with the names of all the fallen. My own military experience had some funny overtones. At seventeen years of age, four of us went down to join the Navy. I happened to be six feet, six inches tall. I was turned down not only by the Navy (twice), but also by the Coast Guard and Merchant Marines because of my height. The Army, however, was not as picky. Six weeks after I turned eighteen, I wound up in the infantry. I shipped overseas to Germany during a fierce North Atlantic storm, and I got so seasick it was unreal. Thereafter I never had had an urge to go to sea. In one way, World War II did some good for the boys of the South Bronx. With the introduction of the G.I. Bill, many men were able to get a college education and go on to a better life they never could have afforded before. Thus was born "The Greatest Generation."

To sum up my life in the South Bronx: I would not trade it for any other. I met my wife there and learned how to be resilient and to appreciate the important things in life—most of all, a fine family.

*Bill is referring to McSherry's on 138th Street and Alexander Avenue, located directly across from the 40th Precinct Police Station. I got to know it well as a kid because my father Mickey was a quick-tempered Irish cop from the neighborhood, and this was his favorite pub. My brothers, and later I, would drive him there for many years so he could drink and reminisce with his buddies. McSherry's was legendary, and stories of all kinds circulated there, especially about the old Irish neighborhood and the fights at the bars. These fights often involved my father and his famous words, "Let's take it outside." Today, McSherry's lives only in memories. It has long since closed and is now a Dunkin' Donuts.

Chapter 3
TWO MARTINS FROM THE GREATEST GENERATION

Martin Teahan (Matty) and Martin Farrell (Mickey) were both poor Irish American kids who grew up together during the Great Depression on 138th Street in the South Bronx. Like so many Irish immigrants in the 1930s, the Teahan and Farrell families landed in the South Bronx to start their new life. As you may have guessed by now, both Martins influenced my life in incredibly different ways. While they shared birth names, a culture, and way of life, their personalities starkly contrasted each other's, and this difference was reflected in their journeys and interactions with the family.

The backdrop to their lives was bleak, and both eventually earned their membership in what Tom Brokaw so memorably termed "The Greatest Generation." Life was cruel, ruled by poverty, in the South Bronx, and many young Irish children like Matty and Mickey were forced to leave school to help support their families. Clothes were scarce; most everything was worn, patched, and hand-me-down. Like many Irish immigrants, both Matty and Mickey's parents and other relatives succumbed to alcoholism, a disease they would pass on to their children. Many Irish drank alcohol as a natural way of life; it was a ritual, a rite of passage. The bars in the South Bronx in the 1930s were a place to hang out with your friends, laugh, cry, share stories, and forget the cruelty of life.

Matty and Mickey's similarities, including their names, were influenced by heritage, culture, and poverty. They were both devoted to the Catholic Church; both the religion and its institution held a defining importance for Irish Immigrants. They played New York City street games, went for a time to Catholic school, and maintained an unbreakable bond and loyalty to family. As much as they had in common, however, they were two totally different individuals, and each would shape my family's life.

Martin Teahan and Martin Farrell, my uncle and my father, represent the Greatest Generation. Uncle Matty, a paratrooper, died in combat in Normandy; my father Mickey, a bombardier, was shot down over Austria and spent nine months as a prisoner of war, but survived. Mickey never talked about the war, and as kids we never thought to ask. Although I never understood my father, and my uncle died before I was born, both Martins significantly shaped my life.

Mickey was a tough, introverted kid with a quick, mean temper. He would fight anyone as if it meant life or death. His brother Larry called him "The Bull," and if anyone messed with Larry, he would bring Mickey in to bat cleanup. Mickey was famous for saying, "Let's take this outside." This tactic diverted many a serious brawl, but it also resulted in a fair share of fistfights. Mickey didn't seem to care which way it went.

Matty, on the other hand, was quite the socialite and could be very entertaining. He sang Irish songs, danced like a professional, and wooed the ladies with gusto. When Matty got on the dance floor, there was no getting him off, and he could get almost anyone to dance. Some of his favorite songs were "East Side, West Side" and "Danny Boy." He was always the life of the party, he never missed a beat with his jokes and stories, and he could make everyone laugh. He was adored by everybody and was known as the joker of the block.

As fate decided, Mickey was my father. He married Matty's sister Ann, who was my mother. Before children, Mickey served in the 454th Bombardier Group in Italy. Mickey was color blind, which made him perfect to be an aerial photographer. On October 7, 1944, while on a mission to bomb the Winterhof Oil Refinery, his plane was shot in the rear and burst into flame. The plane crashed somewhere over Vienna, Austria. Although he successfully ejected, the fire from the plane left him temporary blinded. He had no choice but to surrender. He suffered from October 7, 1944 to June 9, 1945 in the Stalag Luft III Sagan Silesia Bavari German Prisoner of War Camp. He survived, but barely: on arrival home, he weighed less than one hundred pounds. His bravery earned him a Purple Heart and a Bronze Star. After the war, Mickey took a job as a New York City police officer, stationed in the heart of the South Bronx. Irish cops were legendary for their toughness and bravery, and Mickey fit right in.

I remember the great blackout of 1977, when the electrical grid went down in New York City. I was a young kid at home in our apartment on 184th Street and the Grand Concourse. Seconds after we plunged into darkness, the streets awoke, bright with chaos. It was like a bomb had hit the Grand Concourse; more than two hundred cars were stolen from a dealership, stores and shops were looted, and people whooped through the streets like a war zone. My father Mickey began yelling at the looters from our fifth-floor apartment. Finally, he lost it and went downstairs with his gun. All night long, he stood outside the pizza shop below us, he armed with his gun, the owner brandishing his pizza-oven stick. What a pair! No one touched the shop, and it was one of the few in the Bronx that survived unscathed. I'll tell you what—the looters were wise to stay away from Mickey.

Mickey's temperament stayed with him to his final days. A few years before he died, three hoodlums decided they had a quick and easy score with the old man and tried to mug him. Oh, boy—did they figure wrong on this one. Mickey fought them off, with only a few bruises as evidence of the scuffle. When he told me about it, he only had one regret: "I couldn't get to my gun until those punks ran away." Never did he show any fear for safety—he just wanted to get 'em and get 'em good.

Matty was every bit the warrior as Mickey, but he controlled his temper and had a zest for life. I think this is the perfect combination: He had the bravery to fight and the ability to instill fear but also the foresight and character to settle things with the mind rather than the fist. He enjoyed what he could of the life he had, spending time with friends and chasing girls. So many of the girls in the neighborhood, and later in Ireland and England, were crazy for Matty. He was good-looking; he could make you laugh and feel special—and, *oh*, could he dance and sing. These characteristics served Matty well through his short life as he enjoyed what little time he had.

Matty had a different fate than Mickey, although they both served in the war. Matty successfully made the D-Day jump in the Invasion of Normandy with the 508th Parachute Infantry Regiment. After landing, he volunteered to be a forward scout, a highly dangerous position, to try to spare the married men from such a risky job. During his mission, Matty was shot in the leg and captured. Shortly after, a German soldier shot him dead. As his friend and fellow paratrooper

Arthur (Art) Jacoby put it: "He was wounded and captured and was using his rifle as a crutch. He moved his hand, and the dirty Kraut shot him."

I've been asked if I carry any resentment toward my father; he was a mean drunk with a quick temper. My siblings might say, "Yes," but I've learned to let things go. Maybe I take after Matty in this way. I learned from all the stories of his life, his antics, his bravery, as well as his cool and collected demeanor. There is no doubt I admire my father and uncle's courage, but I also admire my Uncle Matty's level-headedness and his choice of laughter as the remedy to the tough cards he was dealt.

Chapter 4
UNCLE MATTY'S FAMILY

Uncle Matty survived growing up in the rough South Bronx, endured the brutal paratrooper training that earned him those coveted silver wings, and, despite the machine-gun fire all around him, successfully made his D-Day jump into Normandy on June 6, 1944. He was all of twenty years old. Courageously, he survived getting shot in the leg, despite profuse bleeding. There was no one to listen to him complain about being hungry, wet, cold, and in great pain. Even getting captured and going without medical treatment did not do him in. It took a point-blank assassination bullet by the gutless German soldier in charge of him as a prisoner of war to end his life.

How did he hang in there, all but knowing he would be killed? Where did he get such great survival qualities? To understand this, we need to understand his family, the hardships of their upbringing, and what they did to survive. Uncle Matty and his family grew up during the Great Depression. His parents had emigrated from Ireland to escape the potato famine and the complete lack of economic opportunity in their homeland. For Matty and his siblings, things were tough growing up. Bellies often went hungry, opportunities were few and far between, the future looked nothing but bleak, and children as young as twelve were pulled out of school to help with family finances.

Nothing in or out of the household was wasted, and I mean absolutely nothing. If you had a meal, you finished it, hungry or not, because you didn't know when you might get the next one. If anything was broken or torn, you fixed it, and if you didn't know how to fix it, you learned. If you still couldn't fix it, you did without. Understanding Uncle Matty and his remarkable survival skills starts

An Irish-American family in the South Bronx (also known as the 33rd county of Ireland). Father Richard, mother Nora, brother Jimmy, and sisters Ann and Francie lived through the Great Depression and World War II, and managed to handle everything else the world threw at them.

with knowing his large family and how they succeeded in overcoming such seemingly insurmountable obstacles.

Martin (Matty) Teahan was born in the South Bronx, the third in a family of four children. Matty's parents were Richard (Papa) and Nora (Maime) Teahan. He had an older brother, Jimmy; an older sister, Ann; and a younger sister, Francie. Nora was christened Honour Flynn but later changed her name. The practice was common among Irish immigrants, and many, like the O'Farrells on my father's side, dropped the "O" in their family name upon arrival at Ellis Island.

Born in Tuam, County Galway, on May 10, 1883, Honour Flynn immigrated to the United States on the RMS *Lusitania* in 1912.* She departed Queenstown on September 29, 1912, and arrived in New York City on October 4, 1912, where she changed her name to Nora. She was a third-class steerage passenger, nineteen years old at the time. She traveled with her cousin, Delia Burke, who had earlier immigrated to New York and had returned to Ireland to bring Maime to the United States. Delia had sixty dollars in her pocket, and Maime had twenty-five. Like most Irish immigrants, she came to America hoping for better financial opportunities and would send back nearly her entire pay to support her family in Ireland. To the desperate Irish immigrants of the day, the survival of the family was the one thing more important than the Catholic Church.

Richard (Papa) Teahan was born in Tralee, County Kerry, on August 7, 1888, into a land-owning family. His father, Michael Teahan, however, developed a serious gambling habit, which caused him to lose his land, horses, and home. Like most of his fellow Irish immigrants, Richard came to America before World War I in hopes of finding work and making a better future. Although he had family in Boston, he settled in the South Bronx to make a living at his chosen trade. More fortunate than many Irish who swelled the ranks of unskilled labor, Papa came to the New World as a skilled draftsman and experienced carpenter. He served in the Army during World War I and was stationed down South. The Army put his drafting and carpentry skills to good use in the shipbuilding industry, and he never left stateside.

Once the Great Depression hit, Papa lived a tough life. No one needed a carpenter, and his means of earning a living ceased to exist. Like many Irish, he felt an obligation to drink and hang out in the bars, and, with no work in sight, he became an alcoholic. His wife, Maime, my grandmother, had to take a job as a maid to feed the family. Papa and Maime were also the supers for an apartment building at 435 East 138th Street, where they themselves lived. Papa wound up drinking heavily, and alcoholism contributed to his death—sadly, a common occurrence in the Irish South Bronx.

MATTY'S MOTHER, NORA (MAIME)

Nora Teahan had very little education and grew up poor in Ireland at the time the country was still devastated by the long-lasting effects of the potato famine. She was sent to America to find employment so she could help support her family back home. In this she was representative: In the early 1900s, many of the Irish poor like Nora immigrated to America to join relatives who had fled in the mid-1800s at the peak of the Great Hunger, as the famine was called in Gaelic.

A lively young woman, Maime so loved to dance that she often wore out her shoes. It was at a dance, too, that she met her future husband. They married in Manhattan on February 11, 1920. When Papa fell to drinking after the Depression, Maime, no drinker herself, would take his liquor bottle and pour it down the sink, to Papa's great aggravation. Papa had another way of getting beer: he would tie a string to a cup, put a dime in it, and let it down from the window to a young relative standing outside, who would go to get him a pint. On return, the relative would put the pint of beer in the cup and Papa would hoist the bottle up to the apartment. Did he fool Maime? We will never know. Eventually, she threw him out of the house, and they separated.**

By the time I was old enough to remember her as a kid, Maime had fondness for Wilson Irish Whiskey and smoked two packs of Winstons a day. These habits, which continued unabated for the rest of her life, never got the best of her indomitable determination to thrive and protect her own. Although she lacked a formal education, Maime always spoke her mind and was always able to find, keep, and thrive at her jobs. She worked very hard as a maid for the Statler Hilton Hotel in New York City, where she became the maid for Sammy Davis, Jr. and many other celebrities. Maime had such an uplifting personality and could tell so many stories that she apparently made an irresistible impression on Sammy Davis, Jr. I remember well the story she often told of how he once gave her a kiss on the cheek.

Maime spent everything she earned on her children and grandchildren, sacrificing her own pleasures and luxuries to be able to give her family more. She somehow, for example, managed to have a piano at the apartment on 138th Street. Uncle Matty, who learned to play piano by ear, used to play it all the time. I have no idea how Mamie paid for it, and it may be she never did—but I do know that piano enlivened many an evening when Matty played and led singalongs for gatherings of family and friends.

In addition to her clever money-management skills, Maime was very astute and adept at dealing with people. A hard worker who knew the value of customer service, she earned more in tips than she did in salary. Because she so well knew how to survive and took such good care of the people who were important to her, Maime also became the go-to person for her siblings and other relatives when they immigrated to the United States. I don't know if Uncle Matty inherited his mother's survival skills or learned them from daily observation as a child, but he made good use of them and thoroughly absorbed her values, including hard work and total loyalty to the family. These helped him to excel at the exceptionally demanding training the army required of its elite paratroop forces.

Uncle Matty's code was that of a paratrooper born and raised: he viewed his fellow paratroopers as brothers and was so loyal he would—and did—put his life on the line and die for them. Like his mother, Uncle Matty also sent money back home to his family. In fact, the fifty dollars extra jump pay due a qualified paratrooper was a key reason Matty, like many other underage soldiers in the original U.S. paratroop forces, volunteered to undertake the risk at the ripe old age of seventeen. I am sure his ability to buckle down and do the hard work before him was a real asset on all those long hikes with full gear in the heat, rain, and cold. Also like his mother, he spoke his mind openly and was determined to meet his goal. Although Maime sternly forbade him to enlist in the Army, like many other adolescent patriots, Matty forged his parent's signature and enlisted anyway. Nothing was going to stop him from becoming a paratrooper.

MATTY'S OLDER BROTHER, JIMMY

Jimmy Teahan was born in May 1920. The most charismatic of the Teahans, he grew up to be the favorite of all the girls. His good looks and charm had many a lass chasing after him, begging for attention. Believe me, he knew this well and took maximum advantage of it. I often remember the look on my Aunt Mary's face whenever she talked about Jimmy. "Oh, my God—he was *gorgeous*. I mean, *really gorgeous*. All the girls were crazy over him," she would say with a dazzled look in her eyes. There was no hiding that she, too, had a huge crush on Jimmy. Every time I saw her, Aunt Mary told me again how *gorgeous* Jimmy was, repeating it over the years with increasing passion. Weddings, funerals, parties, family reunions—it didn't matter: The story was always the same. I guess, since I'd been named for him, I triggered memories for her.

I got to know a little of what Matty must have been like by spending lots of time with his brother Jimmy. Jimmy Teahan time was party time! Fun-loving, with a zest for life, he would take all his nieces and nephews on trips and to ball games, and buy us all our favorite eats. He was pretty much a best friend and playmate to us all. Uncle Jimmy was also a gambler and late-night type of guy. Whenever he won a bet, we all won. The moment the game or horse race was over, it was time to yell, scream, and order up pizza. This was followed by a call to the local liquor store, and the message that one of us kids would be right over to pick him up a bottle of whiskey. In those days, with one phone call from an adult, I could pick up any liquor they wanted when I was barely ten years old. I often made that trip to the liquor store, sometimes for Uncle Jimmy, for grandmother Maime, to fetch her favorite Wilson Irish Whiskey. But when Jimmy lost his bets, watch out. He became grumpy and irritable, no longer wanted us around, and kicked us out of his apartment. If we were smart, we just stayed away. Thus was I introduced to the life of a gambler.

Looking back on Jimmy now, I don't know how he managed it. He always seemed to have a scheme to make money, a big score. But even when he succeeded, he blew through his money as quickly as he got it. Jimmy was also a small-time numbers runner. Although I didn't realize it as a kid, I guess you could call him a low-level mobster. Normal hard work held no appeal: he preferred to chase the next easy money that came along. He never had a steady job. How could he, boozing all the time, out with women till the wee hours of the morning? His style of life was considered glamorous, or at least that was the impression I got from the people who knew him. Jimmy was not your typical guy of the era who'd gone to war and come back wanting only normalcy—to settle down to a stable job with benefits and to raise and support a family.

Jimmy's Aunt Helen introduced him to the Irish mob at a very early age. His mother Maime did not like him hanging around with Helen, but it was already too late for her to stop it. Helen was a wild one. She operated a hair salon for the mob and got Jimmy his job as a numbers runner, a low-level mob job that was nevertheless very profitable back in the day. The mob was notorious for trying to set people up so they would owe them for a lifetime, and to his great misfortune, Uncle Jimmy fell prey to the scheme.

It went down like this: Jimmy was told that a certain long-shot horse was in the fix to win a race, and he should bet the house on it. He borrowed $10,000—a fortune at that time—and bet to win on this horse. My Aunt Francie was present when Jimmy discovered he had lost; she said he screamed as long and as loud as possible. She instantly knew something terrible had happened, something far greater than losing an everyday bet. Jimmy was in trouble big time with the mob, who would expect him to do some dirty work, besides paying heavy interest to the Shylocks every week.

While Jimmy liked to act the big shot, he was actually a very small fish in the mobster world. Yes, he lived off ill-gotten gain, but he was only a low-level numbers runner—not the killer, or the enforcer, or the thief that he would need to be to get out of his terrible predicament. When the enforcers came knocking at the door, Maime covered for Jimmy and said he wasn't home. Meanwhile, Uncle Jimmy hid out on the back fire escape. "What the hell can I do?" he asked himself. He ran and hid out in Atlantic City with a trusted friend, where he was indeed safe—at least for a time. Although no one really knows what Helen's role may have been in setting Uncle Jimmy up, she ran away to Florida to hide from the mob right after Jimmy hightailed it out of town.

On September 23, 2016, my sister Liz and I met so I could interview her about anything she recalled about our Uncle Matty. To our mutual surprise, we discovered that we both had fragmented memories of this incident that we were able to piece together to complete a much fuller picture than either of us could remember on our own. I knew my father didn't like Uncle Jimmy or the way he was living. On numerous occasions, he got Jimmy a steady job, but to my father's great frustration, Jimmy never kept any of them. I told Liz about a scene that occurred when I was about five at our grandmother's house at 2780 Grand Concourse. Our mother, father,

Uncle Jimmy, and eight or so other adults were there. As my wife will tell you, my memories are sporadic, but this one is vivid, something I have played over in my mind my whole life.

Something very serious was going on. Even as a little child, I could feel the tension in the apartment. All I knew was that my Uncle Jimmy had asked my mother to ask my father for help to get out of some trouble. He could not ask my father directly, because he feared him greatly, and with good reason. As it turned out, the mob had no choice but to make an example of my uncle: He lost the bet, owed money, and ran. In short, he embarrassed them, so he had to be killed.

My father was well known in the South Bronx for his brutal fights outside the bars—fights in which, if need be, he would fight to the death every time. *He* was feared, but he feared literally nothing. I vividly remember my father looking into Jimmy's eyes that day, and instilling a look of fear no bookie or loan shark could ever match. That look was the look of a prizefighter staring into his opponent's eyes just before the starting bell of a championship fight. I can still see that look of fear in Uncle Jimmy, a look I will never forget as long as I live.

My father, however, was one of the very few people who could actually get Jimmy out of this life-or-death dilemma. Neither Liz nor I know what my father did. He was a cop, an ex-POW, and the all-around neighborhood tough guy. He did not give a damn if you were a mob enforcer—you had better watch what you said and how you said it to him. But whatever he did, he made sure that Uncle Jimmy was permitted to live and was no longer indebted to the mob. In fact, he even got his job as a numbers runner back.

His Aunt Helen was not so lucky. Everyone presumed her dead. Some say her body was never discovered. Others, like Liz, heard that Helen had been found somewhere in the swamps of Florida, literally dead in the water. Was this part of the deal? That she would get whacked? Liz and I still don't know the answer to that one, and we're not sure we really want to know. As it is, we are grateful to our father for saving Uncle Jimmy, who'd given us both so many wonderful childhood memories.

No matter what else he may or may not have been, we kids loved Uncle Jimmy because he always entertained us and treated us like we were special. We grew up so poor that we had to walk to most places and could only occasionally afford a bus or train. But with Jimmy, it was hail a cab and go any place you please! His philosophy was, "Let's live for today! Who knows what tomorrow will bring?"

Uncle Jimmy was born with rheumatic heart disease, which may at least partly account for his "live for the day" approach to life. His bad heart also made him ineligible for the armed forces—a hard blow to a young man in the World War II era. The country was so patriotic that most young men were volunteering for military duty, passionate to defeat the evil of Germany and Japan. I later found out my father despised Jimmy because he'd never served in the war. Many other people also held hard feelings against men who'd never served, no matter that, in Jimmy's case, this was no fault of his own. To make matters worse, it was Jimmy who opened the door and received the telegram from the US Army notifying the Teahan family that their much-beloved, youngest son Matty had been killed in action—a double blow and burden to his older brother safe at home, unable to serve his country.

One of our relatives, Margaret Lacey, who was present when Jimmy got that knock at the door, wrote to Liz to say that he was so terribly upset when he read the telegram that he ran outside and started breaking windows. Jimmy did calm down and realize his obligation to be strong and hold it together for the Teahan family. But while he may have kept up a brave front, that telegram always haunted him and led to a lifetime of guilt over Matty's early death. Jimmy and Matty had been very close and shared similar personalities. The terrible pain that Jimmy carried throughout his whole life may also help explain why he always lived for the day and gave no thought to the morrow.

Jimmy was nevertheless so much fun that we kids loved him, faults and all. He was often reckless, yes, but he was also very smart, and he could turn on the charm at any moment. Jimmy graduated from LaSalle Academy, a prestigious high school, and loved to read books. His nephew Danny remembers Jimmy's bookcase bursting with books, and recalls his uncle as a great reader who was constantly educating himself. In my own recollections, Uncle Jimmy is reading the daily papers. *The New York Daily News, New York Post,* and *The Journal American*—he devoured them all, cover-to-cover. I'll never know if this habit was due to intellectual curiosity or if his interest was simply job-related. Maybe he was looking for clues in the news, hoping to hit the combination to the jackpot at the end of the rainbow. I do know that numbers were always on Jimmy's mind. He even talked numbers in his sleep!

Jimmy's life was not all bad breaks and worse decisions. He got a few lucky breaks as well. In a sense, you could even say his death was one of them. Uncle Jimmy died on Christmas Day, 1968, at a time the Feds were on hot on his trail, searching to arrest him for illegal gambling activities. Shortly before our mom passed away, she and Liz had a heart-to-heart talk about Uncle Jimmy, and mom told Liz that the Feds were closing in. Had Jimmy lived, he would have gone to jail for many years for whatever it was the Feds had on him.

In my correspondence and interviews with Uncle Matty's fellow paratroopers, all of them to a man described Matty as the life of the party and the dreamboat of all of the women. After watching Uncle Jimmy all those years, it's easy for me to imagine the same characteristics in his younger brother. Paratroopers had to use force, smarts, and even charm—whatever they could think of to survive. The very execution of their mission behind enemy lines required that they take great risk—literally, a leap into the void. In my mind's eye, I can just see Uncle Matty applying Uncle Jimmy's charm and derring-do, and his ability to talk his way out of almost anything to the benefit of himself and his paratrooper brothers.

Uncle Matty's closest Army buddy, Jim McMahon, told Liz in a letter that Matty had such a strong premonition that he would die in the war that he showed no concern about the future. Remembering Uncle Jimmy, thinking back to our childhood, Liz and I recalled how, even when we were little, we knew he would not live very long. Jimmy found out when he was just a kid that he had a rheumatic heart, and he suffered from ill health his whole life. He even had a number hanging over his head. His doctor told him he would not live to fifty—he died at forty-nine. It is almost surreal to remember now how strongly these two very close brothers, Jimmy and Matty, shared the belief they must live for the day. Both thought they were bound to die young, and both were correct in their belief.

MATTY'S OLDER SISTER, MY MOTHER, ANN

Born on September 28, 1921, Ann Teahan grew up as a child during the Great Depression. When she was just a girl, she was hit by a truck going down the street the wrong way. It broke her leg in several places, leaving her hospitalized for months and immobile for many more. It sent her spiraling into a depression to see all the other kids from the block playing outside her window. How she longed to join them! Eventually, she was able to walk and play again, but the accident was only one difficult event of many in her very hard life.

My mom, Ann, was so smart she received a prestigious full scholarship to Mount Saint Ursula, a big deal for a poor girl from the South Bronx. At the time, Mount Saint Ursula received funding to create jobs for some of the few poor kids who had received scholarships. Ann and her best friend, Margaret Lacey, each got one of the available jobs, dusting books in the library. Both felt very embarrassed about being poor and were afraid of being teased because they had to work, so they tried to hide the fact by pretending they were looking for books whenever anyone came into the library. They would go back to dusting after the person had left. Poor girls were not considered equals at Mount Saint Ursula, a prejudice prevalent from top to bottom of the institution that filtered down from head administrators to teachers to better-off students. Mom and Margaret often walked all the way home from Mount Saint Ursula to 138th Street to save the five-cent fare for the El train. They used the nickel to go to the movies. The show cost ten cents on the weekend, but your dime also got you a voucher to see another movie during the week for five cents.

Like her brother Jimmy, my mother was influenced by her Aunt Helen. Helen took my mother around to some seedy bars and introduced her to the mobsters. Liz thinks Mom's familiarity with underworld types caused her to lose her fear against real tough guys like my father. One of the reasons they got married, Liz believes, is because our mother's guard was down. The two met at a festive event, the wedding of a mutual friend, and perhaps she found my father's tough-guy, war-hero good looks intoxicating. But once they were man and wife, his drinking and fighting made mom's hard life even harder.

Ann and Martin (Mickey) Farrell had five children, Marty, Jackie, Pat, Liz, and me. Mom was the go-to person for us all. One day in the early 1960s, my cousin Noreen and I were playing together at grandmother Maime's apartment. Noreen liked to have fun and could laugh and run like crazy all day long. Her lifelong dream was to become a nurse. Obsessed with this desire, she read up all about it and would watch anything and everything on TV remotely related to nursing. She was motivated, determined that nothing would stop her! (Sounds like Uncle Matty to me!)

On the day in question, Uncle Jimmy got us all sugared up on candy, and we started raising Cain, ripping and racing all over the apartment. All of a sudden, *BOOM! BAM!* The Venetian blinds fell down amidst the chaos and sliced off nearly my entire left middle finger. Blood was spraying everywhere, Noreen was screaming and crying, and she finally keeled over in a faint from shock. The whole apartment was in panic mode.

Someone had to step up big, or this was going to end badly for me. Mom stayed calm, grabbed a towel, wrapped my finger in it, and rushed me to the nearest doctor's office. The person who answered the door rudely informed her that the office was closed, but Mom refused to accept no for an answer. Luckily for me, the doctor complied with her demand and sewed my finger back on. Thanks to my mom, my finger was saved intact. It healed, with only a little scar remaining to remind me of the incident.

Poor Noreen did not heal so well. She was so traumatized that she gave up on being a nurse. For better or worse, she had me to thank for her change in career focus. This episode typifies our mother's ability to always solve the whole family's problems and stay cool and calm while doing so. Mom was the family rock for my brother and sisters and me. She lived until 1982, when she succumbed to lung cancer at age sixty-four. You could say our mother was on the front line of every family crisis. Paratroopers were legendary for their ability to solve sudden, unexpected problems on the fly in the midst of chaos and maintaining their focus in life-or-death situations. I see Uncle Matty as sharing his sister's way of courageously maintaining control in the trenches—be they metaphorical or, in his case, all too real.

MATTY'S YOUNGER SISTER, FRANCIE

Francie Teahan was born on July 4, 1925. Her birth name was Ella Francis—Ella after one of her grandmothers and Francis for Saint Francis. Francie almost died at birth and had to have one of her lungs removed. Much distraught, her mother Nora prayed to Saint Francis and promised God she would name the baby Francis if she lived.

Aunt Francie was also a gifted motivator of children. She always came up with a thoughtful, neat new gift to cheer you up through the tough times. When I was still a young kid, I needed eye surgery. I remember being very scared during that long wait in a hospital bed for the surgery to begin. A feeling of hopelessness came over me as I was wheeled into the operating room, unsure of what was about to happen. They strapped a gas mask to my face, and the surgeon started counting back from one hundred. I was out cold before he got to ninety-five.

When I woke up after the operation, the very first thing I saw was a smiling Aunt Francie with one of her thoughtful gifts, a G.I. Joe action figure—a toy I'd long wanted. This memory is so vivid I can picture it anytime I think of Aunt Francie. She just had a way of making you feel comfortable. Somehow she always got you laughing and made everything seem better. No matter how bad your predicament, no matter how low you felt, she would bring you back to practical reality and end up making you feel good again, in spite of yourself.

Aunt Francie was one of the sweetest, kindest people God ever created. If you needed it, she would literally give you anything and everything she owned. She never dwelt on the poverty of the Depression, her difficult childhood, or the rampant alcoholism that devastated her family. She married a German American, Willy Werner, who was also a drinker—and a fighter, too. My father Mickey tried to get Willy jobs, but he was just as bad at hanging on to them as Jimmy was. Yet never once did I hear Aunt Francie complain. She was always happy and positive and quick to smile her contagious smile.

My mom and Aunt Francie were very close and shared everything with each other. With a drinker and brawler for a husband, the lot of breadwinner and sole provider for the family fell to Francie. She not only made the best of it, she had a long and successful career at the Federal Reserve Bank in New York City—no small feat for any woman in her day, let alone one who was married. Francie, moreover, had four children to care for: Billy, Richie, Danny, and Noreen, the cousin whose nursing career my chopped-off middle finger abruptly cut short. Aunt Francie passed away in 2008 and was much mourned. I remember how she always described Uncle Matty as a happy, fun-loving, kind, and giving person. And indeed, she showed me a shining example what he must have been like, as she herself was graced with an abundance of the same marvelous qualities.

The discovery of Uncle Matty's rifle and the process of bringing it home have been the project of a lifetime. I've racked my brains for memories, interviewed family members, extensively researched the family ancestry, joined the 508th Parachute Infantry Association and any other organization I could think of. I obtained my uncle's Army records and read books about his unit and the Normandy drop. I twice traveled to Europe and reached out to everyone and anyone I could think of on both sides of the Atlantic who might have known Uncle Matty or otherwise be associated with his story—long-lost family members, fellow 508th veterans, the lovely French woman who tends Matty's grave, tour guides, families abroad who could possibly identify Matty's mysterious girlfriend Kitty—you name it.

History is a living, breathing thing, continuously evolving and growing. The "Greatest Generation" lived largely in silence about the effects of World War II, but the cost of their silence about that war, as well as the effects of the war itself, continue to seriously affect us. Even now, seventy-two years after the Allied Invasion of Normandy, the effort to understand this cost has only just begun.

I'm grateful to say my research and publications so far have received an abundant, generous, and very moving response: Memories, both painful and wonderful, and oral and written historical accounts that otherwise would have been lost are now on record. And the process is still ongoing! Nearly every day, significant material flows in, demanding to be recorded.

On a personal level, bringing Uncle Matty home has led me to understand how the history of our family is inextricably bound with that of our country and its course in World War II, and how this story, beyond its specifics, resembles and evokes the experience of so many others whose sons were on the front line in World War II. Our family, like many others from World War II up until our day, suffered the loss of the ultimate sacrifice, the death of a young son killed in action. But as part of our grieving, we also take pleasure in the idea that someday—be it fifty, a hundred, or even two hundred years in the future—a descendant of a veteran who fought in Normandy, or a World War II buff, or an historian of the Irish-American experience, or a researcher studying the history of the Bronx will discover this book in the process of writing another book.

Meanwhile, my research has yielded a collateral, yet highly gratifying result: I can now tell family stories as well as my brother Jackie!

Uncle Matty, thank you. May this book be a living, growing legacy for the Teahan/Farrell family, and continue to interest and help other readers, writers, researchers, veterans, and their families and friends—anyone down the line trying to comprehend what it was like for the select and fated few who jumped into Normandy or otherwise battled in front line combat, no matter where or when their service and engagement occurred. Please shine down on researchers of the future. Together, through your story, may we help keep history alive.

*The RMS *Lusitania*, the ship on which my grandmother sailed, was torpedoed by a German U-boat two years and seven months later, on May 7, 1915. The attack occurred eleven miles off the coast of Southern Ireland, inside a declared war zone as the ship was returning to Liverpool from New York Harbor. The ship sank in just eighteen minutes, resulting in the death of one-thousand, one-hundred, ninety-eight passengers and crew, including three-hundred, seventy-five passengers in third-class steerage, just as Nora had traveled. Many women and children were among them. The destruction without warning of an unarmed, commercial ship caused an international outcry and contributed to the decision of the United States to declare war on Germany on April 6, 1917.

**Maime and Papa's daughter Ann, my mother, remained close to her father. She visited him regularly in his rooming house in Harlem and attended to him during his final days. He died of pleurisy on December 5, 1945.

Chapter 5
MY FATHER MICKEY

As most of my friends and family know, I believe Uncle Matty's story was destined to be written, and for whatever surprising reason, I was meant to write it. What? Me write a book? That was my first response when I first heard the calling. As a beginning writer, little did I suspect how stories can alter and expand during the writing process. Uncle Matty's awakening, the discovery and return of his rifle after seventy-two years, also "woke up" forgotten family memories, reestablished connections, instigated new events, and indicated further pathways to explore. Not until I was closing in on my last chapter did I realize I'd written on just about everyone and everything related to Uncle Matty, with one glaring exception—my father. The blind spot was all the more remarkable, given my concentration on our immediate family and the intergenerational effects of the war. How had I gone so long without seeing it?

I now felt I needed to write that chapter. But I was worried that I wouldn't have anything to write. I really did not know or understand my father. Only through writing this book did I discover that my father's silence was typical of veterans who'd been in action in World War II. Drinking, hostility, undiagnosed depression: This was the dark side of the Greatest Generation, who regarded the show of emotion as a weakness and the subject of the war taboo. My father so rarely opened up on anything that writing one chapter about the man who had puzzled my life and thoughts for thirty years would be more of a challenge than writing a whole book on Uncle Matty, who died before I was born.

My father Mickey, all-around tough guy from the Irish South Bronx, famous for saying "Let's take it outside." Mickey loved his beer and his dogs! Here he is with Spanky, his beloved Dalmatian, and my brother Jackie at McSherry's Pub on 138th Street and Alexander Avenue. Spanky's drinks were always on the house. Mickey was a prisoner of war in Stalag Luft III, the camp for airmen depicted in the film, *The Great Escape*. Liberated at the end of the war, he became a cop in the Bronx. Like so many other veterans from the Greatest Generation, he turned to drink as his personal means of escape.

So, I asked myself, who was my father? I spent days just sitting and staring into space trying to remember things about him. I reached out to my brothers and sisters for help. I would feel uncomfortable calling him *dad*. We were taught to call him *Mickey*. To us kids, it was no big deal. He didn't care, and it meant no disrespect. It was just what he was called.

Finally, I realized I knew only three things definitively: Mickey loved to drink, he loved to fight, and he loved dogs. From what my siblings told me, I've blocked a lot of things from my memory, perhaps for good reason.

The facts about Mickey Farrell are: He was the oldest son of Irish immigrants, a World War II hero, and a prisoner of war for nine months at Stalag Luft III, the prison camp for airmen depicted in the famous movie *The Great Escape*. Mickey was color blind, so he was put to work as an aerial photographer on a B-24 bomb crew in the Army Air Corps. He was perfect for this duty, because the color blind are not fooled by camouflage like those with normal vision. It was easy for Mickey to spot targets, and he was very valuable to the crew. Mickey witnessed the death of his Army buddy when his helicopter was shot down, just one of many tragic deaths he would see. Later, Mickey himself was shot down over Austria, temporarily blinded, and captured. Ironically, it was the last of the twenty-five combat missions he needed to complete his service as an airman and go home. The German soldiers who captured him debated whether to kill him or let him live. He got to live by a one-vote margin.

After the war, my father became a New York City policeman. Doctors told him to deal with what is now known as Post Traumatic Stress Disorder by going on long walks. *Suck it up and be a man* was the standard prescription. Let's add this up: in WWII, POW, PTSD, NYPD, Irish descent. A perfect recipe to make an alcoholic. Maybe being an alcoholic was pre-determined, my father's destiny.

As I've been writing this book, my brothers Marty and Jackie and my sisters Pat and Liz and I have been talking together about the family and what we remember from our childhood. We all came to realize from these talks that none of us really knew or understood our father. Unfortunately, we did know that he was not a good one. He was abusive to my mother and never cared much about his five children. He had a fierce temper, and anything could set him off. I guess all of us carry some level of resentment—speaking only for myself, however, it's not that strong. I just wish I'd had a father who cared a little more. Oddly enough, I can say this: He was not the worst father of his era. There were plenty of alcoholics, but very few of them were able to keep a steady job like Mickey did.

On the other hand, my sister Liz carries a great deal of resentment even today. Her experience with Mickey was far different from mine. Growing up, Liz repeatedly heard Mickey say he wished he'd had another boy instead of her. What can be more devastating to a little girl? Liz was born on January 19, 1958, on the day of a terrible snowstorm. When our mother went into labor, Mickey was not to be found. We had no telephone, so she went to a neighbor's to call the usual bar. The bartender who answered was shocked to hear that Mickey was married and was having a kid. Amazing! In all his drinking at the local bars, Mickey rarely, if ever, mentioned his family. My mother was forced to take a taxi to the hospital. Luckily for Liz, she made it just in time, sparing Liz the notoriety of being born in a New York City cab.

By 1981, Marty, Jackie, and Pat had married and moved out, and I was away at college. Liz, the youngest of the siblings and the last to leave home, was still living at the apartment at 2355 Grand Concourse. Mickey's verbal abuse was escalating, and his drinking was even worse, if that's possible. Liz described it as "out of control" and said she thought at times that Mickey would kill her if she dared to open her mouth. Our mother, too, rightfully feared for her life. It took Liz an entire year to convince her, but, in December, mom finally agreed to move with Liz to an apartment in Queens near my sister Pat. They were so afraid, they did not even tell Mickey they were leaving. They told him only after the move, saying it was just temporary and in order to help Liz.

Once she'd moved in with Liz, our mother became a different person. She was happy, wanting to socialize with more people and get out and experience things. In a cruel turn of fate, she was diagnosed with lung cancer just two months later, and in February 1982 she underwent the torture of chemotherapy. Mom passed away on April 12, 1983. I will always be grateful to Liz that our mother was able to experience a few months with the monkey off her back and have some happiness. Rest in Peace, Mom.

I've racked my brains but cannot remember Mickey saying one thing to Liz while we were growing up. Liz respected him greatly for his military service, and, later in life, she attended some reunions with his unit, the 454th Bombardier Group. I think Liz probably understands or knows who Mickey was even less than the rest of us do. "I'll never understand him," she told me. "I'll always honor him for his service, but lots of other veterans experienced even more horrible things in the war and still were loving and caring toward their family."

From there, Liz went on to recount a horrifying story that happened when she was five years old. She was hurrying, trying to get to the bathroom, and fell hard on the floor. As she lay, hurt and crying, Mickey came down the hall, stepped over her, went into the bathroom, came back out, and walked back over her, never once looking at her and ignoring her crying. She remembered he wasn't drunk, because he wasn't weaving down the hall, bouncing from wall to wall as he usually did. This is not normal parenting—it was neglect, and it took quite a toll on Liz's psyche and self-esteem.

MICKEY'S FIRST LOVE—ALCOHOL

To say Mickey loved to drink is a huge understatement. Drinking is *all* he did, what he lived for. This may be hard to believe, but as far back as I can remember, my father drank twenty or more beers every day of his life. He was the walking definition of an alcoholic.

My brother Jackie became sort of a caretaker for Mickey during the last year of his life. Every Saturday morning like clockwork, Mickey called Jackie at 5:30 am to wake Jackie up to take him shopping for a little food and a lot of beer. Jackie also had to drive Mickey to his favorite local bar, the Tiebout Tavern on 188th Street, a block or so off the Grand Concourse. Jackie would drive him there, have a drink with him, leave him for a few hours, come back, have another drink with him, and then drive him home.

In the last year of his life, Mickey had to be admitted to the hospital several times. He always went to Union Hospital on 188th Street, conveniently located near the Tiebout Tavern. On one occasion, he was admitted for heart problems and gout complications. He had an Indian lady doctor—and, boy, did she yell and lecture him! I heard her tell him, point blank: "Keep this up, and you'll soon be dead. *You cannot drink anymore, sir!*" What she did not know was that the night before, Mickey, lying in his hospital bed, had ordered his brother Phil to sneak him in a six-pack of beer. This was like a candy bar to a hungry kid, and it lasted just as long.

"Is he going to listen to her?" I wondered as I drove my father home that day. Well, the ride from Union Hospital to 2355 Grand Concourse was short. Before we got home, Mickey ordered me to get him a six-pack from the bodega across the street. Of course, I complied.

In April 1986, Jackie was getting ready to move to a new house, and Mickey was going to move in with him. The Saturday just before the move, there was no 5:30 wake-up call. Jackie immediately thought, "Oh, my God—he's dead!" Jackie had been very good about taking care of our father that year, but he was so busy packing that he called to ask me to go check up on Mickey.

My sister Pat and I went to Mickey's together. When we got to the apartment, she went right, into the living room, and I went straight down the hall. A second later, I heard her scream, "Oh, my God! Mickey!" We found him dead on the floor. Next to him was a ladder with several untouched pizza slices on one of the steps. Funny, pizza would be my choice as a last meal. I guess it was Mickey's, too, but he never got to eat it.

Just to be certain, Pat reached down and touched Mickey. He was cold as ice. We called the police, and they came soon enough, but we waited a few hours on the coroner. Mickey's .38 was not in its usual place on the windowsill. The responding cops, Pat, and I searched for it intensely, but to no avail. The apartment was in a terrible state—filthy, stinking, a total mess, with cockroaches running everywhere. When we finally got home, Pat and I both had to take showers.

Pat and I still have vivid memories of this day and that horrible search through the apartment. From time to time, we have nightmares about it. We later found out that Mickey had given up his gun, which was probably a very wise decision.

Ironically, finding my father dead was not the hardest part of the day for me. It was our old, beloved dog Mugsy crying over Mickey's body. Mugsy and my father had a special relationship. They loved each other and would have conversations together. Mugsy was seventeen years old and in very bad shape. The day after Mickey's death, I had to take Mugsy to the vet to be put to sleep. It broke my heart.

MICKEY'S SECOND LOVE—FIGHTING

My father grew up a tough New York City street kid, comfortable fighting anyone who stood in his way. Most of the time, he won his fights. Nothing scared him. Even as a cop, he was famous at his police station for dropping his gun belt and telling anyone foolish enough to argue, "Let's settle this outside." Once on front desk at the five-two precinct, he saw some young cops tossing a football outside. This, for some reason bothered him, so he went outside. "Keep throwing that football," he warned, "and I'll come out and kick your asses." They stopped.

Mickey lived by the street code of the Irish South Bronx. This would come in handy for me one night in 1973, when my friend Jimmy VanDoran and I wound up in handcuffs at the four-six precinct in the Bronx. We'd been drinking at the Western Tavern on 183rd Street and Crescent Avenue. I'd recently turned seventeen, and Jimmy was fifteen. Being underage in the 1970s rarely stopped an Irish American kid from being served in neighborhood bars.

Jimmy and I were having a blast drinking the night away, listening to bar patrons' stories, laughing at all the jokes, and singing to the Irish music. At one point, I went to the bathroom and returned to find Jimmy cursing and screaming at some guy. "What's wrong?" I asked. "This fucking guy grabbed my ass and propositioned me!" he exclaimed. Well, this was definitely a new one for me. Jimmy and I talked and agreed to tell this dude, "Let's settle this outside." Young as we were, underage, drinking in a bar, to us this was clearly the only sensible action.

So Jimmy and I went outside and walked halfway down the block toward the Grand Concourse. The guy came out of the bar and followed us. All three of us were all liquored up. Something bad was about to happen. The guy who'd grabbed Jimmy's ass was belligerent. "Who the fuck do you guys think you are?" he yelled. "I will fuck you up." There was no doubt in my mind that we were going to have to fight. Then the asshole pulled out a switchblade. "I'm gonna cut you motherfuckers up!" he announced, waving and angrily pointing the knife at us, as Jimmy cursed and yelled at him nonstop.

Now was the time to act and make my move. If there is one thing I learned growing up in the Bronx streets, it's that cursing and threatening without action makes you vulnerable. I was not an aggressive person and did not get into a lot of fights, but my father's blood is in me, and it was about to show.

The guy confronting us stood about five feet, eight inches, was a little chubby, and was waving his knife about like crazy. I was about six feet tall, one-hundred-ninety pounds, and in very good physical condition. To be sure, the code of the Irish streets would not allow us to retreat. We would be the laughing stock of the neighborhood for the foreseeable future, and Jimmy and I could not have lived with that. My split-second analysis told me our adversary was not expecting me to charge. After all, this asshole felt confident waving and pointing that knife at us.

I decided to bull rush him to the ground in a football tackle and get the knife off him. I went at him hard, easily knocked him down, and his knife fell off to the side. I can still hear the sound of the metal, *tin, tin*, as it hit and bounced on the sidewalk. The guy's head made that distinctive noise that a head makes hitting the New York City pavement, a noise and vibration you know from fighting or playing rough in the neighborhood. The pervert was stunned all right—getting the knife off him had been easier than I thought.

Adrenalin and instinct drove me to start punching him in the face, and I let loose with everything I had. The funny thing was, Jimmy just stood there cursing through the entire scene.

So here I am on top of this asshole, whaling away at him with punches, with the knife I just knocked off him right beside me, shinning brightly under the street light. And guess what? Just my luck—a cop car pulls up. The cops pull their guns, and assume that Jimmy and I are the aggressors. I can't blame them—it certainly looked like we were committing a crime. One minute I'm protecting Jimmy, and here I am the next in big trouble. The whole fight probably took only a minute or two. It was just my dumb luck!

The cops handcuffed all three of us, pushed us into two separate patrol cars, and took us to the station to figure this out. Throughout the whole ten-block ride, Jimmy still kept yelling and cursing. I just kept quiet. All I was thinking was, "I am really fucked." Jimmy told me later he'd felt so violated by the guy who'd grabbed him that he couldn't control his anger.

At the four-six precinct, the cops separated Jimmy and me from the pervert. Somehow Jimmy slipped out of his handcuffs while we were waiting to get interviewed. I don't know how he did it, but it broke the tension, and we cracked up laughing. One of the cops came over, and we stopped laughing. He uncuffed me, looked strangely at Jimmy, and took away both pairs of handcuffs. Of course, Jimmy and I started laughing again because the cop hadn't realized Jimmy had slipped the cuffs on his own. Jimmy should have been a magician.

I told our side of the story to the cops and let them know my father was a policeman from the neighboring five-two precinct. They wanted proof, so they called him at home and told him all about what happened. They also called Jimmy's father and requested both of them come to the four-six precinct to figure out what to do. Jimmy's family lived on the fourth floor of our building, just one floor down from us. Mickey and Mr. VanDoran met in the hallway but didn't say a word on the way to the station. Mickey, ever the alcoholic, stopped on the way for a beer at Sullivan's on 183rd Street. He also stopped in for a beer on his way home.

By the time Mickey reached the station, the guy with the knife had concocted some story in which we were to blame. The Precinct Captain told Mickey the perv was going to press charges against me. Just like Mickey, the Captain was royally pissed off that a man had made an aggressive sexual pass at a minor like Jimmy as he innocently sat enjoying his beer in a neighborhood bar.

For cops at the time, a sexual predator, and especially a same-sex predator, was about the worst person on the planet. In fact, the cops at the precinct were enraged. The Captain told Mickey he would talk to the perv *privately* in a room and inform him that Jimmy would press steadfast charges against him. He then would describe the disdain for sexual predators on Rikers Island, where the perv would be spending the night. The Captain was forceful and deliberate in delivering the message. Bad things were going to happen to our ass-grabber at Rikers. I am pretty sure he was explicit about what those bad things would be.

Honesty soon prevailed, and all concerned agreed to make believe that the night had never happened. When they let us all go, the perv bolted out of there with the look of fear in his eyes. I'm not sure if it was me, the four-six Precinct Captain, or both of us who scared him.

Somewhere along the line, Dezi Clarke, the bartender at the Western Tavern, where Jimmy and I had been drinking that night, had come down to the precinct to back up our story. Or maybe it was someone else from the bar. But before the cops let us all go, they pulled Jimmy and me aside. "Guys," they said, "don't be idiots. Next time take the guy down an alley where no one's watching." Good advice. It was a different time, and things were handled in a way that would make people scream bloody murder today. Who is to say which era handled it better? What I can say is, back then, you pretty much knew where you stood, with none of today's so-called *political correctness.*

My friend Jimmy and I walked the ten blocks home from the four-six precinct. The whole way home, Jimmy was laughing. I was thinking: *My father is going to kill me.* Jimmy didn't have to worry. His father, like Mickey, was an alcoholic, but he was the mellow type of drunk who would probably laugh at it all the next day. Jimmy and I walked up the steps together, parting company on the fourth floor. He wished me good luck with my father, and I slowly trudged up the last flight of stairs, dreading every step to our apartment.

Time to face the music. My only hope was to sneak into the bedroom unnoticed. It was close to midnight, but somehow I just knew that Mickey would would be waiting for me in the living room. I was scared, but I opened the door. The dogs went ballistic. "Jimmy!" Mickey barked out. "I need to talk to you right now!"

Mickey was sitting on the couch in his underwear and a badly torn white tee shirt. Oh, man, did he reek of booze. But he had sobered up a little and was coherent enough to talk. His loaded .38 revolver was in its usual place on the living-room windowsill. The dogs went back to sleep in one of the other rooms, so I couldn't lean on them for help. *Oh, my God—here it goes*, I thought, *At best, I'm going to get a beating. At worst, who knows?*

"What the hell happened?" Mickey sternly asked, just slightly slurring his words. I told him things from my point of view. He pondered, looking up at the ceiling, while I stood waiting. *One Mississippi, two Mississippi*—the wait was killing me! *Just give me my beating, and I'll go to sleep*, I thought to myself. *Anything but weighing my fate like this in silence!* I guess he must have stared at the ceiling for five or six seconds. Then, looking me straight in the eye, he blurted out: "I'm very proud of you." I was dumbstruck, in total shock. *What?! Did Mickey just say what I thought he said?*

There was a little smirk on Mickey's face that I had never seen before. "You did the right thing, sticking up for your buddy," he said, his odd little smirk starting to spread. "You showed real guts confronting that fucking sexual pervert." *Holy cow! For the very first time in my life, I think Mickey is proud of me!* His acceptance, with this little odd smirk I think is pride, leaves me speechless.

In Mickey's mind, in this one instance, I had followed his precious Irish South Bronx street code. You must stick up for your friends no matter the danger, even—and especially—if it means a fight. Mickey started ranting, cursing out the sexual predator, his disdain growing larger and louder in a long string of words that are better left to the imagination. After about ten minutes, I went to bed. I was ecstatic the night was over but so exhausted it took me more than an hour to fall asleep. All I could think of was my shock at Mickey's reaction. The next morning, Jackie, as usual, went around the whole neighborhood telling everyone what happened. Again, as usual, Jimmy and I had to repeat the story at least a dozen times.

To really convey the extent of Mickey's fearlessness and love of fighting, I need to tell the story of his interrogation by Internal Affairs, right after the shooting in 1967, when he killed the Puerto Rican guy who made the mistake of trying to rob a bar where Mickey was having an off-duty beer. Internal Affairs took a look at the case and decided to sweat Mickey, implying a sinister motive for the shooting. Picture a dark room in the back of the station, with one bright light hanging from the ceiling, just like the TV cop shows. That's the room where they took Mickey. They had five Internal Affairs officers, all intent on breaking Mickey and forcing him to admit to wrong. Now, the shooting was clean. He'd pulled his badge out. The robber was armed and had lunged at him with a knife. This made no difference to Internal Affairs. Their officers were bound and determined to break Mickey. Pardon me while I chuckle to myself.

One by one—and then all at once—they threw Mickey questions, accusations, threats. *Do you know what you did? Why did you do that, not this? You made a big mistake, buddy! Confess, and we'll go easy on you! As of now, you're on modified duty! Give us your gun! With the trouble you're in, you'll never get it back!*

"Let's take this outside," Mickey replied. He then slammed down his gun and told them all to go fuck themselves. Or he could also kick their asses then and there, either one at a time or all at once, however they preferred. The five of them stood dumbfounded. "You motherfuckers don't have a pair of balls between all of you!" Mickey exclaimed. Yep, that was my father. Dead serious, he just physically threatened five Internal Affairs officers. I can't stop laughing while I write this—incredibly, the officers backed off. I don't know if Mickey scared them off, or if they just could not believe what they'd just heard.

Two weeks later, they called him in again and informed him he had to move to Brooklyn, where he had a family. They showed him a map where he was supposed to go. Guess what he said to them! Yep, you're right: *Go fuck yourself* again. My god, he was fearless. He then took a compass with a pencil from a nearby desk and drew a circle on the map. The compass pointed to Fordham Road in the Bronx. "That's where I'm moving," he informed them and turned and walked out the door.

MICKEY'S THIRD LOVE—DOGS

Mickey and dogs—perfect together!

I never saw Mickey show the least affection to my mother or any of my brothers and sisters, and he never showed any to me. In fact, except for anger, he rarely showed any emotion at all. But when it came to dogs, he was a totally different person.

Almost everyone on both sides of my family has always had an affinity to dogs, including Uncle Matty. But Mickey's love for dogs was on a whole different level. Whenever Mickey came home or woke up, he seldom said anything to any of us, but the dogs he kept got the royal treatment. We always had two or three of them: Mugsy and Molly were smart mutts, Barney was a dumb German Short Hair Pointer, and Spanky was my cousin Billy's spectacular Dalmatian. Spanky was Billy's dog, but he often stayed with us for weeks. Mickey really loved Spanky. He'd have Jackie or me drive him and Spanky to

McSherry's on 138th Street and Alexander Avenue. Spanky, like my father, was a regular at the bar. It was here that Spanky got fed, and all his drinks were on the house. Funny thing—most of the time, Spanky was the only one sober in the place.

When Mickey was a POW at Stalag Luft III, he and a few of his buddies had a German Shepherd they took care of and called their own. Mickey loved that dog. Why Mickey and his friends were allowed to keep the dog is a mystery. The so-called "Great Escape" had happened at this camp before Mickey was captured, and the Germans had since cracked down hard. Finally, food was in such critical short supply that the Germans shot the dog. It was devastating to Mickey, and probably one of the reasons for his great love of dogs. By the time he was liberated in June 1945, food was so scarce that he was under a hundred pounds.

Every morning when Mickey woke up, he made himself tea and toast. But first he made three pieces of toast for the dogs. He would butter them up to the maximum, walk to one of the bedrooms with all three dogs close behind, and lock them in with the toast as a treat so he could eat his breakfast in peace. After breakfast, he would take the dogs up to the roof to pee, shit, and play. Once he got back to the apartment, it was time for Mickey to drink his first of many cans of beer for the day. The first was no later than 7:00 am. My brother Jackie and I were often hung over from a night of drinking ourselves. I still cringe when I remember the sound of Mickey opening a Schaefer or Rheingold early in the morning.

When Molly died, Mickey wanted her to have a proper burial. He decided I should drive the dog to his sister Bridie's house in Brooklyn and dig a grave in her backyard. He wrapped Molly's body in a blanket, showing no emotion, as usual. I had a station wagon, so my brother Jackie, being smart, darted out of the apartment, leaving me as the designated driver. Jackie was always good at getting out of such situations. My sister Pat took pity on me and came along to help. Mickey stayed home.

I don't know why it was funny, but every time I went forward or stopped, it jarred Molly's dead body and shifted it around. You could hear the *bump, bump, bump* of her cold body sliding around in the back of the station wagon. Pat and I cracked up, and to this day we laugh about poor Molly bumping about. When we got to Bridie's house, my cousins Tara and Theresa had already dug the grave. It took them hours to get it deep enough. Tara laughs when she recalls how hard the ground was—no matter what they did, Molly's legs would still stick out. But despite the many challenges, Tara and Theresa gave old Molly a royal burial, including flowers and a eulogy.

Tara was afraid of Mickey. During the last few years of his life, he'd bring the dogs to stay a night or two at Bridie's, Tara's Mom's. In our conversations, Tara recalled times when Mickey was so drunk he would bounce off the walls, or sway from side to side in his chair. She does not ever remember him sober. Bridie got really angry because the dogs would shit and pee all over her house, but my father didn't care. He had a close relationship with his sister Bridie, so it worked. I can see why Tara would have been afraid of him, and I understand Mickey's love of dogs. I am the same. What I don't understand is why he never showed any love or affection to anyone else. The only thing I remember him saying to my mother is, "What's for supper?"

One early evening in the late 1970s, some idiot up on our roof was throwing bottles down into the street. The Grand Concourse was almost always full of pedestrians, so this was quite dangerous. Mickey and I ran up to the roof with the dogs to confront the bottle-thrower. Whoever it was must have caught on and run away because the roof was empty. Then one of our neighbors, a Puerto Rican guy, ran up, armed with a huge machete. For a second, Mickey and I didn't know if he thought we were the ones throwing the bottles. After a few tense words, we all figured out we were on the same side, pursuing the bottle-thrower. We laughed with the guy and parted shaking hands.

It never dawned on me until I sat down and wrote this, that when that guy with the machete appeared, Mickey was more concerned about the dogs than he was about me. After the fellow left, Mickey looked at me and said, "Fuck, the one time I forgot my gun, I needed it. I would never forgive myself if he hurt the dogs." This is as close as I ever got to bonding with my father.

Marty, the oldest of my siblings, saw and remembers much more of the bad stuff, including the treatment of my mother. Mickey rarely spoke to, or even deigned to recognize, my sisters Pat and Liz. So maybe it's not surprising that Jackie and I, the youngest male children, bear Mickey the least resentment.

Jackie himself has a good memory and helped me a lot in recalling things about Mickey. One day, when Jackie was drinking in the White Heather Pub, he had his South Bronx Irish Street Code moment with Mickey. The White Heather was right across the street from us on 184th Street and the Grand Concourse. A real nasty guy named Bear used to hang out there from time to time. He was taller and heavier than Jackie and had a tough reputation for picking on people.

On the day in question, Bear was picking on a friend of Jackie's at the bar. Jackie got up in his face. "Let's take this outside," he said to Bear. "I'm going to kick your ass." Bear yelled back, "Hey, man— I've got a gun."

What to do? Jackie, always calculating, replied, "Just stay here a minute." He then ran across the Grand Concourse to our apartment and asked Mickey to help him confront Bear. Mickey, of course, would not—for anything—pass up a fight.

So Jackie and Mickey go into the bar, and Jackie says to Bear, "OK. You have a gun, and I've got someone with a gun. So, now let's take it outside." All of a sudden, Big Bad Bear was frightened. He looked Jackie in the eyes. Then he took in Mickey's mean stare. Most probably, he knew that Mickey was a cop.

The upshot? Bear backed down, darted out of the bar, and never again caused trouble at the White Heather Pub. Jackie followed the Irish Bronx Street Code so dear to Mickey and had his bonding moment with his father. Bear was later arrested for assaulting children. My own Irish Bronx Street Code moment with Mickey involved a guy trying to sexually assault a minor, Jimmy VanDoran. For Jackie, it involved a guy who was later arrested for assaulting children. Coincidence?

In late March 2017, my sister Pat and I got together to reminisce about Mickey. The consensus: Mickey was an heroic member of the Greatest Generation but a horrible father and husband. Pat cracked up remembering when her husband Ralph first met Mickey. Ralph is a pure gentleman—always has been and always will be. A lover of tradition, he insisted that Pat dance with her father at their wedding. Pat tried to talk Ralph out of it, but he refused to listen.

The day of Pat's wedding, Mickey snuck away to the bar every chance he got. The wedding photographer was puzzled and annoyed. Why were we always looking for Mickey? By the time the father-daughter dance came around, Mickey was so sloppy drunk he could barely stand up. Pat laughed, recollecting how she struggled to hold her father up during her debut as a married woman.

Pat's recollections of our father killing the guy in the bar in 1967 confirmed what Liz had told me about our mother's friend, Joe O'Brien. Mom had once dated Joe's brother John. She would have married him, except that one of her relatives would have none of it. Joe and John's sister had some mental issues, and the objecting relative did not consider John a suitable mate.

As Pat remembered it, many Puerto Rican parishioners of St. Jerome's Church were up in arms and hell-bent on killing us in retaliation because Mickey had shot one of their own. Monsignor Albert Pinckney of St. Jerome's intervened and saved us. Well-liked and respected by most St. Jerome's parishioners, Monsignor Pinckney proffered magic words of healing: "We are all Catholics. Let's get along with each other." Just one year later, in 1968, Monsignor Pinckney retired. We are so fortunate that he was there for us.

Mom told Pat about hearing the howling scream of a wife who had just received the notice her husband had been killed in action. Many St. Jerome parishioners had loved ones who had died in World War II, including good friends of Matty and Jimmy. Our mother felt strongly about this. She wrote postcards to all her brother's friends overseas and saved all the letters that came back, including replies and letters returned unread. Pat recalls playing with these postcards as a kid, which were very important and sentimental to mom. One day Mickey, in a fit of jealous, alcoholic rage, made our mother throw all these letters out.

A drinking tradition that Mickey established with Marty, Jackie, and me is the perfect send-off to this chapter about our father. Irish had to show up at wakes. Whenever anyone died, Mickey would make a short appearance and then tell Marty to take him to the nearest bar. Marty could hold his own, but even for him, a short time drinking with Mickey was enough. Marty then went back to the wake and sent Jackie to the bar for the next shift with Mickey. Jackie, too, could hold his liquor, but he, like Marty, soon discovered that a short time boozing with Mickey equaled a whole night out of serious drinking with friends.

According to tradition, when Jackie got back to the wake, he would send me down for the closing shift to drink with Mickey. By this time, Mickey was sloppy drunk and drinking vodka and orange juice to close out the night. Don't get me wrong: Even drunk, he drank a lot.

I was thankful to be the last shift. I struggled to keep up with him, knowing he would give me his usual dirty look if I could not match him drink for drink. So it was, it took three young Irish American sons all their effort to keep up with a normal night of their father's drinking. A sad statement, but a reality that shaped all our lives.

Mickey passed away on April 15, 1986. Thus ended the tradition of keeping our father company as he drank at wakes.

Mickey was waked on April 16 and 17, 1986, at Hodder Funeral Home in the Bronx. Sadly, no cops attended. Mickey had not stayed in contact with the police community, preferring to split his time between the Tiebout Tavern and McSherry's Bar. It did not feel right to me without a fellow brother in blue, but this is the way Mickey lived his life. Some of his drinking pals did make it to the wake. From the look on their reddened faces and the reek of booze, it would not be long before they, too, wound up in a coffin.

Wakes and funerals were usually times when family feuds or fights would be renewed, but I don't remember anything like that at Mickey's wake. Aunt Francie and Aunt Mary were there, as were some of our cousins. Our Uncle Phil ordered Jackie and me to go get a flag to drape over Mickey's casket. He was very insistent that we go to the Veterans Administration Hospital on Kingsbridge Road, where we could get a flag for free. We darted out to the VA Hospital and discovered Phil was right. We got the flag, and Phil felt so much better.

Mickey's funeral mass was at Saint Barnabas on McLean Avenue. The U.S. flag was draped over his coffin, as was befitting a veteran. He was buried in Calvary in Queens. After the burial, we had a family meal at McMenanim's Pub on McLean Ave. As usual, it was a time for reflecting, a little drinking, and telling a lot of stories.

Chapter 6
A SOLDIER AND HIS RIFLE

Like my father and uncle before me, and their fathers before them, I did a stint in the U.S. Army. I remember well the culture shock of basic training at Fort Dix in the winter of 1974. Yes, the drill sergeants immediately made their presence known and reinforced it every moment thereafter. *What the hell did I get myself into?* we all wondered. Back in the day, drill sergeants did not worry about how they affected your feelings. As a matter of fact, the worse they made you feel, the better they were doing their jobs. But you know what? Most of us understood. We knew they were making us stronger, building character, and instilling discipline so we could be good soldiers.

After about a week, you were introduced to your rifle. Your rifle was now your best friend, and you'd better never lose sight of it. Lose a rifle that gets found, and you'd be lucky to be docked only a rank and some pay and to pull some extra duty. Lose a rifle that doesn't get found, and it's *goodbye, soldier.* It meant dishonorable discharge and maybe worse. Clean it daily, take it apart and put it back together ten times a day or more, sleep with it, kiss it—nothing is more important. This is the start of every soldier's love affair with their rifle.

Here I am in 1976 at Yakima Training Center, on duty for the 9th MP Company Training Mission. A soldier has a life-or-death relationship with his rifle—mine never left my side for the entire week at Yakima.

There are many versions of the "Rifleman's Creed," but I remember this as the one our drill sergeants made us memorize.

> *This is my rifle. There are many like it, but this one is mine.*
> *My rifle is my best friend. It is my life. I must master it as I must master my life.*
> *Without me, my rifle is useless. Without my rifle, I am useless. I must fire my rifle true. I must shoot straighter than my enemy who is trying to kill me. I must shoot him before he shoots me. I will.*
> *My rifle and I know that what counts in war is not the rounds we fire, the noise of our burst, nor the smoke we make. We know that it is the hits that count. We will hit.*

My rifle is human, even as I, because it is my life. Thus, I will learn it as a brother. I will learn its weaknesses, its strength, its parts, its accessories, its sights, and its barrel. I will keep my rifle clean and ready, even as I am clean and ready. We will become part of each other. We will.

Before God, I swear this creed. My rifle and I are the defenders of my country. We are the masters of our enemy. We are the saviors of my life.

So be it, until victory is America's and there is no enemy, but peace!

There are few feelings as good as marching with your rifle, singing cadence with your platoon, company, or battalion. Your rifle is strapped on your shoulder, and you're singing one of the "Jody Boy" cadences. *Watch out, world! There are over a hundred bad-ass soldiers marching past!* Having been at the firing range, you knew your rifle like you knew your best friend, and you knew it would never fail you. Maybe you even had a name for it. At the firing range, you were taught how to shoot, how to relax and squeeze with no tension. *Do it right and you are hitting that target, baby!* Hold your rifle like you hold your girlfriend, and she will never let you down.

After basic training, my friend George and I went on to Military Police School at Fort Gordon, Georgia. There we were introduced to another new friend, the .45 automatic pistol. George was a great guy, but for reasons unknown to me, he did not qualify on the .45. What that meant for him was a new specialty: instead of 95B, Military Policeman, he was classified 95C, Prison Guard.

The funny thing is, George went on to be an expert marksman who could outshoot me with the .45. But he could not compare to me with my girlfriend, my rifle. I was one of the best shots with the M-16, and the .45 handgun could never take the place of my one true love. After MP school, I was assigned to the 9th MP Company in Fort Lewis, Washington, where we took part in field maneuvers and training. My girlfriend, my rifle, and I always took care of each other on maneuvers. If ever something was not right with her, I made sure to make it better.

At Fort Lewis, I also had another friend, or more of an acquaintance, I should say—the M-67 .90mm recoilless rifle. The M-67 fired a ten-pound round. Man, was that one macho piece of equipment! I was the crew leader of a two-man team. The back blast would kill you in a second, so you had to lie sideways on the ground when firing. The effective range was three-hundred-twenty-eight yards, about three football fields in length. I found it very accurate at three-hundred yards or less.

At the shooting range, we practiced on old tanks and armored personnel carriers, which the M-67 was designed to destroy. We had fun hitting the targets and seeing them blow up and start on fire. The M-67 was a bad-assed girl all right, but ours was a brief affair. After I was certified, I got to fire her on three different exercises at the firing range. As much as I enjoyed this, I stayed true and loyal to my girlfriend and best friend, my rifle.

From 1976 to 1977, I was assigned to Camp Ames, Korea, 110th MP Company, where I guarded a missile-storage base. Here I was again introduced to a new friend, the M-60 machine gun. The M-60 was a rifle on steroids. It could fire more than five-hundred rounds per minute, with an effective firing range of one-thousand, two-hundred yards. Believe you me, you would not want to be in its cross-hairs. My duty was to man guard towers circling the missile-storage silos. Towers that had M-60s were two-man teams. The M-60 was pure pleasure at the firing range. But if you had only one shot to take and could choose your weapon, my choice would be my rifle. I believe most soldiers would agree.

Uncle Matty's M-1 Garand was heavy at ten to eleven pounds, but the advantages were plenty. First and foremost in World War II, the M-1 gave the paratrooper a huge advantage in firepower. One of the first semi-automatic rifles, the .30 caliber M-1, firing an eight-round clip, was superior to German bolt-action rifles. It was accurate to three hundred yards, with a maximum effective range of five hundred yards. All you had to do was pull the trigger. *Bang, bang!* Eight rounds fired in seconds. "One to put 'em down and seven to keep 'em down," as I once heard a D-Day paratrooper say.

So what did Uncle Matty's M-1 mean to him? For paratroopers and front line soldiers, your rifle was everything. It always had to be cleaned and ready. Your life depended on it. You'd better have it zeroed-in and know all the nooks and crannies of it. Your bayonet had better be sharp and easy to fasten for hand-to-hand fighting.

Even though rifles are mass-produced, most soldiers can tell their particular rifle from others. Uncle Matty engraved his name on one side of his rifle stock and the name of his British girlfriend, Kitty, on the other. I imagine him doing this shortly before D-Day, after the 508th was sealed in at Folkingham Airfield. Perhaps he engraved it on the night of June 5, sitting on his cot, surrounded by fellow troopers nervously waiting to hear the word *"GO!"* Whatever the circumstances, he must have felt very strongly about the engraving, and we in his family are so happy he did.

On a magical day, May 29, 2016, I had the opportunity to see and feel Uncle Matty's rifle for the very first time at the home of Brigadier General Patrick Collet in Paris. The General had discovered Matty's rifle in Normandy and managed to trace it back to our family and notify us. Monica and I had been dreaming of this day for over a month. I got to meet my hero, General Collet, and to hold, take apart, and contemplate Uncle Matty's rifle—the very arm he had in his hand when he was killed on D-Day. The wood of the stock was warm, the metal of the barrel cold in my hands. Holding so much history—my family's, my country's—overwhelmed me. It was a once-in-a-lifetime experience.

Thank you, Uncle Matty, for coming home in spirit as your rifle after all these many years.

Chapter 7
I OWE YOU BIG TIME, UNCLE MATTY

Uncle Matty and I both grew up on 138th Street in the South Bronx, went to Saint Jerome's Church, and attended Saint Jerome's School. His era was the 1930s; mine was the 1960s. To be a good Catholic, you were taught at Saint Jerome's to say your prayers at night, especially for anyone in your family who had passed away. I always thought this was a little weird, but I followed the tradition, maybe out of fear of getting in trouble with the priest and nuns who drilled this practice into us at a very young age. I said my prayers every night, but a secret I've kept to myself until now was who it was I prayed for. The very first time I said a bedtime prayer it was for Uncle Matty, and I have continued this prayer every day of my life. Over the years, my grandparents, mother and father, uncles, aunts, and others would be added to my prayer list, but Uncle Matty was the first and only one I have said a prayer for every night of my life. Uncle Matty and I have a special connection, maybe because we both left the Bronx and served in the Army. Whatever the reason for our connection may be, one Hail Mary and one Our Father is mighty nightly medicine.

I salute you, Uncle Matty! At Saint Jerome's School we were taught early on to pray for family members who had died. Believe you me, the nuns who taught us did not fool around! At the time, Uncle Matty was the only person I knew of who had died in my family, so I began to pray for him when I was very young. Thus began a tradition I continue to this day. Prayers to Matty have helped me handle some mighty tough situations!

One day in the summer of 1978, my father assigned me such an impossible task that I desperately prayed not *for* but *to* Uncle Matty, as if he were my personal patron saint. I can still remember saying, "Oh, my God, Matty—I need your help big time on this one." Call it divine intervention, dumb luck, whatever you want—this prayer helped me accomplish a feat that few people outside of our family believe I ever performed and most believe to be impossible. So just what was this Herculean task my father so imperiously assigned to me? To drive a car in reverse all the way from 184th Street and the Grand Concourse to 204th Street and Webster Avenue—a distance of about two miles—and this in the midst of daytime weekend traffic!

My father Mickey and Uncle Matty both grew up during the Great Depression, and nothing they had was ever wasted. Few people had automobiles back then, and those who did took such good care of them that they lasted forever. In my day, we drove more often but did not begin to drive until we went to college or started working. I myself learned to drive when I joined the Army. I was ordered to take a driving test in a jeep with a manual transmission, but I had never driven a stick shift. I ground the gears so badly that the instructor passed me on the test simply because he felt so sorry for me! Later I came to love driving a stick shift and especially enjoyed maneuvering in reverse with various army vehicles. My training included learning to go in reverse with a trailer hitched to my jeep—no easy feat. On a night-time training mission in 1975 at the Army Training Center in Yakima, Washington, we practiced going in reverse in pitch-dark desert conditions. Luckily for me, I excelled at these skills, because I later had to call on them big time when my father's old white Ford broke down.

My father would never get rid of a car. He would always have it fixed, no matter how old, no matter what part was *kaput.* If the shocks were going, he'd wait until they were completely shot. If the tires were going, he'd let them go bald. If the brakes were going, he'd squeeze another thousand miles out of them. His cars would have to be literally ready to explode before he would get rid of them. On one occasion when the brakes needed repair, my father was driving my sister Pat and cousin Noreen someplace around Yankee Stadium. He literally had to assist his deceleration down the hill at 161st Street by opening the door and sticking his foot out on the street to help slow the car. Poor Noreen was so traumatized that she never rode in a car with him again. She still tells me this story almost every time I see her. She laughs about it now, but you can hear in her voice how it affected her.

My father's mechanic was a charismatic guy from Ireland named Kevin, who had a repair shop on 204th Street and Webster Avenue. Many a time Mickey had his cars pushed, towed, or otherwise delivered by any means possible to Kevin's shop to be repaired. He would never give up until Kevin finally said in his heavy Irish brogue, "Martin, my friend, it is time for a new car."

During the summer of 1978, my father's old Ford was often on the blink. The car was actually my brother Jackie's, but my father paid for the repairs so he could get transported to his favorite drinking hole, McSherry's Pub on 138th Street and Alexander Avenue. And so it was one day, the old Ford would not drive forward. The transmission had gone bad. At the time I didn't know that a car with a bad transmission can still be driven in reverse—something my father knew all too well and was all too ready to enlighten me about. You may be getting a hint of where I'm going with this. Hang in there—it gets more interesting.

On the day in question, I overheard a conversation between my brother Jackie and my father, who was trying to get Jackie to drive the car in reverse from our apartment building on 184th and the Grand Concourse to Kevin's repair shop at 204th and Webster Avenue. They sounded like two Irish mobsters concocting a dumb scheme. Jackie was definitely the instigator in thinking this was a viable idea. *What the hell are they talking about?* I remember wondering to myself. *Why would anyone drive a car in reverse on the crazy streets in the Bronx? Surely, I must be dreaming.*

Jackie always had a way of not getting in trouble. Me, I always got caught. The next thing I knew, Jackie was making up some nonsense excuse that he had to be somewhere right away, so he could not take care of the task he'd so cleverly designed with my father. As he made his expedient exit, he uttered the fatal words that set me up: "Why don't you ask Jimmy?"

Oh, no! Mickey's not going to order me to do this, is he? Yes, you guessed it—this was not going to be good for me. My father came into the next room, where I quickly fell into a shammed sleep, but not even this could stop him from "asking" me to take the car to Kevin's. "Oh, yeah," he added as if it were an afterthought, "you can only drive it in reverse."

"Why would I need to do that?" I innocently asked. And so I was informed that the transmission was blown, but it would still drive in reverse, and Kevin could fix it. All I had to do was get it there. The pitch of my father's voice said: *You were in the Army—you can do this.* After Jackie had encouraged and then slickly ditched him, the tone of his message was: *I am not asking—just get this thing done.* Maybe I have too much deference for authority, or maybe I'm just plain dumb, but I said "OK." What the hell was I getting myself into? I was about to find out.

Now that it was established I was going to drive Mickey's car in reverse, he had two points to discuss with me. "Listen up," he said. "One, you have to make it past the Fordham Road underpass on the Grand Concourse. Once you see Poe Park, you're safe. That's the 52nd precinct." My father, you see, was a cop in the 52nd precinct, and these guys were like brothers to each other. "If you're caught in the 52nd, just mention my name, and they'll give you an escort to Kevin's," he said. This would be an easy favor for any of his brother officers. "If you get stopped before Poe Park, that's the 46th precinct. I don't know all the guys over there, so tell them to give me a call at McSherry's."

What!? I could only hope his second point made more sense. This was: "Here's a dollar for bus fare home. We'll drink some beer when you get back. Don't waste any time." *So, my fate is set on this one*, I said to myself. *Freaking Jackie, you did it to me again. Uncle Matty, help me!*

So here I go. The car is parked on Creston Avenue, just north of 184th Street, which runs parallel to the Grand Concourse. Mickey took the last spot before the water hydrant, so at least I have some room to back up. When I turn the ignition key, I'm hoping it won't start. No such luck—it starts up like a new car. I put it in reverse, left hand on the steering wheel, head and eyes turned toward the rear window, and down Creston Avenue I go to make a left onto 184th Street.

Driving a car in reverse is not a natural position. Your senses and motor actions are set up for driving forward, landmarks are pictured in your head that way, and the act of going left, right, forward, and back is deeply ingrained in your brain. Reverse is designed for very short distances, meant only to maneuver out of a specific area. For longer distances and in the normal flow of traffic, driving in reverse is abnormal, illegal, and something I'd never done before, except during Army training. Never did I think I'd be called upon to do it in civilian life.

But leave it to Mickey. Here I am, thinking in opposites—my right side is now my left. It's a Saturday morning around 9:00 am, so the traffic is not so bad. *Thank you, Uncle Matty! Stay with me!* I'm able to make the turn in reverse on 184th Street, and down the block I go to get on the Grand Concourse. Now a guy starts beeping his horn at me. "Are you crazy?" he yells out the open window. I ignore everything and just march on. I am viewing this like an assignment in the Army. Maybe I don't agree with it, but I'm going do my damnedest to succeed. So, I'm about fourth in line at the light at 184th and the Grand Concourse, waiting to make the left turn to head north. My good friend Joe sees me. "What the freak are you doing?" he asks, astonished. "Not now, Joe. Can't talk. See you later." I say. He looks at me puzzled, as if he were wondering if I were mad at him, and kind of throws his arms up. "Hey, dummy—you can't drive a car in reverse!" shouts some Irish lady sitting out on her fire escape. Everyone is staring at me. And now the moment of truth: the light turns green.

So I make the left and finally get going north in reverse in the express lane on the Grand Concourse. The local lane may be easier, but this is the 46th precinct, and there are always cops at Fordham Road and the Grand Concourse near the Army recruiting station, so express lane it is. I'd prepared and planned as best I could in the fifteen minutes I'd had to prepare before I undertook this suicide mission. I'm now driving about twenty miles an hour on the inside express lane, and the horns are honking. Some guy who sounds like he's stoned on pot yells, "Yo, man! Whaddya doin'?" Others shout worse. "You freaking, crazy nut!" "Pull over!" "I'm calling the cops!"

Ignore everything. That is my strategy. Laser-focused, I cruise past Lowe's Paradise, which is strangely on my right side while driving north. Strange because the Paradise is on the southbound side, so if you were driving north, normally, it would be on your left. Now driving at what I think of as the amazing speed of twenty-five miles an hour, I just miss the light at 187th and the Grand Concourse.

And so the wait begins. Now I really start to feel the stress. A cop on the beat is usually somewhere around here, especially at the newsstands and the entrance to the D train. At least I get to realign my head, neck, and eyes back to their normal positions. *Man, does that feel good!* There's no shortage of motorists at the light eager to drop a dime on me, and more of the same comments keep coming. *Focus on the mission*, I tell myself. *Thank you, Uncle Matty—so far, so good*, I pray.

If only I can get to the 52nd precinct, I can stop stressing out. Tick, tock, tick, tock. *C'mon light! I've been waiting for hours! Are you still with me, Uncle Matty?* Finally, the light turns green. It's back to left hand on the steering wheel, eyes, head, and neck turned to the rear-view window. I keep getting evil looks, honks, curses, and wisecracks. At this point, I'm almost immune.

"Here we go again" is a very popular Army cadence I've sung over and over in my head ever since basic training, especially when I'm trying to accomplish something difficult. It goes like this:

Here we go again,
Same old shit again,
Marching down the avenue,
A few more days, and we'll be through.

Anyone who's served in the Army knows this cadence by heart. I credit it along with Uncle Matty for helping me succeed in my Mission Impossible. At every step I managed to progress in reverse, I repeated in my head, *Here we go again.* The second part, *Same old shit again,* is the next thing I said in my head, as the comments kept raining down. The next part, *Marching down the avenue,* to me meant forward in reverse, heading north on the Grand Concourse. *A few more days, and we'll be through* became *A few more blocks and I'll be done.*

In one of the most rewarding moments of my life, I start down the Fordham Road underpass as fast as the car would go in reverse. I have to be going at least twenty-five miles an hour. I'm thinking, *At this point, no one can stop me until I'm in the 52nd precinct, and then I'm in the clear.* I pass the legendary Alexander's Department Store on the southbound side, and the Dime Savings Bank on the north side. I am cruising, baby, and feeling so good. All of a sudden, I'm out of the underpass, and the sweet sight of Poe Park is on my left. *I made it!* If I get stopped now, just like Mickey said, the 52nd brothers in blue will give me an escort. At this point, I start thinking, *I have to get smarter like Jackie and stop taking these risks.* Jackie loves telling all the family stories, but he's smart and stays out of the firing line. For the moment though, as long as I don't get into an accident, I'm miraculously in the clear. *Thank you, Uncle Matty!*

Now that I'm in friendly territory, my next objective is to get into the local lane. It's easier, and I'll need to make a right turn when I get to Mosholu Parkway in order to get to my destination on Webster Avenue. My thoughts now are how to approach the entrance to the local lane before I hit Kingsbridge Road. My Army training comes in handy, and I make a split-second decision. I gun it as fast as I can to get through an opening into the local lane. Any slower would cause a commotion and possibly an accident.

I go through that opening like a race-car driver. I'm in the zone, it's perfect, no swerving out of any lane. My cool maneuver does not go unnoticed. I get a few horn beeps with thumbs up, and a bus driver smiles with what I think is admiration. *Wow! I'm getting encouragement from motorists! Uncle Matty, you are one cool dude.*

Now I'm going almost as fast as the traffic flow. *This feels so damn good!* I'm proud of myself and feeling more confident that I'll make it to Kevin's garage. I have to stop at the light at Kingsbridge Road. *Too bad.* I'm feeling so great, I think I could drive in reverse forever. On the other hand, *What a relief!* Finally, another break for my neck, head, and eyes.

So here I am, smiling to myself at the light, and these two beautiful girls pull up next to me in a Volkswagen Beetle. They start laughing, saying, "You're crazy! Where the hell do you come from? We love you!" I'm stunned but laugh along with them all the same. *Is this what it takes to pick up girls?* I wonder. To them I say only, "My father made me do this." Oh, my God—did that make them laugh!

The light turns green, they smile at me, I smile at them, and off they go in forward, and off I go in reverse. My neck, head, and eyes turn back to the now-dreaded back window. I pass my grandmother's house on 196th Street, heading for the next critical point at Mosholu Parkway. I am really into this now and almost feel normal driving in reverse.

Here we go again, I sing in my head for the rest of the drive to Mosholu Parkway. I only recall thumbs up and shouts of encouragement from other drivers on the remaining stretch up the Grand Concourse. Don't get me wrong, I'm sure plenty of horn-blowing, cursing, and yelling was still going on—I just don't remember anything but the good stuff. This is a trait of mine that my wife calls "selective memory." By the time I get to Mosholu Parkway, I'm confident, singing, and happy, positive I will accomplish Mickey's mission. Right turn (for a demented nut driving in reverse) coming up on Mosholu Parkway? *No problem, perfect turn! Now, onward to Webster Avenue!*

My one thought at this time is, *Make this turn, and you're home free.* Kevin's repair shop is just up the road. *Oh, my God—what a sweet sight!* Now I see the shop. I'm about to cross home plate with the walk-off homer. Suddenly, I realize how many horns are blowing. I must have blocked them out for a while, but they're not about to stop me now. Luckily, Kevin's is on the northbound side, so one last easy turn, and into his shop I go. *Thank you, Uncle Matty! We did it! It's a miracle!*

You can imagine the reaction I got pulling into Kevin's garage. Everyone from the turn on Mosholu Parkway was watching. Apparently all the horns and yelling tipped Kevin off that I was coming in. He met me with a puzzled look, but he was laughing. His Irish brogue was so heavy it was hard to make out his words. "Lad," he asked, "where did you come from?" When I told him I'd driven in reverse from 184th Street and my father made me do it, he laughed as hard as he could for what seemed like an hour. At first he did not believe me, but I guess after knowing my father for all those years, he finally came to the conclusion I was telling the truth. Finally Kevin said, "Give me the keys. I will have a look at it. Dear Lord, your dad is crazy."

I don't know how I looked to Kevin, but I could sense he was concerned, and it seemed like he even felt sorry for me. "Come on in for a drink—you look like you really need one," he said. *What does he mean? It's 10:00 in the morning and I look like I need a drink? Do I really look that pitiful?* "Let me get you some good Irish whiskey I have in the office," he said. I was mostly a beer drinker. I rarely ever drank whiskey, but I'd just spent about 45 minutes driving in reverse, looking mostly out the back window, never thinking about what this would do to my neck muscles. This is not the way neck muscles are meant to be used, and when I got out of that car, my neck was killing me. At that moment, I realized this was the price I was going to pay for this mission. I took Kevin up on his offer. That Irish whiskey was probably the best drink I ever had in my life. It was so strong that it even, momentarily, helped me forget the pain in my neck.

Kevin did not want to let me go. He said to hang around and help myself to his whiskey, and he would drive me home when he closed up. I was way too fired up on adrenalin to hang around, so I told him thanks, but I had to get going. I don't know if this was a good decision, but I decided to walk home, partly to save the dollar bus fare, but also to try to walk off the pain.

The walk home took a little longer than two hours. This was not a problem; I used to walk everywhere. I kept replaying in my head the crazy stunt I'd just pulled, laughing and wincing from neck pain both at once. *That was crazy, but fun*, and *I am going to kill Jackie* were the main thoughts floating in my mind. I probably should have stayed at Kevin's and drunk his whiskey. From what I can remember, I got back a little after 1:00 pm. I recall Jackie standing across the street outside the White Heather Pub, laughing and calling out to me, *Jimmy, Jimmy, Jimmy!* I ignored him. I already had a pain in the neck, and Jackie would just be another one. What I really needed was some aspirin and a warm bath.

My father was still drinking with his buddies at McSherry's and had no idea if I'd been successful. This is the place he'd said to call if the cops in the 46th precinct stopped me. Fortunately, I never had to learn how that one would play out. If I told you how much beer my father drank every day, you would not believe me. He'd been shot out of the sky in World War II and served nine months as a prisoner of war, so this was his way of escaping.

Jackie came home from the pub across the street and sat on my bed, laughing, trying to pry every single detail out of me as I lay there with my painful stiff neck. Jackie was going crazy about it, asking me the same questions over and over again. I could not get him to leave me alone. I yelled and cursed, but he just went on nonstop. "Tell me more! Tell me again!" He was like a reporter on a breaking story.

Finally, my father got home. "Did you get the car to Kevin's?" he asked in an undramatic tone. I told him I did, but he'd have to ask Jackie for the details. It did bring a chuckle to him, and I think for a moment he was proud of what I'd done, a rare emotion he never showed to anyone. Mickey decided we should have some beer to celebrate, and wise guy Jackie egged him on. The only thing I wanted was to rest my stiff neck, but I wound up drinking with Jackie and Mickey until all of us drank ourselves to sleep.

Waking up the next day was a painful experience. Eventually the pain in my neck went away, but the memory of it stayed forever. I don't tell this story very often, but Jackie tells it all the time. No family function ever goes by that he doesn't tell it again. It's a good thing he asked all those questions—I needed his help to write this all down. Once again, Jackie proved to be the smarter one, staying out of trouble, but getting all the enjoyment of telling the story.

The marching song "Here we go again" still plays in my head sometimes, and I'll always remember how it helped me drive the old white Ford to Kevin's in reverse. I also believe Uncle Matty answered my prayers that day and was pivotal to the success of my mission. Or perhaps I inherited some of his cunning paratrooper instincts. I like to think it was a little of both.

Chapter 8
BEYOND DYING—KILLED IN ACTION

Accoring to a well-known saying, "Death and taxes are the only two things certain in life." We all have to learn how to cope with the death of family members, friends, and loved ones. Some of us learn very early in life; the lucky ones learn much later.

Of course, there are many kinds and causes of death—accidents, diseases such as cancer, and the natural course of old age, for example. Such deaths are always difficult to come to terms with emotionally for the loved one's survivors, but in the vast majority of cases, we pass through the various stages of grief, cherish the memories of the loved one in our hearts, and eventually move on with our lives. The emotional shock and grief that result when a loved one is killed in action are different. The feelings, the trauma are so intense that they occur on a whole different plane.

It has been my experience so far that families, especially those members closest to the deceased—mothers, fathers, spouses, brothers, and sisters—never get over the death of loved ones killed in action. I have seen it in my grandmother, my mother, my aunts, my Uncle Jimmy, and in the Gold Star Mothers I have met in

Seventy-three years after he was killed in action, Uncle Matty's legend lives on! Connor Regina proudly points to his great-great uncle's name at Saint Jerome's Church in the South Bronx on June 4, 2017, at the first annual Martin Teahan Mass. This is the plaque to the parish war dead that prompted me to learn more about Uncle Matty and the circumstances of his death in Normandy.

the course of writing this book. Whole lives are destroyed, and survivors become totally consumed for the rest of their days with honoring the loved one who was killed in action. They become fixated on getting answers to unanswerable questions: the details of when, where, why, who, and how, or chasing down conspiracy theories—and the list goes on.

Sometimes, too, that fixation is passed down to the next generation, as my mother's and grandmother's grief was passed to my sister Liz and, in a certain measure, to me as well. Why else would Uncle Matty be the first and only person I have prayed for every night of my life since childhood? Thus, the reason I am writing this chapter: To try to convey—if even just a glimmer—what it is like for a family to be notified that a loved one has been killed in action, and the effects or repercussions this death can have as it ripples through not only one but often two or even more successive generations.

My most marked experience of the death of a loved one occurred when I was an adolescent. It was a very spooky one and remains the most haunting still. This was the death of my paternal grandmother, Elizabeth Farrell, whom we called "Nannie." She passed away on February 8, 1971, when I was just fourteen. The spooky part was that she was waked in her house in Brooklyn. Right there, smack in the living room, was her casket. And her body was in it!

Although the practice is no longer allowed, from what I understand, it was not unusual back in the day to be waked in your home. As a kid, all I could think of that day was my dead grandmother's body in the next room, while everyone congregated in the kitchen of her house. Talk about being spooked out! It felt like a ghost was watching me. My father's brother, Uncle Phil, must have noticed I was white as a sheet. He came over to talk to me and try to make me feel better.

At this point, Uncle Phil asked if I'd ever had a drink of alcohol. I told him I had not. Then Phil said, "Now's the time for your first drink. Do you like orange juice?" Of course, I did, and he proceeded to pour me a tall glass of comfort consisting of 75 percent vodka and 25 percent orange juice. "Drink up!" he said, lifting his glass. Who was I to question? So I drank it down.

At the time, it was not all that surprising in Irish-American families that a fourteen-year-old kid would have a drink at a wake. I noticed that my brother Jackie, who was a year and a half older than me, had a drink in his hand, too. Uncle Phil was right about one thing—that drink was so strong that I forgot about my grandmother's dead body for a while. He stayed with me until I finished it; I could tell that he wanted me to drink up fast, which I did. "Do you want another?" he asked. "No," I said, feeling dizzy. I was afraid I'd pass out if I drank another one.

Most of the adults were drinking quite a bit—again, not uncommon in Irish-American families at the time. Although the vodka did temporarily divert my attention, the spooky feelings came back. Thinking back now, I can remember only that I could not look into the other room, there, where Nannie's body lay, and so I left to wait outside. I will never forget the huge rush of relief I felt when the rest of the family emerged from the house and we finally left. This spooky experience haunted me for many years, and to this day, I have never forgotten it.

Nannie's wake was not my first experience of the death of a loved one. This occurred in 1968, when I was eleven years old. My uncle Jimmy, whom I was named after, died on Christmas Day. He was waked at Walter B. Cooke funeral home on Jerome Avenue, just north of Fordham Road in the Bronx. My maternal grandmother, Maime, took his death very hard. "First my Matty, now my Jimmy!" she screamed. "I can't take it!" Her tears seemed to flow in an unending stream as she hugged and kissed Uncle Jimmy right in his coffin in front of everyone. Even as a child, I could feel she was going through a terrible emotional shock, and I absorbed her pain. This was her second son to die, and in the natural course of life, it is not supposed to happen this way.

In 1976, I was stationed with the U.S. Army in Camp Ames, Korea, serving as a Military Policeman. Our function was to man the guard towers surrounding the storage of missiles and other offensive weapons. Just as it is today, North Korea was then an unstable regime, and we were there to protect South Korea and the interest of the United States. Our work schedule often demanded three full consecutive days of manning the towers. Platoons took shifts on the towers but had down time on guardhouse duty, where we could catch up on sleep, but were still on call for duty on the towers. One particular early afternoon when my platoon was off duty, goofing off on base with not much of a care in the world, the company officers came running though our housing yelling, "Quick! Stop what you're doing! Get dressed for duty, ASAP!"

We immediately understood that something terribly wrong had happened. We quickly complied, dressed, got our weapons, and took over for the on-duty platoon. My fellow platoon members and I went up in the towers, covering all of them with the exception of one. We could see many of our officers congregated at this particular tower, but we had no idea what was going on.

Not until the end of our shift did we find out what had happened. A friend of mine in the original on-duty platoon had gone on guard duty that day and climbed up his tower with his rifle and equipment. When he got to the top, he put his M-16 in his mouth and pulled the trigger. Even if you have never seen what an M-16 bullet can do, you still can probably well imagine the effect.

My friend blew his brains out in the tower that day. We were all in shock, often speechless. The investigation was quick: All of us in the 110th MP Company were interviewed for any scrap of information about why our brother soldier had decided to end his life. Afterwards, the Army provided counseling to help us cope with the sudden death of our comrade. We never did find out why he committed suicide; all we knew was that he had family problems back home and was depressed. None of us had seen him as depressed—I guess he hid it well. This was my first experience with the traumatic, sudden death of a friend. After a while, the pain went away, but the experience of writing about it now, for the first time, has brought that pain to the fore again.

I've written here about some of my experiences of coping with death, both from natural causes due to age and from out-of-the blue, traumatic events. At some point in our lifetime, we all experience the death of people we know—and deal with it, for better or worse. But my research into Uncle Matty's history and the process of writing this book has left me with a puzzling thought. How does someone cope with receiving a notice that a loved one has been killed in action?

Uncle Matty was deployed in combat, and I am certain that my family knew that he was engaged in a dangerous mission. But how do you prepare for a telegram that tells you that your son or your brother was killed in action? I don't think it's possible. Even if you are a person who always expects the worst to happen, receiving a letter from the War Department has to be one of the most dreadful things that can ever happen in the course of civilian life.

On July 29, 1944, this is exactly what happened to the Teahan family. My Uncle Jimmy received the letter and had to tell his mom and the rest of the family. Previously, it had also been Uncle Jimmy who answered the knock on the door when the official telegram informing us of Matty's death arrived. Our family still has that terrible telegram and the official letter that followed. No matter how many times I've read that letter, I always get emotional. It was signed by the founder of the 508th Parachute Infantry Regiment, Colonel Roy E. Lindquist. This, for me, is particularly important, as I have read that Colonel Lindquist and his 508th commanders hand-picked all of the initial recruits to the regiment. They wanted the best of the best, and apparently Colonel Lindquist saw that in Uncle Matty.

This is the text of the letter my grandmother received:

Headquarters 508th Parachute Infantry
APO 230, US Army

Pvt Martin J Teahan 12155370   *29 July 1944*

Mrs. Nora Teahan
435 E 138th St.
New York, N.Y.

My Dear Mrs. Teahan:

You have been informed of the death of your son, Pvt. Martin J. Teahan, who died in action in Normandy, France during our invasion of the Continent. No words can adequately express our feelings of sympathy with you in your loss. I can only impart to you as a partial consolation the fact that your son died as a soldier, a hero, performing his duty as only a paratrooper can for his regiment and his country. It will comfort you to know that every soldier of this regiment while in England and France was able to attend regularly the religious services of his own faith, and those we lost were buried by a minister representing their own church.

This regiment has been awarded the Presidential Citation for "Extraordinary heroism and outstanding performance of duty in action against the enemy in Normandy, France 6 June 1944." In every engagement thereafter, the members of the regiment, without exception, conducted themselves in such manner that our battle accomplishments will go down in military history as outstanding and extraordinary. In your sorrow you can also be proud of his participation and performance as a soldier.

It was inevitable that many of the fine men of this regiment were to pay with their lives for our successes and accomplishments. Only fighting soldiers such as your son could have made possible the breaching and penetration of the continental defenses. Those who gave so much were memorialized in a service here on 28 July. A copy of our memorial service program is enclosed.

I am not permitted at this time to give you the information I know you wish, or to disclose the exact burial place. At some future time, the War Department will send this information to you. In the meantime, your son's personal effects, including military decorations, will be sent to you. If you desire any further information regarding his military affairs, I suggest you write direct to the War Department.

In closing, may I reiterate that the regiment most sincerely joins you in the sorrow of your recent bereavement. If I can be of any assistance to you in the future, please feel free to write to me.

Sincerely yours,

Roy E. Lindquist,
Colonel, Infantry

I can only imagine the shock, sorrow, and overwhelming sadness my grandmother, Uncle Jimmy, Aunt Francie, and my mother experienced. To make matters worse, the notifications and burial were confusing, and information took a long time to arrive, greatly adding to the family's grief. In July 1944, some of Uncle Matty's personal items were mailed home to my grandmother at 435 E. 138th Street, Bronx, N.Y. This included his dog tags, lighter, parachute pin, and souvenir coins.

Not until a year later did my grandmother receive the following letter, informing her that additional personal items were being mailed:

RTB: WN:vw

193326   *September 25, 1945*

Mrs. Nora Teahan
435 East 138th Street
New York, New York

Dear Mrs. Teahan:
    The Army Effects Bureau has received some additional property of your son, Private Martin J. Teahan.
    The effects, contained in one carton, are being forwarded to you. If delivery is not made within thirty days from this date, please notify me so that tracer action may be instituted.
    As previously indicated, personal property is transmitted by this Bureau for distribution according to the laws of the state of the soldier's legal residence.

Sincerely yours,

P.L. Koob
1st Lt., QMC
Officer-in-Charge
SJ Branch

I can only begin to imagine the sadness and confusion our family felt each time one of these letters appeared. There were many other letters relating to the burial, some of which I see my grandmother just ignored. These letters refer to previous letters, stating there has been no response. Eventually, the box of Uncle Matty's personal effects arrived. This is the official list of its contents:

3-backgrounds
1-rosary
1-Fame ribbon
1–1/2pence
1-cup
1-mouth organ
1-cigarette case
1-spoon
1-wallet
1-belt
18-snapshots
8-negatives

Today, many Americans have become spoiled and complain about the most mundane things. Writing my Uncle Matty's story has made me realize that most people I know, and I, myself, have very little to complain about. Truly we are blessed and living the good life in ways that our forebears never could have imagined, even in their dreams.

PART TWO

UNCLE MATTY'S WAR: D-DAY, NORMANDY THE 508TH PARACHUTE INFANTRY REGIMENTIN COMBAT

Chapter 9
THE PARACHUTIST'S CREED

*A*lso called the Airborne Creed or the Paratrooper's Creed, the vow below has evolved over time, but the core values, beliefs, standards, and pride of the airborne soldier this early version expresses remain unchanged in all the variations I have encountered. I believe the creed as it here appears to be the official creed used in World War II, and the vow that Uncle Matty and all his early airborne brothers-in-arms would have known and pledged to follow.

I volunteered as a paratrooper, fully realizing the hazards of my chosen service; and by my actions will always uphold the prestige, honor, and rich esprit-de-corps of the only volunteer branch of the Army.

I realize that a paratrooper is not merely a soldier who arrives by parachute to fight, but an elite shock trooper, and that his country expects him to march further and faster, to fight harder, to be more self-reliant and to soldier better than any other soldier. Paratroopers of all Allied armies belong to this great brotherhood.

I shall never fail my fellow comrades by shirking any duty or training, but will always keep myself mentally and physically fit and shoulder my full share of the task, whatever it may be.

I shall always accord my superiors my fullest loyalty and I will always bear in mind the sacred trust I have in the lives of the men I will lead into battle.

I shall show other soldiers, by my military courtesy to my superior officers and noncommissioned officers, by my neatness in dress, by my care for my weapons and equipment, that I am a picked and well-trained soldier.

I shall endeavor by my soldierly appearance, military bearing and behavior, to reflect the high standards of training and morale of paratroopers.

I shall respect the abilities of my enemies, I will fight fairly and with all my might. Surrender is not in my creed.

I shall display a higher degree of initiative than is required of the other troops and will fight on to my objective and mission, though I be the lone survivor.

I will prove my ability as a fighting man against the enemy on the field of battle, not by quarreling with my comrades in arms or by bragging about my deeds, thus needlessly arousing jealousy and resentment against paratroopers.

I shall always realize that battles are won by an army fighting as a team, that I fight and blaze a path into battle for others to follow and carry the battle on.

I belong to the finest unit in the Army. By my appearance, actions, and battlefield deeds alone, I speak for my fighting ability. I will strive to uphold the honor and prestige of my outfit, making my country proud of me and the unit to which I belong.

XVIII Airborne Corps
Airborne Procurement
Fort Bragg, North Carolina
"Home of the Airborne"

Chapter 10
MY NORMANDY INVASION EXPERIENCE
by O.B. Hill

*N*o one has done more for paratroopers and their families than O.B. Hill, the founder of the Family and Friends of the 508th PIR Association. A legendary 508th World War II paratrooper himself, O.B. served as 1st Battalion Message Center Chief in Headquarters Company, where Uncle Matty also worked in communications. On his many visits to Normandy after the war, O.B. faithfully visited the gravesides of his fallen 508th comrades, including his friends Matty and their Commanding Officer, Captain Gerard Ruddy, who was killed jumping into Normandy. It was on one of these visits to the American Cemetery at Collville-Sur-Mer that O.B. so famously heard his Captain's call to "do something to get the men together." As we all know, O.B. heeded that call, ever "present and ready for duty."*

O.B. Hill passed away in June 2002 after leading a very full life dedicated to the service of others. His magnificent legacy to us and future generations includes "My Normandy Experience," his vivid account of the first three days of brutal fighting in the infamous "Hell's Half Acre." Never published in its author's lifetime, O.B.'s riveting account is now available on the 508th Association website. I thank O.B.'s son, Joe Hill, for the great pleasure and privilege of publishing it here in print for the first time.

Prior to the jump into Normandy, my battalion was at Folkingham Air Strip in the Midlands of England. As I remember, we were there about five days preparing for the invasion. Before that, we did not know when or where we would be involved in combat.

At Folkingham, we studied sand tables prepared by our intelligence crew, known as S-2 people. The buildings, fence rows, hedgerows, rivers, and other features on the table gave us a good view of the area where we were to land. We also spent our time packing equipment bundles, cleaning our rifles, playing cards, shooting dice, attending movies in the hangar building, going to church services, and writing letters. The area was secured, and no one was permitted to leave for any purpose. We were fully ready to take off on June 4, but the weather forced a delay. Finally, we blackened our faces and loaded into the planes on the evening of June 5.

Every man was fully loaded with everything he thought he might need. We were taking

Uncle Matty's good friend and a true World War II hero, O.B. Hill, has a street named in his honor at Beuzeville-la-Bastille, which he fought to liberate on June 6. O.B. and Matty both served in Headquarters Company, 1st Battalion, 508th PIR; their company commander, Captain Gerard A. Ruddy, was killed on the D-Day jump. The idea to start the Family and Friends of the 508th PIR Association first came to O.B.'s mind at the grave of his beloved Captain Ruddy in the American Cemetery above Omaha Beach. He founded the Association in 1975 and served as its Chairman until his death in June 2002. *Photo courtesy of Joe Hill, son of O.B. Hill.*

rations and ammunition for three days. There was ample ammunition, so many of us took several bandoliers over the allotted amount. This proved to be a worthwhile move. Most of us landed far from our scheduled drop zones and were behind German lines for days before we got back to our unit. We also carried land mines, Gammon grenades, hand grenades, maps, radios, smoke grenades, phosphorous grenades, and much more.

I was the 1st Battalion Message Center Chief, with a rank of Buck Sergeant. Normally I would have jumped behind my company commander, Captain Gerard A. Ruddy, but he and my platoon leader, 1st Lieutenant Charles J. McElligott, were very good friends. McElligott wanted to jump behind Ruddy, and so I traded places with McElligott and was the last man to leave our plane. This proved to be a lucky break for me, because Captain Ruddy was killed almost immediately after landing, McElligott was shot through the stomach and captured, and all but the last four of us in that plane were either killed or captured.*

We left Folkingham on June 5 at about 9:30 pm. To be honest, this is a pure guess. At the moment, I was not wondering about the time. Many of us left our reserve chute, Mae West vest, gas mask contents, and rifle case in England. We were still carrying far too much equipment and had to have help getting up the steps to the plane. Finally, we were all aboard. We flew around for about four hours, getting into formation, and could see the planes going in all directions.

At last we were on our way to Normandy. As our formation was crossing over the Guernsey Islands in the English Channel, flak started exploding in the air around us. By this time, we were standing; we had hooked up and checked our equipment and were waiting for the green light, our signal to jump. When we hit the French coast, much more flak showed up, and the formation hit some clouds. The planes started veering right and left in order not to bump into each other. When the green light came on, we were out of the door in a few seconds. The combination of flak, clouds, and the fact that our pilots were making their first combat flight was at least part of the reason for our biggest problem after jumping: we did not know we were not over our drop zones.

On the way down, we received machine gun and rifle fire, and it looked quite bad. My chute opened with a very hard jerk. The extra weight made the opening shock quite rough. I looked up to check my chute and saw numerous holes from small-arms fire. I looked down and saw tracers coming up at me. Instinct caused me to raise my feet, but I quickly put them back down again to get in position for landing. We were not very high for the jump, but it seemed forever before I reached the ground.

I could see I was going to land in water. I figured that this must be the Merderet, because that was the river closest to where we were supposed to land. Later I learned it was the Douve, and I was miles from the proper drop zone. I'd left my gas mask in England but had filled the case with cigarettes. It was rubber, so I figured it would keep my cigarettes dry if I landed in the water. Some of the machine gun fire hit the case and ripped it open, causing me to spin around. I then figured if I landed in the river, I wouldn't be able to get out of my chute and all my equipment before I drowned. I did land in the water, but it was only waist-deep. They were still shooting at me, so I went back down under and stuck my nose out just enough to breathe. I remained in that position for some time after the shooting stopped. When I stood up again, there was no firing, so I started toward dry land. After organizing all my gear, checking my rifle, and getting out of my chute harness, I headed away from the water.

It was quite dark. I could hear lots of action. There was a lot of fire at the planes, which seemed to be coming from all directions around me. I kept walking in what I assumed to be the right direction. Our objective was to secure the area and prevent the Germans from reinforcing their beach troops. The 508th was to destroy some bridges in the area, and we prevented many Germans from retreating from the beaches.

As I was making my way, I heard the sound of men walking to my left. I didn't know if they were enemy or friendly, so I stopped and lay flat on the ground. I then realized I was at the edge of a ditch about four or five feet deep. The men were walking in the ditch toward me. I remained very quiet. I was sure they could hear my heart pounding, but they did not. There were about twenty-five of them. At the end of the column, one of the men spoke to another in German. I could have reached out and touched their helmets as they passed.

I jumped the ditch and was continuing down a path when, suddenly, someone said, *FLASH!* I said, *OH, SHIT!* This was not proper password. I had completely forgotten it! Lucky for me, the challenger was one of my corporals, William P. Brown from Detroit. We compared notes and decided we must be going in the right direction, and so continued on the path.

We soon discovered we were not the only troopers who'd been dropped in the wrong place. Along the way, we picked up men from the 505, the 508, and even two from the 101st Division, who were many miles from their drop zone near Carentan. We met our first resistance at the first crossroad, where we engaged in a fierce fire-fight. My guess is that it lasted about twenty minutes. We eliminated this problem but were challenged again before we reached one of the main roads. This time, we were seriously outnumbered. The only explanation for why we came out ahead is that we were more determined and perhaps better trained.

The memory of that experience will stay with me forever. It was our first experience, and it was not good. Along the way, we lost some of our men. We had been trained for this, but nothing can prepare you for seeing friends and comrades falling around you. We also had some wounded, but they were able to keep up. We had no medics, but we each had a first-aid kit, and we all took turns treating the wounded.

I guess it was about 10:00 a.m. when we arrived at a village we later learned was Beuzeville. Across the river was the village of Beuzeville-la-Bastille. We were going down one side of a road when we discovered S/Sgt. Ray Hummel was on the opposite side. There were some houses on his side and two buildings on ours, both of which had German troops in them. We went to the one on our right to secure it. We encountered only a few Germans in it, and we assumed that our troops now occupied the other building. I attempted to cross the bridge and was immediately met with artillery fire from the opposite side of the river. The explosion blew me off the road and into the ditch. It also discouraged me from making another attempt.

I returned to my group, and we crossed the road to join forces with S/Sgt. Hummel. At this point, Melvin Beets said he'd go get the rest of the troops from the other building. It was filled with Germans. Mel was captured, but he later escaped and got back to the company.

S/Sgt. Hummel and I compared notes. Together, we had about fifty-two men and had lost about twenty-five. Our best guess was that we had twenty-six still able to fight. We'd secured ammunition from all the men we'd lost, and, at the time, we were in fair condition. We had no heavy weapons, no officers, no medics, no radios, and we were not sure where we were. We could see where the two rivers came together and decided that the village must be Beuzeville. We were surrounded on two sides by floodwaters from the rivers. We knew there were numerous Germans at the crossroad just ahead, so we decided to go to a higher spot to try to see our surroundings.

We were behind a house. I knocked on the door but got no response. I then shot the lock off and discovered people were inside. The mother was just about to open the door when I'd shot the lock off. They were badly scared but did not interfere and seemed glad to see us. Hummel and I went up the stairs, followed by Jim McMahon, who waited at the top to notify us of any action from below. Hummel and I went to two large windows at the front and looked in all directions for signs or any other things that might help us, but we saw nothing to aid our escape.

At this point we heard tanks approaching from the bridge I had earlier tried to cross. One passed the building, and the second stopped immediately under the window where Ray was standing. The turret opened, and a German stood up to look around. I handed Ray a Gammon grenade. He dropped it in front of the man in the turret and knocked the tank out of action. The other two tankers tried to figure out what had hit them, but didn't see either of us at the window. We left the building and rejoined the men in the fields behind the houses. With no heavy weapons, we couldn't have stopped the tanks if they had pursued us. An M-1 rifle will not stop a tank.

We soon learned that we could cross neither the river to our west nor the floodwaters south of us. There were machine guns in both directions, plus the .88 across the river that had knocked me into the ditch. Our only hope was to move east across the hedgerows. We had a 101st man shot through the stomach. We didn't think he could do much hedgerow jumping, so we gave him a supply of morphine and some sulfa powder and promised to send him help if at all possible. We placed him in one of the outbuildings and started across the fields and crossroads.

Hedgerows are not easy to cross. Plainly visible from the road, we jumped across, two men at a time, while the others kept watch for resistance from the road at each field. Everything went fairly well until we made it to the next road. This, we found, was one of our objectives, the causeway going into Chef du Pont. We were now sure we had gone the right direction after landing in the water. There was firing around us in all directions. The battles sounded quite fierce, but, for the time being, it was quiet in our area, for which we were thankful. We quickly learned to distinguish the sound of German guns from our own.

We were in this last field only a short time when we were again pinned down by German fire. Hummel and I had the men spread out along the two hedgerows. The rows faced in opposite directions, so we were protected regardless of where the Germans hit us. During pauses in the firing, we dug foxholes along the edges.

Hummel and I were on the north side, closest to the road. There were a barn and a barn lot in front of us and a two-story house on the corner, occupied by Germans. We fired on it in force. As long as they were in that house, we could go no further. In the middle of the firefight, an American voice yelled out for us to stop shooting. Some of our men were being held prisoner, and if we didn't stop, the Germans would kill them.

We stopped firing at the house but were still being fired at from the road. August Labate was killed by a burst from a machine pistol. Our ammunition was rapidly disappearing. If we hadn't taken the extra supply from the airfield and the ammunition from those who'd been killed, our supply would already have run out. Hummel and I discussed the problem and decided to ask the other men if they wanted to surrender or stay until the end. Every man said the same thing: *We have come this far, and we don't intend to give up now!* There would be no surrendering from this group.

After the war, I met the Cotell family, who lived in the corner house where the Germans were holding our prisoners. Their son Pierre was fourteen at the time, and over the years we've become close friends. One day, I had lunch with his mother and learned through an interpreter that I had almost killed her! During a lull in the fighting, I'd seen a few Germans in the farmyard. I threw a hand grenade up in the air, hoping to get them about the time it hit the ground. It was still in the air when they walked behind the barn, and a lady appeared from the opposite end! I was sure she would be killed, but fortunately, she wasn't even injured. I asked Mme Cotell if she was scared when that grenade went off, and she replied that she'd had to change her skivvies! She proved to be as much of a joker as her son Pierre. As of this writing, I've enjoyed their friendship for several years.

Going into our ordeal on June 6, we had about fifty-two men. We lost half of them along the way, and others were wounded. We were pinned down in that field for five days, frequently challenged by the Germans, but we proved to be a stubborn group and held our ground against every attempt to get us out. Ray Hummel and I agree we did quite well with what we had. Our crew was from a variety of units; we had little equipment, no medics, officers, or heavy weapons, and no chance of being supplied with ammunition for our small arms. We did, however, slow down the retreat of enemy from the beaches, kept reinforcements from advancing past our corner, and certainly caused problems for those opposing us. In *Night Drop*, S.L.A. Marshall refers to us as "a pack of strays." I suppose that's a good description of our group. In my opinion, our crew from various units is a good example of Airborne Spirit.

Many other things happened during those five days behind German lines. The 101st man who'd been shot through the stomach and left behind came into our field. We continued to give him sulfa powder and morphine. C.P. Reynolds was shot in the head but didn't know he'd been hit until he took off his helmet and wool knit cap. We treated him, too. George DeCarvalho was hit in the ankle by a German rifle grenade. The grenade didn't explode, but it did severe damage to his ankle. Hummel buried Labate where he'd been killed. One night we were visited by a Frenchman. He brought us some cheese, bread, and wine, and told us how many Germans were around us and where they were located. He risked his life doing this. We nearly killed him ourselves.

By the late afternoon of the fifth day, we were practically out of ammunition. A lot of firing was coming from the causeway into Chef du Pont. It was getting closer all the time, and that promised to be help for us. It kept approaching, and finally we knew for sure that it was some unit from our own Army. The first words we heard were the orders of a Master Sergeant from the 90th Division: *Bring up that dammed bazooka!* At this, we all stood up and cheered. He yelled for us to get back down, which we did. Remarkably, none of us were shot. The Germans were now running from our corner, and we had been found by friendly forces.

The Master Sergeant got our wounded on their way back to an aid station and sent our one prisoner back to a POW compound. He gave us a guide to get us through the minefields, and we then headed back on our way to the unit.

When we arrived, we learned that our battalion commander, Lieutenant Colonel Batcheller, had been killed. My plane had been hit hard, too. Captain Ruddy was killed, Lieutenant McElligott shot through the stomach and captured, First Sergeant Earl Smith was killed. First Lieutenant Abbott [81mm mortar platoon leader] and many others from my platoon were killed. This was a severe shock to all of us who'd just returned. I cannot explain the feeling I had that day. We'd seen many killed along the way, but these men were very close friends. Captain Ruddy was a great platoon leader and the finest man I had ever met. All of his men would have followed him through the fires of Hell. McElligott was a very good man and a good friend, and all the others from the platoon were top-notch. I felt very sorry for all of them and their families.**

Those of us who had been in that field still refer to it as *Hell's Half Acre*. It most certainly did qualify as Hell. I still feel very close to those of us who survived those five days. I feel closer to them than I would if I had brothers. They are a special breed. They were Airborne. They became full-grown men in the first few minutes of our experience in that field. I will always remember everything that happened during my first five days in Normandy.

*Captain Gerard A. Ruddy, Company Commander, 1st Bn 508th PIR HQ. KIA June 6, 1944.
First Lieutenant Charles J. McElligott, 1st Bn 508th PIR HQ. WIA, POW, June 6, 1944. Died May 27, 1994.
PFC William P. Brown, 1st Bn 508th PIR HQ. WIA Oct 5, 1944. Died April 21, 1998.
Pvt. Melvin Beets, 1st Bn 508th PIR HQ. WIA/POW, June 6, 1944. Died June 16, 2001.

S/Sgt Raymond J. Hummel, 1st Bn 508th PIR HQ. WIA Sept 17, 1944. Died November 14, 2001.

Cpl. Jim McMahon, 1st Bn 508th PIR HQ. Died March 7, 2006.

PFC August D. Labate, 1st Bn 508th PIR HQ. KIA June 7, 1944.

PFC C.P. Reynolds, 1st Bn 508th PIR HQ. WIA Dec 1944 and Jan 1945. Died July 10, 1961.

PFC George DeCarvalho, 1st Bn 508th PIR HQ. WIA June 6, 1944. Died April 25, 1994.

T/5 Andrew H. Hritzko, 1st Bn 508th PIR HQ. Died June 6, 1944.

Sgt. Joseph F. Gagnon, 1st Bn 508th PIR HQ. POW June 6, 1944. Died Dec 15, 1972.

Cpl. John J. Marshall, 1st Bn 508th PIR HQ. POW June 6, 1944. Died Mar 2, 2009.

Sgt. Earl J. Smith, 1st Bn 508th PIR HQ. Died June 6, 1944.

PFC Arthur B. Jacoby, 1st Bn 508th PIR HQ. Still living.

Pvt. Garfield Wilkinson, 1st Bn 508th PIR HQ. WIA January 8, 1945. Died Jan 15, 2003.

T/5 Robert A. Marchese, 1st Bn 508th PIR HQ. WIA June 8, 1944. Died Dec 1977.

Pvt. Otis Eugene Hull, 1st Bn 508th PIR HQ. Severely wounded in action (SWIA) June 6, 1944, Evacuated (EVAC) July 3, 1944. Died January 30, 2000.

PFC David M. Jones, 1st Bn 508th PIR HQ. WIA July 3, 1944. Died Oct 9, 2004.

T/4 Owen B. Hill 1st Bn 508th PIR HQ. WIA June 6, 1944 and January 25, 1945. Died June 10, 2002.

**McElligott survived the war, and we remained friends until his death in 1996. I always thanked him for trading places with me. Mel Beets [d. 2001] attended many of our reunions and made the trip back to Europe for the 50th anniversary of D-Day.

Chapter 11

A CONVERSATION WITH ROCK MERRITT, "MR. 508TH"

A legendary 82nd Airborne paratrooper, Rock Merritt, fondly referred
to as "Mr. 508th," served in World War II, Korea, and Vietnam.
While retirement after thirty years was mandatory at the time, he retired
after thirty-five years of service, one of only five Command Sergeant Majors
who had ever been selected to serve beyond the terms of retirement. Rock
was nominated as Sergeant Major of the Army in 1963, 1970, and 1973.
He served twice for a position he created, the Command Sergeant Major
of the XVIII Airborne Corps, made more than two hundred parachute
jumps, was awarded the Bronze and Silver Stars, and received numerous
other distinctions and awards. When you meet him, there is no question
you are in the presence of someone special.

On D-Day and throughout 1944, Rock served in the same platoon of
HQ Company, 508th PIR as my uncle had. Rock only vaguely remembers
Uncle Matty, because they were in different squads. But he did say that
when Matty had guard duty, he knew for sure he would man his post,
no matter what. On a funny note, he remembers that Matty was usually
called last at roll call because his last name, starting with a T (Teahan),
fell at the end of the alphabet.

Rock has met with every president since he first became Command Sergeant Major, including President Trump, whom he met at the 2016 Army-Navy game in December 2016. Here US Army Chief of Staff General Milley also told him about an historic M-1 rifle recently recovered from Normandy that once belonged to a Martin Teahan. Imagine his surprise when the General learned that Rock had known and served with Matty Teahan!

I had the distinct pleasure of meeting Rock in 2016 at the annual 508th reunion. To my knowledge, Rock is one of only two people still living who knew Uncle Matty, so I was eager to document his thoughts and glean any information possible about my uncle. While I'll never know what Uncle Matty was thinking during his brief, historic days as an active-duty paratrooper in World War II, listening to Rock was an experience I will cherish forever. Our January 6, 2017 telephone interview is below.

Hey, Rock! This is Jim Farrell, Martin Teahan's nephew. How are you doing?

"Mr. 508th," retired Command Sergeant Major Rock Merritt, at the 2016 Annual 508th Family and Friends Reunion with Jan Silver, widow of Captain Walt Silver, and me. Everyone wants to talk with Rock! A World War II hero and legend in his own time, Rock was in the same HQ Company as Uncle Matty and served for thirty-five years!

I'm pretty good! I just got back from Florida yesterday.

Good for you! What were you doing in Florida?

I was having my regular two-week vacation during the Christmas holidays. Looks like I should've stayed another week, with this snow-storm coming in here to North Carolina!

Yeah! I'm in New Jersey, so we've got snow here, too. I wanted to ask you a few questions, if that's all right with you.

OK.

First of all, I had a good chuckle when I saw you'd met General Milley at the last Army-Navy game. He started telling you about Matty's rifle—and you knew whose it was! That's so funny!

Yeah, how about that! Your uncle was in my company! In fact, he was in my platoon, but he wasn't in my squad.

My uncle's title was "Communications." Would that be a lot like what Jim McMahon did—running wires and that type of thing?

Well, it could be. Or it could be taking the radio messages that come in from Regiment or Battalion, and things like that. I have no idea what his role was. I remember at roll call he was one of the last four or five standing every time because the name "Teahan" came near the end of the alphabet. Personally, I didn't know him, but I knew he was in our company. We were a heavy-weapons company, so I recognized everyone—we had one-hundred, thirty-three men, whereas a rifle company had one-hundred, ninety-eight.

We had a "commo platoon"—a whole communications platoon. They had the wire section, the radio section—they're the ones who received all the communications. And there was a colonel's radio operator, an executive officer's radio operator, and a company com-mander's operator, all of them with SCR-300 radios. Your uncle could have been one of the 300 radio operators for the battalion commander or the battalion exec, or what have you, because the battalion commander's staff, the commo platoon, supported all the commo for him. Then, of course, they had the line section that had EE-8 Field Telephones. He could have been any one of those.

Would he also have been a machine gunner?

I told the chief of staff that your uncle was in my company, and then someone called me and said he was in the machine-gun platoon. I don't recall that. If he'd been in my squad, I would've known, because I still have pictures of my whole squad, and he wasn't in any of them. I'm not downgrading any of the machine gunners or mortar men, but the people who had the high IQs went into the S-2 section and the commo section, and the rest of us were in the machine-gun platoon and the 81-mortar platoon. Your uncle must have had a pretty high IQ. Too bad that O.B. Hill's not still around, because he was a sergeant, and he had the radio section of the commo platoon.

My Uncle Matty and O.B. Hill were very good friends.

Well then, I bet he was in the radio section with O.B.

OK—that would make sense.

Also, Jim McMahon, the commo platoon, and O.B. Hill were all in that plane where the battalion commander and the company commander got killed. That was on the first day. A lot of them lived, and a lot of them got killed a few days later, you know?

Yeah. We think Matty got killed either on D-Day or the day after.

What does his report show?

It's kind of strange because the report shows June 23. But then I've seen a different date, and a couple of people who served with Matty told my mother that he got killed pretty quick, on D-Day or the day after.

On the 23rd of June things were quieting down quite a bit. With soldiers being killed every damn week, I guess they did the best they could when things slacked up and there was no one around to figure out the date of death. Graves Registration comes and picks them up, and they might just mark the date of death as the day they found him—who knows?

I think that's what happened. A couple of people have told me that.

Hey, Rock! I liked what you told Trump at the Army-Navy game: "The 82nd will be ready when you ask!" Right?

Yeah, that's what I told Trump. I said to him, "Sir, I represent the 82nd Airborne Division, and I just want you to know when you're Commander-in-Chief, the time's gonna come when you need the 82nd, and, Sir, we'll be ready." He said, "I know you will, Sergeant Major. Thank you very much."

And General Milley almost jumped out of his seat when you told him you knew who Martin Teahan was, right?

Yeah! He said, "I want the Sergeant Major to come up to my office!" His aide, a big, tall guy, a Colonel, said, "*Yes, Sir!*" About five minutes later, we shot some kind of a newsreel with the both of us, and when it was over, the General looked at his aide again and said, "Did you make a note that I want the Sergeant Major to come to my office?" And he said, "*Yes, Sir!*"

That must have been really interesting.

General Milley looked at me and said, "You know, they gave me the rifle, and I'm going to present it to the Army Museum." Well, they've got an Army Museum up there pretty close to the Pentagon. There's a little Army base up there. I guess that's the Army Museum he was talking about.

How it happened, Rock, is that General Milley had my wife, Monica, and me come to a ceremony. The French Army Chief of Staff presented the rifle to me, and then I gave it to General Milley. They're building a brand-new museum in Virginia at Fort Belvoir that's going to open in 2018. In 2019, the General wants to take the rifle from his office, drive it to the new Army Museum, and donate it.

What kind of condition was the rifle in?

It wasn't bad. I think you could still fire it.

You could? After seventy-two years, lying out in the sand!

I know! It's absolutely amazing! I'm writing a book on the whole thing. We went to visit Folkingham, England. It was fascinating. Do you know Glyn Shipstone or Graham Lawson? They're really nice guys and great guides. They drove Monica and me all around.

Yeah, I know the Lawsons from England. He's come to our World War II, 508 reunions. I know him well.

They got the keys to the airport at Folkingham, and we actually drove down the runway that you and my uncle took off on. Then they showed us Wollerton Park and the memorial tree that O.B. dedicated for the 508th Association, thanking friends of the regiment in Nottingham. It was very interesting!

Yeah, I bet.

So, Rock, briefly, what was the mission of HQ Company?

First, it's called Headquarters Company, 1st Battalion, 508th. It supported the whole battalion—A Company, B Company, and C Company. That's four companies and a battalion. They had an

1944 Corporal Kenneth "Rock" Merritt. Rock stepped up big-time after his entire chain of command was wiped out on D-Day. As German machine gun fired non-stop at the 508th PIR, Rock told his company platoon leader: "I'm going out there to knock out that damn machine gun." Rock was as good as his word, and was awarded a Silver Star for his heroic action.

81-mortar platoon and a heavy machine-gun platoon—four 81 mortars and eight water-cooled machine guns. The machine-gun platoons were normally attached to a specific company that was under or going into attack.

I was attached to A Company, so I flew into Normandy with A Company, not Headquarters Company. My section was machine gun, which was the first section. Each section had four machine guns. The second section was attached to B Company or C Company—I forget which one. The mortar platoons were very seldom attached out to one of those companies because they had those 81s—that's a heavy mortar—in support of the battalion, so they'd be pretty close to the battalion CP. Whatever company needed support would call the 81 platoon leader, who was a First Lieutenant. Of course, they also had an observation man out of the 81-mortar platoon who'd be with those three companies. He's the one who would call back to the 81-mortar platoon and say, "Hey, we need such-and-such coordinates, and I'm with B Company, or A Company, or C Company."

The rifle companies always had a forward observer with them, but, normally, the whole four guns stayed back with the battalion commander, and the 81-mortar platoon leader also stayed with the mortars. You usually also had a Second Lieutenant, who would go with one of the attacking companies of his choice. Normally, you never had all three companies, A, B, and C, on line at the same time: you had two attacking and one in reserve. One of the observers could be a Lieutenant, and the other could be a Sergeant. He'd be the one to call back to the company and direct the fire on the hill or the coordinates.

Then you've got the commo platoon—you have your radio section, your wire section, and your runners in there. There's a runner for each company who sends out information to the companies about where the lines are broken and need to be spliced. The battalion staff was also assigned to Headquarters Company—a Lieutenant Colonel, his Major, his Exec, and right on down—his S-1, 2, 3, and 4. They have an intelligence section in there, also. You put them all together and wind up with one-hundred, thirty-three men supporting the three rifle companies. That was their mission, one-hundred percent.

So Rock, what did you think when you heard about my uncle's rifle being found?

[Laughs.] Well, they're finding stuff like that all the time over there, but they never determine who it belonged to. What shocked me was his name written on one side of the stock and his girlfriend's name on the other. I don't know the history, but they found out right away who it belonged to. That just didn't happen over there!

We found a lot of helmets with somebody's last name in them. You might have been somebody named, say, *Jasper*. Well, we might have had ten *Jaspers* in the regiment, you know? We'd never know whose it was. But to find out! That's the first weapon that we ever found out about in the war. Not only in the 508—I'm talking about the *thousands and thousands* of Americans who went in on D-Day. As far as I'm concerned, that was the first.

Wow! Rock, he could have got in trouble for that, right? If they had found out?

No, I had my wife's name on my own machine gun.

Really!

Yeah, I had it in red paint—*Sally*. And the people on the guns, on the mortars, put some of their girlfriends' names on them. The Army was real lenient on that. As long as you didn't hurt the function of that weapon, I don't think they would have said anything at all.

You know, Rock, like they always say, "A soldier and his rifle have a special relationship." Did you feel that way?

I threw mine away first chance I got. I had a carbine. I didn't like the carbine—I wanted my own damn rifle. So anyway, I found one on a soldier who was killed on D-Day when it got daylight. I just dropped my carbine and took his M-1 rifle.

But yeah, a lot of people had their markings on their rifles. You're the first person I've heard ask if it was legal to do something like that. I suppose the Army figured if a man cared that much about his rifle to put his name on it, or his girlfriend's name on it, or like me, to put his wife's name on a machine gun, then he's going to take care of that machine gun, he's going to take care of that rifle. I never heard a word about defacing a weapon or anything like that. I'm not saying that some platoons didn't forbid it, but I don't think our company did.

Interesting! What do you remember about your time in Nottingham?

Well, the big chateau—or whatever you call it—up on the hill is still there. There's no doubt about that. Of course, we were in squad tents and had shower tents outside, and all that good stuff. I guess what I remember the most is going through the fence at night and into the little surrounding towns. Everyone had their own bar. Some of the 508th pubs were the Hand & Heart, the Jolly Higgler, and the Jerusalem. Once we found a bar, we kept going there until we got out of England.

I enjoyed Nottingham more than any of the other towns, including those in Ireland and Soissons, France—all of them. Most of them were all friendly to us, and what have you. If you didn't get in trouble, if you weren't restricted, you could go to town at night. One thing I remember about it was when they hollered *"Time, please!"* The sun was still up! It was daylight, and the sun was up, and they closed at nine o'clock! When they hollered *"Time, please,"* you could drink your beer that was on the table, and that was about it.

[Laughs] I think when you visit General Milley, you're going to have a great time. It's very special.

When I got back from Florida, I got a call from a Colonel in Protocol, 82nd Airborne Division. He said he had a group out of Chicago who wanted to come here to Fayetteville and do a DVD or something on my military history, including the war and what have you. I didn't know if it might be connected with General Milley. Before I'd left for Florida, he'd called and said he had a group that wanted to do an oil painting of me. I said, "Jesus Christ, I don't know what that nonsense is all about." So now I thought maybe they wanted a video, or that they'd seen a picture of me and Trump in the news, or something like that. So I just said, "You just tell them that after January 6, I'll be available. I'm not committed to anything." I just signed three hundred copies of Dietz's *Fury from the Sky*, showing the battle of Hill 30.

I've got one, Rock!

I guess they're doing good. They've got the oil painting on display at 508th Headquarters, and they had five-hundred, eight copies made. They've already sold three hundred of them at $115 apiece. Well, as I was signing them, I asked the Sergeant Major, "By the way, who's the lucky person to get number 508?"

Oh, yeah!

He said, "Ho, ho!" And then the Major shook his head, like, "Don't answer him!" Finally, the Sergeant Major said, "Rock, we can never keep the secret from you. It's been framed, and we're going to donate it to you."

Oh, that's nice!

They didn't have to do that, you know? But anyway, they've got it framed, and they're going to give it to me. That's nice. I was on Hill 30, but I got there late. I was with Captain Adams' thirty-seven people. It was only about two miles from Hill 30. We were pinned down with a whole damned battalion of some outfit because we had one of their Prisoners of War. He was on a listening post, and we overran him. He stayed with us until we got up on Hill 30. Then some sorry bastard killed him.

How was your visit with Valérie from France? *[Valérie Gautier Cardin tends veterans' graves, including Martin Teahan's, in the Normandy American Cemetery and runs a non-profit organization to fund trips for World War II veterans returning to visit France.]*

Oh, bless her heart! She stayed four days and nights with me here! Yeah, I took her all around. She saw every military museum we've got here in the Fayetteville area and the whole of Fort Bragg. She was tickled to death over it. That's a great, great woman and a real patriot for what she's doing for all our soldiers and veterans.

She's amazing. She and I became very good friends. She helped me when we did our trip in June. She's just unbelievable. And she cares so much for all the veterans! She told me she had a great time with you.

Yes, she did. I was glad to have her. Another veteran dropped her off here, and he was just as nice as he could be. I'm not sure about it, but I think he was a bombardier on a B-17. Valérie knows them all. Not just all of our boys—she knows any veteran who went into Normandy. Or, hell—even people who went into the war after Normandy. She takes care of all of them, you know?

She does. And she has an organization, "Veterans Back to Normandie," where she pays for their trip to go over there, too.

Oh, yeah. Have you met Gene Garren?

Yeah, I like him.

He and Valérie run the committee getting veterans over there who can't afford to pay their way. Gene Garren runs it here in the United States, and Valérie runs it over in Europe.

What a remarkable thing to do. Listen, Rock: Thanks so much for talking to me. I can't wait to hear about your visit to General Milley!

Well, it better be pretty soon. I'll be ninety-four in August!

You sound like twenty-one, though!

Thank you, partner! I appreciate it.

Stay safe in the snow, and I'd love to have another chat, maybe in a month or so. Can I give you a call?

You call anytime you want to. I'll be glad to talk to you.

Thanks so much, Rock. You have a great day now!

Chapter 12

DISTINGUISHED UNIT CITATION, 508TH PARACHUTE INFANTRY DIVISION*

*T*he following is an excerpt from the General Orders conferring honors on the 508th Parachute Infantry Regiment for outstanding performance of duty in the first three days of fighting in Normandy. That fighting significantly included the Battle for Hill 30, located in the vicinity where our investigations so far have led us to believe Uncle Matty was killed. The Citation was, and remains today, the highest honor that can be bestowed on a unit for heroism in action against the enemy. The award is now known as the Presidential Unit Citation.

Army unit decorations date from World War II and, in order of precedence, are: the Presidential Unit Citation (established in 1942 as the Distinguished Unit Citation); the Valorous Unit Award (established in 1963); the Meritorious Unit Commendation (established in 1944); and the Army Superior Unit Award (established in 1985).

Colonel Roy E. Lindquist, first commander the 508th Parachute Infantry Regiment, commanded the Red Devils throughout World War II. Uncle Matty was one of the original paratroopers assigned to the regiment, which made its first combat jump in Normandy. For its performance from June 6–9, its first days in battle and some of the bloodiest of the entire war, the entire 508th PIR was honored with a very rare Distinguished Unit Citation for extraordinary heroism in action against an armed enemy. The degree of heroism is comparable to actions warranting the award of a Distinguished Service Cross to an individual. The award is now called the Presidential Unit Citation.

Criteria: The Distinguished Unit Citation is awarded to units of the Armed Forces of the United States and co-belligerent nations for extraordinary heroism in action against an armed enemy occurring on or after 7 December 1941. The unit must display such gallantry, determination, and esprit de corps in accomplishing its mission under extremely difficult and hazardous conditions as to set it apart and above other units participating in the same campaign. The degree of heroism required is the same as that which would warrant award of a Distinguished Service Cross to an individual. Extended periods of combat duty or participation in a large number of operational missions, either ground or air is not sufficient. This award will normally be earned by units that have participated in single or successive actions covering relatively brief time spans. It is not reasonable to presume that entire units can sustain Distinguished Service Cross performance for extended time periods except under the most unusual circumstances. Only on rare occasions will a unit larger than battalion qualify for award of this decoration.

Award: Streamer embroidered Ste. Mere Eglise Headquarters and Headquarters Company, 82d Airborne Division Cited in War Department General Orders 69, 22 August 1944 Division Headquarters and Headquarters Company, 82d Airborne Division, is cited for outstanding performance of duty in action against the enemy between 6 and 9 June 1944 during the invasion of France.

General Orders: The following is an excerpt from the General Orders conferring upon the 508th Parachute Infantry battle honors for the first three days of fighting in Normandy, France. The award entitles every member of the Regiment to wear the Distinguished Unit Badge. [The Distinguished Unit Citation was re-designated the Presidential Unit Citation (Army) per DF, DCSPER, date 3 November 1966.]

Citation: The 508th Parachute Infantry is cited for outstanding performance of duty in action against the enemy between 6 and 9 June 1944, during the invasion of France. The Regiment landed by parachute shortly after 0200 hours, 6 June 1944. Intense antiaircraft and machine-gun fire was directed against the approaching planes and parachutist drops. Enemy mobile anti-airborne landing groups immediately engaged assembled elements of the Regiment and reinforced their opposition with heavily supported reserve units. Elements of the Regiment seized Hill 30, in the wedge between the Merderet and Douve Rivers, and fought vastly superior enemy forces for three days. From this position, they continually threatened German units moving in from the west, as well as the enemy forces opposing the crossing of our troops over the Merderet near La Fière and Chef-du-Pont. They likewise denied the enemy opportunity to throw reinforcements to the east where they could oppose the beach landings. The troops on Hill 30 finally broke through to join the airborne troops at the bridgehead west of La Fière on 9 June 1944. They had repelled continuous attacks from infantry, tanks, mortars, and artillery for more than sixty hours without resupply. Other elements of the 508th Parachute Infantry fought courageously in the bitter fighting west of the Merderet River and in winning the bridgeheads across that river at La Fière and Chef-du-Pont. The Regiment secured its objectives through heroic determination and initiative. Every member performed his duties with exemplary aggressiveness and superior skill. The courage and devotion to duty shown by members of the 508th Parachute Infantry are worthy of emulation and reflect the highest traditions of the Army of the United States.

*The text of the Distinguished Unit Citation and accompanying historical information are cited from the excellent 508th PIR website and used with permission. //www.508pir.org/honors/citations/citation_dist_unit.htm. Accessed: June 24, 2017.

MAPS

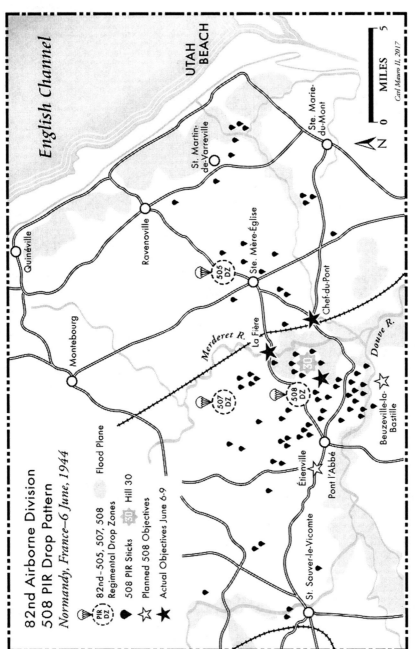

82nd Airborne Division, 508 PIR Drop Pattern, June 6, 1994

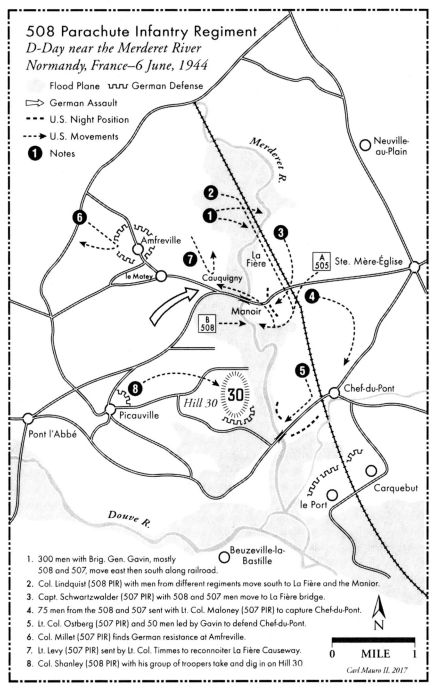

508 Parachute Infantry Regiment
D-Day near the Merderet River
Normandy, France—6 June, 1944

Flood Plane   ᴜᴜᴜ German Defense
⟹ German Assault
▪▪▪ U.S. Night Position
- - → U.S. Movements
❶ Notes

1. 300 men with Brig. Gen. Gavin, mostly 508 and 507, move east then south along railroad.
2. Col. Lindquist (508 PIR) with men from different regiments move south to La Fière and the Manior.
3. Capt. Schwartzwalder (507 PIR) with 508 and 507 men move to La Fière bridge.
4. 75 men from the 508 and 507 sent with Lt. Col. Maloney (507 PIR) to capture Chef-du-Pont.
5. Lt. Col. Ostberg (507 PIR) and 50 men led by Gavin to defend Chef-du-Pont.
6. Col. Millet (507 PIR) finds German resistance at Amfreville.
7. Lt. Levy (507 PIR) sent by Lt. Col. Timmes to reconnoiter La Fière Causeway.
8. Col. Shanley (508 PIR) with his group of troopers take and dig in on Hill 30.

0   MILE   1

Carl Mauro II, 2017

D-Day near the Merderet River

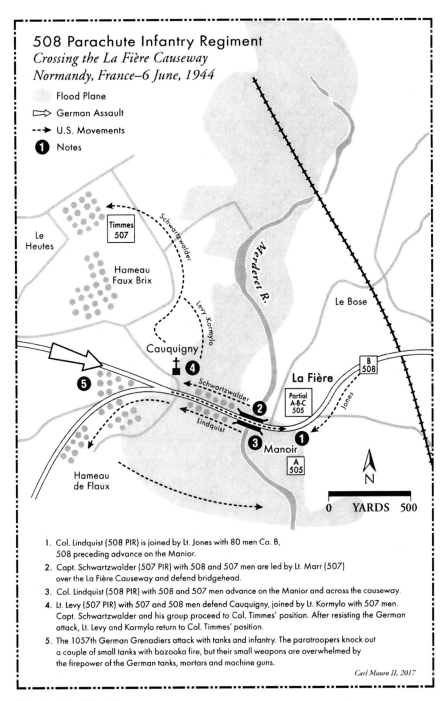

508 Parachute Infantry Regiment
Crossing the La Fière Causeway
Normandy, France–6 June, 1944

Flood Plane
German Assault
U.S. Movements
1 Notes

Le Heutes

Timmes 507

Hameau Faux Brix

Schwartzwalder

Levy Kormylo

Merderet R.

Le Bose

Cauquigny

4

5

Schwartzwalder

La Fière

B 508

Partial A-B-C 505

Jones

Lindquist

2

Lindquist

3 Manoir

1

A 505

Hameau de Flaux

N

0 YARDS 500

Carl Mauro II, 2017

1. Col. Lindquist (508 PIR) is joined by Lt. Jones with 80 men Co. B, 508 preceding advance on the Manior.
2. Capt. Schwartzwalder (507 PIR) with 508 and 507 men are led by Lt. Marr (507) over the La Fière Causeway and defend bridgehead.
3. Col. Lindquist (508 PIR) with 508 and 507 men advance on the Manior and across the causeway.
4. Lt. Levy (507 PIR) with 507 and 508 men defend Cauquigny, joined by Lt. Kormylo with 507 men. Capt. Schwartzwalder and his group proceed to Col. Timmes' position. After resisting the German attack, Lt. Levy and Kormylo return to Col. Timmes' position.
5. The 1057th German Grenadiers attack with tanks and infantry. The paratroopers knock out a couple of small tanks with bazooka fire, but their small weapons are overwhelmed by the firepower of the German tanks, mortars and machine guns.

Crossing La Fière Causeway

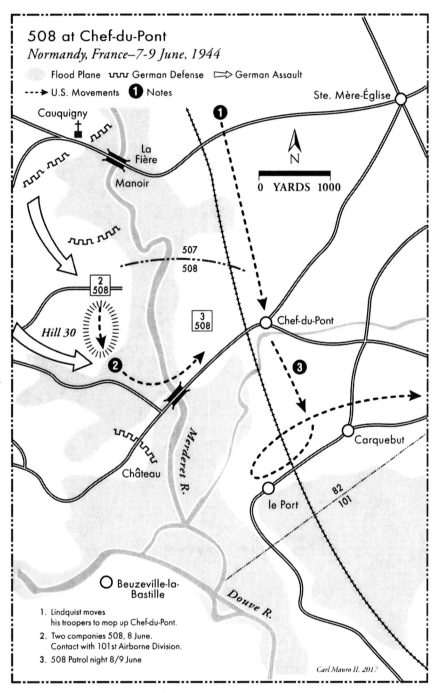

The 508 at Chef-du-Pont

1940 South Bronx, Uncle Matty (left) play-fighting with a friend. In just a few years, Matty and his buddies would be fighting for real for the freedom of the world.

1940 South Bronx. Uncle Matty and a friend humorously "measure up," trying to see who is taller. Matty loved to make people laugh. I hope this picture brings a smile to your face.

1940 South Bronx, 138th Street. Uncle Matty and his million-dollar smile. Always the life of the party, Matty is fondly remembered to this day for his love of entertaining family and friends.

1940 Rockaway Beach, New York City. Always the humorist, Uncle Matty and friends strike a pose for the camera in bathing suits and fake mustaches inspired by Charlie Chaplin. The first of Chaplin's "talkies," the comedic political satire *The Great Dictator* was released in 1940.

Late 1930s South Bronx. Uncle Matty's crew: Bill Burke, back right, with his hand on the shoulder of Matty's best friend, Peter Donahue. Matty does not appear in this photograph, which he may have taken himself. It is captioned on the back in his hand: "The Whacks and their Car."

South Bronx, late 1930s. In back, left to right: Bill Burke, Frank Mooney, Mike Noonan, with friends (unidentified). Bill, Frank, and Mike were in Peter Donahue's wedding party. Had Matty survived the war, they would surely have been in his wedding party too, with Peter as best man.

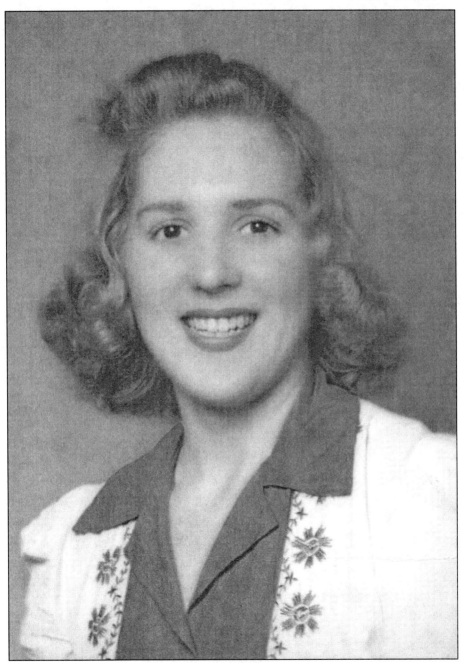

1941 Studio portrait. My beautiful mother, Uncle Matty's sister, Ann Teahan. My mother tearfully watched Matty walk down 138th Street en route to the ship that would take him and his 508th PIR brothers to war in December 1943. She had a premonition in her heart that this would be the last time she'd ever see her beloved brother. Tragically, her intuition was right.

1945 Studio portrait. Aunt Francie, sister to Uncle Matty and my mother, and my sweet, "one of a kind" aunt. Francie and my mother were best friends and did everything together. Uncle Matty loved to sing her favorite song for her, "Ain't She Sweet."

1935 Graduation photo. Uncle Jimmy, Matty's older brother, looking dapper for his graduation from Saint Jerome's School. Always "The King" in the eyes of his mother, Nora, Uncle Jimmy was born with a rheumatic heart, which disqualified him from serving in the armed forces. It proved to be both a blessing and a curse for his entire life.

1940s South Bronx. Uncle Jimmy Teahan looking like an Irish mobster in a car. Uncle Jimmy liked to live large and was considered to lead a glamorous lifestyle. Whenever he won his bets, he showered all his nephews and nieces with candy and other treats. We all loved him as kids, and felt like he was our very best friend.

A Prisoner

Sgt. Martin J. Farrell, Jr., whose parents reside at 351 E. 138th St., is a prisoner of war in Germany, according to a War Dept. telegram which arrived on New Year's Day. Sgt. Farrell was reported missing with a 15th AAF bomber on a mission to Vienna on Oct. 7. His brother, Seaman 2d Class Lawrence, is in the Pacific.

October 1944 Newspaper notice. My father, Martin ("Mickey") Farrell, who was shot down and captured on his last mission with the 454th Bombardier Group. He served nine months in the Stalag Luft III POW Camp for airmen later portrayed in the classic film, *The Great Escape*.

1943 Studio portrait. Private Martin Teahan, 508th PIR, b. December 3, 1923. Matty volunteered to be a paratrooper at age seventeen. Like many underage patriots, he forged his mother's signature on the permission papers.

Late 1940s Family wedding. Standing, left: my mother. Seated, left to right: Francie, Willie Werner, my father, Baby Ann Dolan, Annie Dolan, Patty Dolan, my grandmother Nora. Back wall, left to right: Ann O'Neil Leno, Patrick "Doo-Doo" O'Neil, Mary O'Neil.

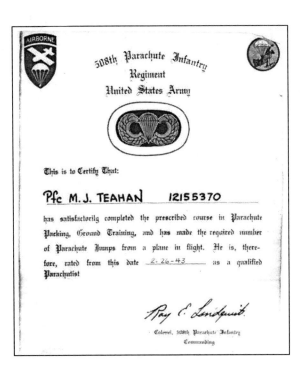

February 26, 1943 Certificate of Qualification. It's official! Uncle Matty's certificate of graduation, signed by Colonel Roy E. Lindquist, the first and only WWII commander of the 508th PIR, who is said to have personally approved every man in the select first group of his newly formed unit. Matty was proud to be one of the chosen and formed bonds with his fellow troopers that made them brothers for life. It has been my pleasure and honor to talk with several of Matty's 508th brothers-in-arms who actually knew my uncle. To this day, all of them remember his sterling personality and honor his ultimate sacrifice.

1943 Camp Mackall, North Carolina. Left to right: Jim McMahon and Martin Teahan ham it up in "uniforms" consisting of long johns complete with helmets and weapons. Inseparable best friends, the two met up at the Army Processing Center in New York City and experienced all stages of training, shipment overseas, and further preparations for D-Day together. First separated when assigned to different planes for D-Day, the two shook hands just before they loaded up and wished each other luck. This was the last time Jim ever saw Matty. Jim survived the war; his buddy was killed in the brutal first days of fighting.

1943 Camp Mackall. Left: Uncle Matty, left, shows off his hand-to-hand combat skills with his 508th PIR buddies. Matty and his fellow trainees kept up their spirits and those of their loved ones by striking exaggerated "action shots" like this that mimicked newsreels played at the cinema. Other photos mocked the slap-stick comedy of the day.

1943 Camp Mackall. Uncle Matty's squad. Top, left to right: L. Green, John Sivetz, Harry Metcalf, Bob Shields. Bottom, left to right: Martin Teahan, Jim McMahon

1943 Camp Mackall. Uncle Matty (lower left) playing guitar. To his right, his platoon sergeant, Bob Shields, also with guitar. Matty's best friend, Jim McMahon, affectionately called him "the Mitch Miller of WWII."

1943 Camp Mackall. Uncle Matty (bottom center) and his buddies take a well-deserved break from training.

1943 Camp Mackall. Left to right: Jim McMahon, Matty. The Inseparable best friends, buoyed up by their relationship, were always smiling regardless of tough circumstances.

1944 Wollaton Park, Nottingham, England. Art Jacoby (second from left), Uncle Matty (second from right) and fellow troopers show off their jump boots shortly before D-Day.

1943 Camp Mackall. Left to right: Jim McMahon and Uncle Matty pose outside their barracks, aiming their M-1 Garand rifles. Notice bayonets are attached.

1943 Camp Mackall. In the driver's seat! First produced for the military, Jeeps went into production in 1941 and became the Army's main light four-wheel-drive vehicle in WWII and the postwar period. Luckily, Uncle Matty passed down his aptitude and early driving skills to me, as I discovered when I learned to drive in the Army a generation later.

1943 Camp Mackall. Left to right, 1st Battalion, HQ Company: Jim McMahon, Henry Luhrman, Uncle Matty, and John Sivertz.

1943 Camp Mackall. Left to right: Uncle Matty and buddy Jim McMahon demonstrate hand-to-hand combat skills, showing off for the camera and the folks back home.

Two great Airborne leaders. Major General Matthew B. Ridgway, Commander, 82nd Airborne Division (right) and Brigadier General James M. ("Jumpin' Jim") Gavin, Assistant Division Commander (left).

A tragic death in Normandy. In the darkness of night, burdened by very heavy equipment and tangled in the harness and risers of their parachutes, many parachutists drowned, sometimes even in shallow water, in the widely flooded areas around the Merderet and Douve rivers.

Picauville, Normandy. The Allied bombing set many buildings on fire, which were still burning when U.S. Airborne forces first encountered German forces.

"Mother of Normandy" Mme Simone Renaud lays flowers on the grave of Brigadier General Theodore Roosevelt, nephew of President Roosevelt and Assistant Division Commander of the 4th Infantry Division, which landed on Utah Beach on D-Day. The tradition of laying flowers has been passed from generation to generation, lovingly tended by volunteers like Uncle Matty's French Angel, Valérie Gautier Cardin.

Matty Teahan, family hero, revered uncle, and the "Mitch Miller of WWII." Uncle Matty died on the battlefield in Normandy in June 1944. Seventy-two years later, the discovery of his M-1 rifle created my calling to tell his story. The ensuing journey of discovery has been an honor and a pleasure. *Photo courtesy of Valérie Gautier Cardin.*

June 2016, Normandy American Cemetery, Colleville-sur-Mer. Army Chief of Staff General Mark Milley and his wife Holly with Monica and me at Uncle Matty's grave. The General took steps to ensure that Matty's memory would live on for future generations.

PART THREE

SEARCHING FOR UNCLE MATTY: THE FAMILY QUEST IN EUROPE ADVENTURES IN NORMANDY AND NOTTINGHAM

Chapter 13

MY HERO,
GENERAL PATRICK COLLET

Let me just do it. I here proclaim French Army Brigadier General Patrick Collet, Commanding Officer, 11th Parachute Brigade, my hero and friend for life. I first heard of (then) Colonel Collet on March 17, 2016—a magical Saint Patrick's Day—when he emailed the following message to my sister Liz: *Found this rifle and helmet of a trooper from the same battalion in the area near Varenguebecq, Bois de Limors.* Included was a picture of the rifle with "M. Teahan," my uncle's name, engraved on the stock, and a helmet that had belonged to another 508th PIR soldier.

Talk about a life-altering moment! Liz and I were elated. We instantly realized the importance of the message. Colonel Collet and I became frequent correspondents, and along the way, we also became good friends. He immediately agreed to our request to repatriate Uncle Matty's rifle. *It's a fantastic piece of history*, he said, and graciously invited Monica and me to visit him to view it.

I will never forget the moment I first saw, and then touched, Uncle Matty's rifle. I felt overwhelmed by happiness and sadness all at once. Sadness, because I knew it was the rifle of a twenty-year-old paratrooper killed in action in Normandy. Happiness, because I knew this was Uncle Matty's way of coming home to his family.

From the beginning, I felt a strong sense of obligation to document everything, including my own feelings. After all, we believe Uncle Matty is returning as his rifle, and this extraordinary journey, both symbolic and physical, is a signal event in the history of the Teahan family. But as the story grew, I came to realize it had wider repercussions. People spontaneously began to reach out. Matty's story had struck a chord that resonated in the silences of their own family histories. They, too, were searching for information, trying to fill in the blanks, seeking closure. Some offered help, others related their stories, many described letters and photographs carefully archived or tossed in boxes pell-mell. All had been touched by Matty's story and wished us good luck for his journey home.

French Army Brigadier General Patrick Collet, Commanding Officer, 11th Parachute Brigade, my hero and friend for life. General Collet located Uncle Matty's historic rifle near Hill 30 in Normandy, the site of fierce fighting for the 508th from 6-9 June, 1944, and moved heaven and earth to bring it back home to our family.

As we soon discovered, repatriating the rifle was a mission in itself. As a weapon used in Normandy in World War II, Uncle Matty's rifle was classified as an historical artifact belonging to the French national heritage. French law thus prohibited its export. *Period.* The only way to bring it back to the States was to go through official US Army channels. I had not a clue in the world how to accomplish this. As far as I was concerned, bringing Uncle Matty's rifle home was as daunting and complicated as planning D-Day in Normandy!

I was about to learn the real meaning of the old saying, *Never tell a paratrooper "No."* It took innumerable phone calls, emails, and face-to-face meetings, and required massive amounts of his time, but General Collet moved heaven and earth to cut through the red tape. The rifle was cleared for export and flown by military transport to the US Army Chief of Staff, General Milley. At the time, General Collet was Chief of Cabinet to French Army Chief of Staff General Jean-Pierre Bosser. Of course, that helped. But well above and beyond the call of duty, he took a personal interest in our story. He even helped arrange for Monica and me to meet General Milley at Uncle Matty's grave in the Normandy American Cemetery on our visit to France in June 2016.

Patrick Collet was promoted to General soon after our visit to France. His father, grandfather, and great-grandfather were all highly decorated French Army officers. Born an army brat in Germany, Patrick already knew as a boy that he, too, wanted to be an airborne soldier. Every year, the Collet family moved to a new location, but, no matter where his father was stationed, Patrick spent summers and holidays in Normandy, where the family had a summer home. He developed an early interest in D-Day, especially when he thought he could apply what he learned to become a better soldier himself. This attachment to Normandy began when he was about fourteen and remains strong today.

Patrick read every book he could lay his hands on about paratroopers, battle strategy, weaponry, and the profiles of the Captains, Lieutenants, and NCOs who had fought in the foxholes of Normandy. D-Day was the largest invasion the Allies had yet attempted, with a massive use of paratroopers dropped in darkness behind enemy lines in a foreign land. Many missed their drop zones by miles. How did they survive? What strategies did they use? How did they overcome such obstacles?

One of the earliest objects of his study was Hill 30 near Picauville. The 508th PIR here fought a horrific battle on June 6–9, 1944, during which the regiment lost many men wounded or killed in action. Uncle Matty was most likely among them—his rifle was found nearby. I had the privilege of walking that hallowed ground with General Collet, who detailed the battle and pinpointed locations with amazing accuracy. Who were the soldiers? He knows. Who performed heroically? He knows. Who died? He knows. In fact, he knows more about D-Day strategies and battles—what worked, what didn't, and why—than anyone else I have ever met.

It takes a special person to become a paratrooper, someone with the courage to jump out of a perfectly fine airplane in full combat gear for the approximately thirty adrenalin-rushing seconds it takes to hit the ground ready to fight. Only the strongest and mentally toughest survive the rigorous training. "The first jump was easy," said General Collet, looking back at his training days. "The second one was hard—but then it got easier again." He completed his qualifying jumps—five day jumps and one night jump—to earn those coveted wings at age eighteen. At graduation, Collet had the great honor of being pinned by his grandfather, a paratrooper with six combat jumps in Indochina, with his father watching the ceremony.

Collet rapidly rose in rank. In 2007, he commanded a regiment of the 11th Parachute Brigade, the elite "first response" force of France, and the French Army's contribution to coalition forces in Operation Enduring Freedom. The six hundred French and one hundred German Airborne soldiers under his command were tasked with the crucial mission of controlling downtown Kabul and areas north and east of the city. This meant keeping out the Taliban, an enemy who knew the terrain, hid among civilians, planted IEDs, and ambushed in the dark of night. Having spent time with General Collet, I was not surprised that he maintained his regiment's morale at the highest level; his men had prepared for their mission for four months and were ready for war. All of them thought of each other as brothers and would die for one another if need be.

General Collet was responsible for assembling teams of his troops to be embedded with two Afghan infantry companies. Their missions were complicated and dangerous. One of his best men, a battle-hardened French sergeant embedded with the Afghans, was killed in a Taliban ambush at an isolated outpost. It is always traumatic when one of your brothers dies in combat, but this man was one of the regiment's best senior NCOs. His death was also the first casualty of a French soldier embedded with an Afghan infantry unit. I would like to think that General Collet's lifelong study of D-Day soldiers gave him strength and contributed to his leadership, as he kept his regiment focused and maintained morale throughout their remaining tour of duty.

General Collet's duties in Operation Enduring Freedom required him to navigate a complicated command structure. He reported to a Turkish General and was responsible for coordinating with troops from many other nations, but the majority of his contact was with the 82nd Airborne Division of the United States Army. It was no surprise to me that he was promoted to General in July 2016. Believe you me, you want General Collet on your team.

Just as he has been a wonderful friend and help to my family and me, General Collet has befriended many 508th PIR World War II veterans and their families, developing friendships with

Chet Graham (1918–2015), Tom Porcella (1923–2010), and Harry Hudec (1922–2007), among many others. His relationship with Chet Graham started in 1992, when General Collet wrote to *The Static Line*, a magazine dedicated to all things airborne, in the attempt to better identify part of a World War II uniform he had and locate the family of the solider who had worn it. The only one to answer was Major Chet Graham. He and Chet began corresponding and eventually became best friends.

In 1994, Chet began to visit General Collet at his homes in Paris and Normandy every year. The two of them flat out enjoyed each other's company—they toured battlefields, enjoyed the beer at their favorite pubs, and attended June 6th and other ceremonies together for many years. Chet even made a special trip to France in 2005, when Patrick was promoted to Regimental Commander. That a friend might fly halfway around the world to witness such a special moment, I can certainly understand. But the amazing thing to me is that Chet flew from Walnut Creek, California, to Paris, took a train to Pamiers in deep southwest France, attended the ceremony, had dinner, and then flew straight back home! Chet thought so highly of General Collet that he undertook a day trip in France that took him two more days to get there and back!

His visits to his friend Patrick continued for ten more years, until Chet passed away in 2015 at the age of ninety-seven. General Collet, who has been collecting World War II artifacts since he was fourteen, has an impressive collection of uniforms, helmets, hats, knives, maps, and many other items from Normandy, but the most special pieces of all are the personal items that Chet contributed as a testimony to their long friendship: his combat knife, silver wings, dog tags, and 82nd Airborne patch. If it is possible to communicate with this world from Paratrooper Heaven—and my experience with Uncle Matty tells me it is—then Chet and General Collet are probably still communicating!

Chet had one wish upon his death—that his ashes be spread over his D-Day drop zone. He trusted only one person to do it right, his best friend, General Collet. Monica and I had the honor and privilege to be present, with Chet's granddaughter, Cyndi, when the General performed a touching ceremony at Picauville in honor of his friend Chet.

As we drove through the French countryside on our way to the drop zone, Cyndi commented that her grandfather had loved horses. Then, at the end of the ceremony, just seconds before General Collet scattered Chet's ashes, one of those incredible, totally spontaneous, happy coincidences that come along only once or twice in a lifetime occurred: A French farmer rode by on a bicycle, leading a horse by the rein. I could see from the look on Cyndi's face that something spiritual had happened.

Chet, General Collet accomplished his mission in style! We all salute you up in Paratrooper Heaven! General Collet, my family, I, and the many others whom Matty's story has touched salute you! Thank you for making my life's mission possible. Because of you, Uncle Matty has come home.

Chapter 14
THE ROCK STARS OF 1944

Some of the biggest thrills and most fun Monica and I had in Normandy happened in our travels with eight World War II veterans who had returned to France to commemorate the 72nd Anniversary of D-Day. They were mobbed, asked for autographs, treated like rock stars everywhere they went. And justly so! Monica and I had the pleasure of attending five events with these very special rock stars of 1944. At the very first one, I discovered the job I was born to do. My dream job was to get girls to kiss World War II vets! Wow! What a rewarding and easy job! No one ever said "No"!

The veterans' return—for many, the first—had been arranged by the French non-profit foundation "Back to Normandie." Founded and operated by Valérie Gautier Cardin, who has arranged return trips for veterans for more than thirty years, the organization is coordinated in the States by retired U.S. Army Sergeant Major Gene Garren, who has accompanied World War II veterans back to Normandy for many, many years to attend the annual June 6 celebrations.

Monica and I first met five of the veterans at Charles de Gaulle Airport in Paris, while they were waiting for the bus that Valérie had scheduled to take them to Normandy. We would join up with three more at later events on the schedule. All but two had fought in the

Allied invasions of June 1944: Cliff Goodall, 7th Naval Battalion, 6th Special Brigade; Jack Hamill, U.S. Navy Coast Guard; George Shenkle, 82nd Airborne, 508th PIR; Erwin Davis, 354th Infantry Division and 89th Infantry Division; Bill Schott, 27th Marine Regiment, 5th Marine Division; Henry Poisson, 150th Engineer Combat Battalion; Bob Noody, 101st Airborne Division, 506th PIR, and Robert Essler, 90th Infantry Division.

World War II veterans Jack Hamlin and Cliff Goodall with me outside a French school in June 2016. What a pleasure it was to see how the people of Normandy honor our veterans and keep history alive in the minds of younger generations! Jack and Cliff answered many questions from the children on our visit to the school and were treated like rock stars everywhere in Normandy.

Now in their nineties, all were in a good mood despite the long flight and eagerly looking forward to the days ahead. Valérie had set up all room and board, transportation, and other arrangements. All they had to do was relax, enjoy the adulation, and follow the program. All knew, too, that they would receive awards in recognition of their service in Normandy; for some, this included the *Légion d'honneur*—the highest award that non-citizens of France can receive for outstanding service to the French nation. There would be plenty of time for personal reflection as well, with visits to former battle sites and to the graves of fallen comrades buried at the American Cemetery at Colleville-sur-Mer.

If you ask Cliff and Jack, they will tell you I deserve a medal for the amount of kisses they got. The two of them had a personal competition going for who would get the most kisses from the girls in Normandy. Throughout our whole trip in Normandy, crowds would swarm around Cliff and Jack, riveted by their every word and priceless smiles. Cliff and Jack, and all the other veterans, too, each had his own special way with the girls. All were dedicated to conquering Normandy all over again, only this time with love.

So, how did they get all those kisses? Cliff's hook was his helmet story. A few days after D-Day, he tripped and sent his Navy helmet rolling down a hill and onto Omaha Beach. All he could do was helplessly watch as his precious helmet rolled far out of reach. Worse yet, it landed on the wrong side of a yellow marker indicating a mine field!

Relying on the wisdom of youth, Cliff, who was only eighteen, decided that he could still recover his helmet, which lay just inside the yellow marker. He descended the hill and surveyed the scene. Spying his helmet, he cautiously stepped over the yellow mine-field marker. Instantly, a loud, cracking noise made him nearly jump out of his boots. Had he stepped on an anti-personnel land mine? Had he only cracked a dry piece of wood? This was no time for reflection! He high-tailed it out of there, to find another helmet and live for another day.

As it turned out, Cliff picked up the helmet of a 29th Infantry Division soldier by the name of W.W. Weaver, who had been killed storming the beach on D-Day. A bullet had hit the helmet, and Cliff had to clean out the blood. So it was, a Navy signalman from the 7th Beach Battalion wound up wearing an Army helmet, and was mighty glad of it. Cliff eventually donated the helmet to the National D-Day Memorial in honor of William W. Weaver, from Roanoke, Virginia. Listening to Cliff's story, Monica, I, and everyone else who had the pleasure to hear it knew that we were hearing history live.

Jack, Cliff's major competitor for kisses, had a major vibe going with the girls. All he had to do was smile, and anyone who saw him wanted to give him a hug! I didn't know at the time about the Coast Guard's involvement in D-Day, so I asked Jack to educate me. The Coast Guard saved innumerable lives. Jack himself retrieved numerous live bodies from the water, loading them up into his cutter and ferrying them to a naval hospital ship. Jack's story was so interesting that I felt as if I could talk forever with him. The people we met in Normandy seemed to feel the same! At some point, I stopped keeping score of the number of kisses Jack and Cliff received. It was all too overwhelming. As far as I'm concerned, they tied for the number of kisses received. Of course, if you ask them, you might get a different answer!

The first event Monica and I attended was at Valérie's school, the Collège André Miclot, in Portbail, Normandy, where eight veterans, including those we'd met at the airport, had traveled to answer questions from the students. The students, all between the ages of thirteen and fourteen, had set up a procession line to welcome the veterans as heroes and create a triumphal entry as they arrived at the school. Some of the veterans walked through on their own; others needed assistance; still others went through in wheelchairs. All of the veterans were smiling as they passed between the double line of enthusiastic adolescents, all cheering and waving little French and United States flags on either side of the walkway up to the school's main entrance.

It was an eye-opening event. It was very revealing to see how motivated the French students were to learn about the history of World War II. Everyone gathered in the school auditorium—students, teachers, politicians, and historians—were fascinated by every word the veterans spoke. On the veterans' side, the need to communicate was almost palpable. Monica and I, and everyone else in attendance, could see and feel the passion and love that the veterans put into answering the students' questions. At ninety years old or older, they were the last men standing. They were the last eyewitnesses to the

Allied invasion of Normandy, and as such, the final living safeguards of history.

The students asked many, sometimes surprisingly acute, questions about the war. The session went well, but certain questions were very hard on the veterans: some cried, and some were left without words. The summary below encapsulates the question-and-response:

Is it hard to talk about the war?

Not anymore. For many years, the memories were hard to relive, painful to talk about. Today, most surviving World War II veterans are constantly asked to speak about the war and feel it is an obligation to keep the memories and history alive. Every World War II veteran understands the importance of documenting what they did in the war. If they do not talk about it, the history will be lost forever.

Have you ever killed anyone?

This was a tough question; some veterans did not want to answer. Not one of the veterans present believed he had directly killed anyone, although one said he had fired artillery and other weapons into enemy territory, likely causing death or injury. Another had shot down a German plane with a 20mm gun.

What do you think of war?

This was the most-answered question, and all the answers were similar: War is an abomination that causes so much pain and damage it should never be repeated. The veterans unanimously expressed their concern about the current glorification of war in the United States.

Where you afraid?

This question produced many interesting answers. All replied they'd been afraid and that anyone who said he was not was a liar! Despite their intense fear, all recognized that they had an important mission to do.

Did you take Prisoners of War?

One of the veterans had helped an injured German soldier who pleaded for his life, saying he had a wife and children at home. He was taken as a Prisoner of War, and the Americans showed great compassion for him. This question was particularly interesting, in that many American and German soldiers both had been ordered to take no prisoners on D-Day.

Did you see a concentration camp?

The one veteran who had indeed seen a camp cried while giving his answer. There were buildings full of dead bodies. The SS loosed their dogs on him and the other soldiers, but they managed to take care of business and help those inmates who'd been lucky enough to survive. This response was by far the most emotional in the entire question-and-answer session.

On June 3, 2016, we attended a ceremony in Carentan, the scene of horrific battles in June 1944. The ceremony was attended by French politicians and members of the United States military, including U.S. Lieutenant General Stephen Townsend, Commander, XVIII Airborne Corps. The 82nd and 101st Airborne Divisions were well represented by active-duty troopers, who stood like Olympic athletes in military uniform as the ceremony took place in the town square. Representatives from the French, Canadian, and German militaries, and many other honored guests from France and abroad were also present, and the United States Navy Band enlivened the ambiance to the appreciation of all in attendance. All of the World War II veterans in attendance received awards: many received the French Senate Award, and three were honored with the Legion of Honor, France's highest award for non-French citizens. Everyone paid the honored guests high homage, and it was obvious to Monica and me that the attention meant the world to the veterans themselves.

The next ceremony was in Ravenoville, where trees were planted in the veterans' honor and a plaque was placed bearing their names and units. In attendance was a German World War II veteran, who wanted to give a tribute to the U.S. veterans. Speaking through an interpreter, he conveyed a message of honor and respect, and the hope that such a war would never again take place. The German soldier saluted, and hugged all of the American veterans, making a very touching scene. Although some people may have mixed emotions about such reunions, as witnesses to the event, Monica and I thought the love, compassion, and forgiveness expressed in the ceremony was very special indeed; certainly it would not have been possible seventy-two years ago.

We also attended events in Ste. Mère-Eglise, the first town liberated in Normandy, where townsfolk and thousands of visitors swarmed the vets to speak with them and ask for autographs. We also attended an 82nd Airborne event, where we were greatly entertained by the fabulous 82nd Airborne Chorus. The 82nd Chorus is so good that I could listen to it all night. I especially enjoyed the performance when they sang and marched to some of the old Army cadences. In attendance was Susan Eisenhower, granddaughter of General Eisenhower. She impressed us with her gracefulness and seemed truly to enjoy interacting with the World War II veterans and the swarm of active-duty 82nd and 101st soldiers in attendance, as everyone conversed and took photographs. Jack and Cliff, of course, took advantage of the event to rack up a good many extra hugs and kisses!

Monica and I stood aside as hordes of active-duty soldiers and other visitors lined up to talk to the veterans. As we watched the veterans reveling in the well-deserved adoration—answering questions, taking pictures, and signing autographs—we were struck by the realization that we were groupies to the greatest rock stars to ever exist: The priceless, one-of-a-kind rock stars of 1944. One message they all repeated was the need to remember all those who had died in World War II. All, too, wanted to hear about Uncle Matty and how his rifle had been found.

What a privilege it was for Monica and me to have the opportunity to spend time with these veterans! What luck, and what an honor! Thinking back on it now, it gives me a glimpse of what Uncle Matty would have been like, had he survived to make the tour of Normandy with his brother heroes. If Matty were still alive on D-Day, June 6, 2016, he would have been ninety-three-and-a-half years old. No doubt he would still be charming the ladies. I bet he'd have given Jack and Cliff a good run for their money when it came time to tally up the kisses!

Chapter 15
OUR JOURNEY TO NOTTINGHAM

M. Teahan: The fact that Uncle Matty engraved his name on the stock of his rifle brought us and many other people, far and wide, together on a marvelous adventure of discovery. Once his rifle was finally discovered, it was clearly identified and very quickly traced back to our family. The identity of "Kitty," the name that Matty engraved on the other side of his rifle, was much more mysterious. What did it mean? Who was this mystery woman? Surely, she must have been important to him. Was she a girlfriend from Nottingham? A sweetheart from Belfast, from the time the 508th had trained in Northern Ireland? A South Bronx girl from back home? Monica and I were fascinated, and felt we owed it to Uncle Matty to find out the answer. On December 10, 2016, we took a trip to Nottingham, where the 508th had trained in England, to see if we could discover the identity of the mysterious Kitty.

Our week in Nottingham introduced us to many wonderful people. Facebook friends Glyn Shipstone and Graham Lawson picked us up at the Birmingham Airport, drove us to our hotel in Nottingham, and planned out our entire trip. Both are dedicated to preserving World War II history, very knowledgeable about the 508th PIR, and were early followers of Uncle Matty's Facebook page. They and their organization, Jump 44 Living History Group, have helped many veterans and their families who've returned to Europe to visit the sites where they fought or were stationed in the war.

Uncle Matty engraved the name *Kitty* on the other side of his rifle. Intrigued, Monica and I traveled to Nottingham, England, in December 2016 to search for this mysterious girlfriend. We there met our guides and wonderful new friends Glyn Shipstone and Graham Lawson, and a family from Radford, near Nottingham, whose mother was called Kitty. Both we and Kitty's family wonder, could she be Uncle Matty's Kitty?

Glyn and Graham have both lived all their life in Nottingham, where both work as bus drivers for the city. Despite their full-time jobs, they had put in months of research to help us learn as much as possible about Uncle Matty's time in Nottingham. All this they did voluntarily, without ever having met us in person. When we protested that their efforts must have cost a lot of time and expense, they replied it was an honor to spend time with us. In short, we had found our "BBFFs"—our "British Best Friends Forever." Thanks to Glyn and Graham, we felt like celebrities! Our week was packed with wonderful experiences, and no one could possibly have done more to help us understand what it felt like for Matty and the 508th PIR in June 1944, in the final days leading up to D-day.

Monica and I, unable to sleep on the flight, were very tired as we stepped off the plane in Birmingham. Sure enough, there were Glyn and Graham, holding up a sign, "Jim and Monica Farrell." Monica instantly perked up: she had always dreamed that someone with her name on a sign would pick her up at an airport. Now she felt as if she'd hit the lottery!

Neither of us had been to England before, and although I knew that everyone in the UK drives on the opposite side of the road than we do, it was a strange experience when Graham got in the right-side driver's seat, and Glyn took the front passenger seat, beside him to the left. Once we were on the road, I was even more confused. Why on earth was Graham shifting the gears with his left hand, while Glyn was driving, looking back at me, his eyes off the road, for five or more seconds at a time? Had I finally gone crazy?

I kept quiet about my reservations, although I was totally freaked out. Finally, a few sharp curves in the road woke me up. *Oh, so that was it!* I realized, after I had recovered my senses. *What a dummy I am! Graham is driving, and I was disoriented.* Once I'd finally figured it out, I told Graham and Glyn about it, much to Monica's embarrassment. All of us had a great chuckle about how my first experience of driving "on the wrong side of the road" had made a fool out of me.

Our trip to Nottingham had originally been sparked by an article in the *Nottingham Post*. The reporter, Andrew Smart, described our quest to find "Kitty," detailed the story of the rifle, and recounted that Uncle Matty had been stationed with the 508th in Nottingham. "It sounds like an impossible quest," he wrote, "but the family of an American soldier killed on D-Day are trying to trace his Nottingham girlfriend, known only as 'Kitty'."

The Straw family of Nottingham responded to the article, offering a possible link to their family, and expressing their wish to pursue it. Their mother, now deceased, was named Kitty, and in 1944, she had lived in Radford, a town a few miles from Wollaton Park, where the 508th had been posted.

The next day, December 11, Glyn and Graham drove us to meet the Straw family at Wollaton Hall. Although it could have gone much differently, the meeting felt natural, not awkward at all. The Straws invited all four of us to the Admiral Pub, where conversation flowed freely over a pint of beer. In 1944, the Admiral Pub had been for officers only, and it made me proud that such a big deal was made over Private Martin Teahan on this day.

The Straws next took us all to the Durham Pub for dinner. Frank Straw, Kitty's son, was a longtime friend of the owner of the pub, who greeted me at the entrance as "the famous American." Never in my life had I been called "famous," and it will likely never happen again. I felt a little embarrassed, but also honored, because I knew Frank was referring to Uncle Matty's story, which by this time had gained considerable local renown. It was very moving to see how Frank and the Straw family talked to their friends in Nottingham about Matty and his possible connection to Frank's mother, Kitty. "I tell everyone I meet!" Frank told me.

I was so engulfed in conversation at dinner that Monica gobbled up my dessert while I was talking! Damn! It sure had looked delicious! And this was not the first time she had done it! The evening ended with an invitation to the home of Kitty's daughter, Sally, and her husband, Greg Antcliff, on the upcoming Wednesday. This meant I could now continue the conversation with Frank, Greg, and Kitty's son, Riclyn. By this time, we knew we could not prove the link between Matty and Frank's mom Kitty, but we had become friends and were greatly enjoying each other's company. There would be no closure that night, but a new friendship had opened up.

The Straws and I had previously been in touch on Facebook, where they quickly learned I am a pizza addict. When we arrived at Sally's house for dinner, Riclyn presented me with a pot of British mustard as a gift, and pizza was on the menu! Our evening together included viewing a World War II movie of their hometown of Radford. I was mesmerized, and now know why the United States and Britain have a special and unbreakable relationship. We would leave with no answer on Kitty but promised to stay in touch and share anything new we learned about Kitty's identity. And I now am hooked on British mustard!

All the Straws were lovely, and treated us like family from the moment that we first met. Our conversations all made apparent how similar our families had been in the 1940s: Both had been very poor, yet fun-loving, with strong survival instincts, and a deep sense of patriotism. In short, the salt of the earth. No matter the personal cost, ours were the kind of families who had fought for the freedom of the world.

Sometimes, but rarely, magical things happen in life. But our journey to Nottingham reaped so many such experiences that I felt as if I'd racked up a lifetime of magic and more! For the whole week prior to our trip to Nottingham, the news had made a big deal about the All-American uniform in the annual Army/Navy game. The uniform looked real snazzy, and the Army was all buzzed about it. Army had not beaten Navy in fifteen years. Would the All-American uniform be Army's secret weapon? Would the spirit of heroes from World War II, and all other 82nd Airborne veterans, combine to will the Army team to victory? Well, go figure. Army beat Navy 21–17 for the first time in fifteen years. Many Army fans, I included, are convinced that the uniform clinched the victory.

Glyn was so excited about the win that he made a sign for Monica and me to hold, and took our photograph by the famous Lion statues in Nottingham City Centre. The sign read 21–17, the score of the game. We all felt special about the win and believed the spirits of departed heroes from the 82nd Airborne in World War II had a role in it. *Airborne All the Way!*

I congratulated General Milley on Facebook, although everyone said he would not respond. Guess what, he did! He felt excited about the outcome, and a photo showed him at the game with the legend-ary 508th paratrooper, Rock Merritt! Both had ear-to-ear smiles. To give justice to their meeting, here are Rock's own words:

> *I spent a lot of time with General Milley, especially when he told me about a farmer in France who found a rifle that belonged to a soldier in the 508th PIR during WWII. General Milley informed me that the weapon (M-1 Garand) was presented to him by the soldier's family, and he was donating it to the U.S. Army Museum. When I informed the General the soldier whose weapon he was donating was in my company during WWII, General Milley jumped out of his chair, and told his aide, "I want CSM Rock Merritt to visit my office in the Pentagon!" So it looks like I will be visiting General Milley in his office at the Pentagon in the near future.*

Lesson learned on this day: never underestimate the power of an 82nd Airborne paratrooper. I must say, it felt special to take a photograph beside the lions, where so many 508th veterans had taken pictures to document their presence in Nottingham in the days immediately leading up to the Normandy Campaign.

One of my life's most spectacular moments will always be when Graham took Monica and me out in his car and drove full-speed down the very same runway from which Matty had taken off on D-day. The airfield had long been out of service, and it was a bumpy ride, similar to being on a C-47 screaming down the runway. It honestly felt like I'd been transported to the moment when Uncle Matty took off. Our trip down the runway took only forty-three seconds, but the memory will last my whole lifetime.

Thanks to Glyn, a remarkable researcher, we now understand that Matty most probably engraved his name and Kitty's on his rifle after the 508th was sealed in at Folkingham and waiting for the call to load up for D-Day. Glyn explained his theory as we were standing on the Folkingham airstrip, his voice fairly exploding with passion and energy. The more he talked, the bigger his eyes grew and the louder his voice became.

June 4, 1944, was a day of deep reflection for the 508th, as it was for all other parachute troopers, regardless of unit, who were scheduled to drop on D-Day. All had been training for this day for years, and had many last-minute thoughts, and final preparations: one more practice run to get on all the equipment—more than a hundred pounds of weapons, ammo, food, a full canteen of water, compass, bayonet, grenades—and the list goes on. Their leaders had studied the sand tables detailing the terrain, helping them to visualize their landing points. Nothing had been left to chance, or so they thought. This was a day when there was no joking around. *Fight at all cost, take no prisoners, failure is not an option*, was the message. Uncle Matty and his buddies waddled like ducks to the waiting C-47s, so loaded up they needed assistance to mount the steps to the plane. The weight of the world was on their shoulders—a very serious responsibility to put on such young men. Many were barely out of their teens, and some of them were even still teenagers.

At the very last minute, the mission was cancelled due to inclement weather. This was a hard letdown. As Glyn pointed out, the troopers were pumped up and ready to accept their fate, but the cancellation of the mission brought their adrenalin crashing down to a new low.

It was then that Glyn surmised that Uncle Matty had coped with this letdown by carving his name, then Kitty's, on his rifle. Glyn had studied the engravings very carefully. Matty engraved "M. Teahan" vertically across the very end of the right-hand side of his rifle butt. "Kitty" was engraved horizontally, and more to the middle on the other side. Matty had likely done both engravings with his pocket knife, possibly with the help of one of his buddies. Uncle Matty must have felt strongly about the engraving, and we hope it brought him some relief in those final, tense days at Folkingham Airstrip as the 508th impatiently waited for the final signal to load up.

Glyn took us back to Wollaton Hall, where the 508th had been tented in Nottingham. Here, my thoughts turned to not only Uncle Matty but also to O.B. Hill, Matty's close friend, and the founder of the 508th Family and Friends Association. A room in Wollaton Hall is devoted to the 508th PIR, and Uncle Matty's name was on the wall. O.B. had been so instrumental in the dedication of this room that Monica and I could feel his presence.

Back outside, where HQ Company had its tent, O.B. had planted a tree in 1976. Here, the 508th had passed the time playing cards and shooting dice. Many had buried their winnings in a jar for safekeeping, hoping to retrieve their stash on return from Normandy. Famously, that jar has not been found to this day. Here, too, Matty would have sung old Irish songs to his fellow troopers, including his favorite, "Phil the Fluter," as recorded in O.B.'s letters to my sister Liz. Standing on that sacred ground, Monica and I could feel their spirits, and imagined them still laughing and playing poker with their winnings.

Like all red-blooded American troopers, the 508th often frequented local pubs. To do so, they often had to sneak out of camp by climbing an eight-foot wall. Staring at this wall on our visit to Nottingham, I imagined Matty and his fellow troopers eagerly climbing over it on their way to court the local belles and down a few drinks at their favorite pub. This meant all were "absent without leave," a serious breach of the rules. According to Graham and Glyn, some of the 508th managed to procure bicycles, threw them over the wall, and speedily returned to camp before their superiors could declare them AWOL.

Our visit to Nottingham had also included an evening with the Straws at the Olde Jerusalem Pub, a favorite 508th watering hole in 1944. Uncle Matty would certainly have been there many a time with his buddies, enjoying a pint of beer and a bit of release from the stress of his upcoming mission. Monica, I, and everyone else could feel the paratroopers' spirits as we enjoyed our drinks. Our visit to Nottingham was an unforgettable experience and a vital link in telling Uncle Matty's story. We still believe that one of these days, we will solve the mystery of Kitty's identity. Whenever that may be, we have vowed to return to Nottingham to visit our newfound friends again and tell them how it has all turned out.

PART IV

UNCLE MATTY COMES HOME:
MISSION ACCOMPLISHED

Chapter 16
UNCLE MATTY COMES HOME

To me, Uncle Matty and his rifle are one and the same. His rifle is him, and he is his rifle. This realization has been the motivation for an amazing journey that has taken me from the South Bronx to the Pentagon, via Paris, the battlefields of Normandy, and Nottingham, England. No, I am not crazy, drunk, or high on drugs. I feel this, I know this, it's real! Bringing his rifle home is bringing Uncle Matty home. *My rifle is human, even as I, because it is my life,* states the Rifleman's Creed.

Yes, Private Martin Teahan died in June 1944, a paratrooper in the famed 82nd Airborne Division. His body is buried in sacred ground, the Normandy American Cemetery, with 9,385 other heroes. When I visited his grave, I promised him to bring him home. He now lives in spirit as his rifle, and my mission is to tell his story.

Life has scripted this to be. I strongly feel it is one of the main reasons that I was put on this earth. Uncle Matty's tragic death in Normandy leaves an incomplete story. He made sure to mark his rifle so his story could be completed. Like all soldiers, he had fears of dying on the battlefield, but unlike most, he engraved his name on his rifle as a last will and testament. His mother, Nora, never accepted his death—he was too young, only twenty. She suffered tremendously from the loss of her son for the rest of her life and turned to Irish whiskey to ease the pain. I vividly recall her hysterical sobbing, and how she cried out his name—*Maaaty! Maaaty!* His brother Jimmy suffered the shock of receiving the dreaded War Department telegram and the grim duty of informing the family that his little brother had been killed in action. This was a heavy burden on Jimmy, unable himself to serve in the war because of a rheumatoid heart. My mother and her sister Francie deeply missed their loveable, fun-loving brother and never got over his absence. "It would be so much better if only Matty were still alive," my mother often told my little sister Liz. Mom believed that handsome, happy-go-lucky, charming, fast-witted Matty would have become a business-owner, the proprietor of an Irish pub, for example, that would have lifted the family out of poverty.

Chief of Staff of the Army General Milley with French Army Chief of Staff General Jean-Pierre Bosser, Monica and me. General Bosser presented me with the rifle at a State Dinner on December 1, 2016. Now it was official—Uncle Matty was back home! No wonder we all have such huge smiles!

I wish my Mom were here today. "Well, Mom," I'd tell her, "you were right. Life is so much better with Matty around. From now on, you can smile, knowing that his rifle will be displayed for the whole world to see. People will honor his memory and learn his story. He has become a man of dignity, a man who stands in spirit for thousands of American front line soldiers who sacrificed their future to safeguard our freedom. Mom, feel proud of your war hero. As wonderful as he was, as tragic as his death was, he has grown to be larger than himself. "

It amazes me how many people have already been touched by Uncle Matty's story. In less than ten months, his Facebook page has gained more than 85,000 fans and still is rapidly growing. Every day, viewers leave messages honoring his service and his memory. To date, more than 200,000 people have written "RIP" on his page. I have received innumerable calls, emails, and texts from veterans, members of military families, and others, young and old, expressing their respect and marvel at the near-miraculous recovery of his rifle and its return. Whenever I tell Matty's story to active-duty soldiers—and I have met many in the course of my journey—their eyes grow wide, and they break out in a grin. "Where can I find more information?" everyone asks. Even Generals, some three- or four-star, are fascinated by his story. Most amazing to me, General Milley speaks fondly about Matty and his rifle. This is the highest level of respect and honor I can imagine. So Mom, Uncle Jimmy, Aunt Francie, and Grandma Nora—stop crying! Your prayers have been answered! I want you to start smiling! Laugh and enjoy the attention people are heaping on Matty. Life of the party that he was, I'm sure he's enjoying it himself.

Uncle Matty, the first leg of your physical journey home began on March 17, 2016—the day we were notified your rifle had been found—and ended on December 1 of that year, when I finally held it—and you—in my arms. The occasion was a grand state dinner honoring the Chief of Staff of the French Army, General Jean-Pierre

Bosser, who formally presented me with the rifle after its arrival on U.S. soil.

Bringing you back in the form of that rifle was complicated, full of metaphorical landmines. There was so much bureaucratic red tape to wade through that many people deemed it impossible. General Collet is my hero—your return would not have been possible without him. Often told that the rifle could not leave France, he never accepted *no* for an answer. When the State Department denied our request to transport your rifle by diplomatic mail, we just kept soldiering on. General Collet, Liz, and I all had known since March 17—that lucky Saint Patrick's Day—that your rifle was a special piece of history meant to make its way home—not only for you and our family but for all the World War II veterans who'd lost their lives in combat.

One week short of December 1, when the Presentation Ceremony at Fort Meyer was scheduled, we still had not obtained approval for transport. Nevertheless, my confidence in General Collet and the destiny of Uncle Matty's rifle was so strong that I had already arranged to take time off to attend the ceremony. General Collet moved heaven and earth and did, indeed, make it happen. "I had the rifle boarding a military aircraft this morning in Paris, thx to the military attaché," he wrote on November 20.

When the official invitation from General Milley did arrive, Monica and I were ecstatic. We felt like we were setting off to see a long-lost member of the family who'd been missing for seventy-two years. On the morning of November 30, our departure date for Washington, D.C., we received an email from Colonel Peter Benchoff, General Milley's Chief of Staff. "General Milley would like to talk to you," the good Colonel wrote. "He will call your cell phone in a few minutes." *Wow! The Chief of Staff of the U.S. Army is calling me!* What an honor. I was nervous, but sure enough, a few minutes later, General Milley was on the phone.

Our conversation is something I will never forget. The General wanted to make sure that our trip was planned to our satisfaction and asked if we would like a tour of the Pentagon the next day. A history buff, he wanted to hear all the details of Uncle Matty's journey since we had last met in Normandy. He was interested to learn we'd soon be going to Nottingham to research Uncle Matty's time at Wollaton Park, where he had been stationed just prior to D-Day. I was moved by General Milley's kindness and his recognition of the rifle as a special piece of history. With great consideration, he would go out of his way to honor it and Uncle Matty.

The dinner was a once-in-a-lifetime night for Monica and me. It had been seventy-two-and-a-half years in the making! I was proud as could be, and my excitement level was off the charts. My sister Liz, steeped as she was at an early age in our mother's grief and stories of Uncle Matty, had undertaken decades of research into the history of his regiment and our family. This special night to honor Uncle Matty was the best thing that had ever happened to her.

On December 1 at 6:00 pm, we arrived at General Milley's Quarters. The house was decorated for Christmas, shining with beautiful lights. They illuminated the flags, both American and French, proudly waving out front. After greetings by General Milley and his wife, I next met Sergeant Major of the Army Daniel Dailey, the highest-ranking enlisted man in the Army. Much more than that, he's the guy who has your back, someone you want to talk to, have a beer with. The Sergeant Major of the Army visits the men and women who guard our freedoms. He runs with them, walks with them, jumps out of planes with them. Having served as an enlisted man myself, meeting him was like a lifelong dream come true. Saying this, I'm sure I speak for all enlisted soldiers, most of whom never get the chance. But here I was, some thirty-nine years after my Army service, meeting the Sergeant Major of the Army. We immediately hit it off. He asked about my time in the service, we shared stories, and it only got better from there.

Sergeant Major of the Army Dailey asked me if I had a "Soldier for Life" pin. I said "No." He himself was all out of pins, so he took the pin off his own jacket and pinned it on me, saying, "You are a soldier for life." Oh, my God—did I feel special now! That's what I mean—he always has your back. Funny, all I could think of at that moment was, "I have to post my picture with the Sergeant Major on Facebook!" I guess, for me, that would make it real. Only then would I know I was not dreaming this.

General Milley called Monica and me over to introduce us to all the other guests. He recounted the story of Uncle Matty's rifle and how General Bosser would be presenting it to me. The passion in his voice was like a bolt of lightning. Uncle Matty, what must you have been thinking at that moment? Seventy-two years after your death, here is your nephew in a room full of three- and four-star generals, and the highlight of the evening is Private Martin Teahan and his trusty M-1! In your wildest imagination, Uncle Matty, I bet you never thought that you would ever *meet* a General, let alone find yourself in such a room, present in spirit through your rifle, with the highest brass possible paying you respect.

General Milley then gave us all a tour of the house where Army Chiefs of Staffs had made so many decisions that, literally, changed the course of history. At dinner, I was placed between General Milley's wife and the wife of Deputy Chief of Staff Lieutenant General Joseph Anderson. Across from me sat the Sergeant Major of the Army and his wife, Holly. Monica had worried I'd embarrass her by not eating properly at the state dinner, but the Generals' wives were so down-to-earth that they put us at our ease. One of them even proposed, "Let's eat dessert with our hands!" This gave me a good laugh and the golden opportunity to tease Monica once we were alone. Monica sat next to General Anderson, and during their conversation, they discovered that one of her best friends, Father Jim, a priest she worked with at Saint John's University, had officiated at the marriage of General Anderson and his wife! What a small world. The majority of my conversation at dinner was with Sergeant Major Dailey. I was fascinated by everything he said, and, to my surprise, he was interested in what I had to say, too—not only about Uncle Matty but my own Army stories as well.

And then came one of the happiest moments of my life. Our dinner concluded, it was time for the rifle presentation. I felt nervous, excited, and very special. Monica's voice ran through my head: "Stand up straight! Say the right things! Don't embarrass me!" Very funny, but not to worry—I had rehearsed for this moment.

General Milley called me to the head of the table, where General Bosser was standing, holding the rifle. General Bosser would speak through an interpreter. I must admit I had no idea what he would say. The speech he gave as he presented me the rifle was elegant and emotionally touching. He fully understood the importance of the moment for my family and me.

General Bosser began by saying how grateful he and his country were for Uncle Matty and other men like him who had given their lives to liberate France. He mentioned General Eisenhower's speech and visits to Airborne units on June 5, and acknowledged that General Eisenhower knew that many young men like Uncle Matty would have to die in combat in order to save the world. The final words of his speech touched me deeply. He said Uncle Matty and his rifle were once one person, one family. He had engraved his name, and now, today, they were one person, one family again, and he was proud to present the rifle to me. He then gave me the rifle. I was on top of the world—cloud nine!

Receiving Uncle Matty's rifle from General Bosser, I felt so proud. I looked over at Monica. Her eyes were shining. Our eyes locked together as we shared this very special moment and everything it meant. I felt the spirit of Uncle Matty while holding his rifle. I could also feel the presence of my Mom, Grandmother, Uncle Jimmy, and Aunt Francie. I was frozen in the moment for seconds, I guess, but it seemed liked minutes at the time. All I know now is that Monica and I did not break our gaze, and we both will remember that moment forever.

What to do next, I did not know. Fortunately for me, General Milley did. He asked me to say a few words. I thanked my hero, General Collet, for making our reunion with Uncle Matty possible. I thanked General Bosser and the people of France, who had been so kind to us on our visit to their country. I thanked General Milley for providing a final resting place for Uncle Matty's rifle. I then presented the rifle to General Milley.

Uncle Matty, know this: General Milley held your rifle, took an infantryman's pose, and said we should be proud—your rifle was back home for good.

Monica and I are deeply grateful to General Milley and his wife for including us in this special night. My final thoughts of the evening were that I wanted my sister Liz and General Collet to have the opportunity to enjoy such a night as this had been. They had worked hard to make this evening possible, and they deserved it. I vowed to work as hard as they had, so one day they, too, might receive the same honor.

Chief of Staff Milley, Chief of Staff Bosser, General Collet, Liz, and Monica—Great Job! Mission Accomplished!

Chapter 17
MISSION ACCOMPLISHED!

We all have moments in life when we reflect on an activity or accomplishment that we've put our entire heart and soul into. On Friday, June 2, 2017, I had this type of moment as I proudly viewed Uncle Matty's rifle on display at the Pentagon in the office of General Mark A. Milley, 39th Chief of Staff of the U.S. Army. It was a priceless moment of pure joy.

The moment was all the more wonderful because it included some of my dearest family members: my wife Monica, who had accompanied me every step of the way on our mission to bring Uncle Matty back home; my sister Liz, who had devoted much of her life to preserving his legacy; and my boyhood playmate and cousin, Noreen, who moved me greatly by accepting the invitation to come with us to Washington, D.C. I was especially happy that two of Noreen's children, Steven and Nicole, Matty's great-nephew and great-niece, were with us as well. Up until this day, Monica and I had been the faces of our family's journey; now, as we shared this very special moment with Liz, Noreen, Steven, and Nicole, two generations were in attendance.

I have always viewed Liz as a partner in this mission. She had also been something of a pathfinder. I had devoted the last fifteen months of my life to researching and writing about our uncle, but she had been at it, selflessly, for *years*. It was Liz who had received the message from General Collet when he first contacted our family to tell us he'd discovered Uncle Matty's rifle. Now, here stood Liz in General Milley's office, soaking it in, looking like she'd just won the Super Bowl. That look, the expression in her eyes, told me that the words in our minds were the same—*We did it! Mission Accomplished!*

June 2017: My sister Liz Farrell and I savor a Mission Accomplished moment at the Pentagon as we contemplate Uncle Matty's rifle in the office of Chief of Staff of the US Army General Milley. Here displayed until 2019, the rifle will be presented for permanent display at the new National Museum of the United States Army, Fort Belvoir, Virginia.

We'd begun planning our "Mission Accomplished" trip with the help of General Milley's outstanding staff in March 2017. Retired Lieutenant Colonel Randy Odom, who had given us our first tour of the Pentagon in December 2016, when Monica and I had come for the rifle-presentation ceremony, was again selected as our tour guide. Randy is extremely knowledgeable, the go-to guy for all the top Generals when it comes to conducting private tours for visiting dignitaries and other lucky guests. Monica and I were delighted to see him again. We knew he would go out of his way to make this very special visit the best it could possibly be.

We met Randy at 9 a.m. sharp at the visitors' gate to the Pentagon, and he helped us get processed and ready for our tour. Once past security, the tour began. As we followed Randy, listening to his every word, I noticed the expressions on Steven's and Nicole's faces. Wow! Just like Liz, they thought they were in paradise. Their mother, Noreen, had been rooting for Monica and me throughout this whole incredible adventure, although she'd been skeptical at first. When General Collet's surprising email first arrived, Noreen had thought it was a scam. Let me tell you: At this particular moment, in the corridors of the Pentagon, it all became real for my amazing cousin Noreen.

As we made our way to General Milley's office, Randy guided us skillfully from one exhibit to the next, building up our excitement. The many historic objects, mementoes, and weapons, all chronologically displayed, represented every war and conflict in which our country has been involved, from the American Revolution to the Civil War, World Wars I and II, Korea, Vietnam, and forward to today. Each and every one of these objects has a fascinating story, and Randy knew them all: For example, when a gold-plated AK-47 understandably caught my eye, he explained that it came from the palace of Saddam Hussein, who presented such weapons as marks of prestige to his favored generals and special VIPs.

The exhibits led up to the official portraits of the thirty-eight former U.S. Army Chiefs of Staff, displayed from first to last on the approach to General Milley's office. The portraits are displayed, Randy explained, only after a Chief of Staff leaves office. Liz was glued to his every word as he pointed out the individuality of each portrait and told us that each subject was depicted in the manner he wished to be portrayed. Some are pictured alone, others surrounded by their families; some appear in dress uniform, others in fatigues—every

Chief of Staff has left his mark and symbolically signaled his values and his character in the style in which he wished to be remembered.

Randy has a unique way about him that makes you feel very special. At the same time, we were totally engulfed by the whole experience. By now, our excitement had reached fever pitch. My head was spinning from trying to take in all the stories and details, when suddenly—*WOW!* There we were, right smack at General Milley's door! My mind sharply pivoted: *This* was what we had come for! Liz's eyes doubled in size. She may have hoped that her devotion to Uncle Matty might be rewarded one day, but she had surely never imagined a reward of this magnitude. In a few seconds, she would walk into the office of the 39th Chief of Staff of the U.S. Army, and behold for the first time her beloved Uncle Matty's M-1 rifle, now hanging proudly on the wall.

General Milley is a four-star General. He can have just about anything he wants to display in his office. That he has chosen Uncle Matty's rifle is pure magic in our family's eyes, and our shared emotion on seeing it there was certainly a "once in a lifetime" experience.

So, there we were, in the General's office, with Randy pointing out one magnificent item after the next and telling us the story behind each of them. General Milley has a big, round table with a glass top. Under the glass are challenge coins from many famous people and military leaders. When we had previously visited the General on December 1, 2016, Monica and I had presented him with a challenge coin on behalf of our friends Bill and Christine Koch. Bill and Christine are from our hometown of East Brunswick, New Jersey, and we had met them thanks to Uncle Matty's Facebook page. The coin was in honor of their son, Steven Koch, who was killed in action in Afghanistan on March 3, 2008, during Operation Enduring Freedom. Steven had served with the same unit as Uncle Matty, 1st Battalion, 508th PIR.

Eyeing the glass table in the General's office, I asked aloud, "Do you think that General Milley might possibly have put Steven Koch's coin on display here?" Eagle-eye Monica spotted Steven's coin in less than thirty seconds. We were awestruck. General Milley, you are a great military leader, but you also have a big heart. It touched us greatly to see Steven's coin on display.

I was allowed to sit at General Milley's desk for a picture. This was where and when it all hit home for me. It felt relaxing, full of peace. I looked around: Liz was floating toward Uncle Matty's rifle—we had not gotten to this point yet. Noreen was staring at Eisenhower's globe. Randy was informing us that General Eisenhower had highlighted in red pen the places he thought Hitler would try to conquer. Noreen, fascinated, was fixated on the red spots all over Europe. She would later tell me it was Eisenhower's globe that made everything real for her that day. Now Randy was explaining something to Nicole, and Steven was reading a handwritten note that General Raymond T. Odierno, 38th Chief of Staff, had sent to General Milley. As tradition has it, the outgoing Chief always writes a note to the incoming Chief on his first day in office. And here was Monica, taking a picture of me sitting in General Milley's chair. And here I am, smiling for the picture, happy my family is caught up in the moment, and realizing that I've actually accomplished the mission Uncle Matty had assigned to me in March 2016. Looking at that picture now, all I can say is, *Oh, what a feeling.*

Finally, Randy brought us all to the point of our visit, Uncle Matty's historic M-1 rifle. Displayed in a classic glass case with a handsome black frame, the rifle hangs above "The Shot Heard 'Round the World," the famous painting by Domenick D'Andrea that depicts the first shots of the Minutemen as they fire at the British on Old North Bridge in Concord, Massachusetts, on April 19, 1775. I was overwhelmed by the powerful juxtaposition of Uncle Matty's D-Day rifle with this depiction of the start of the American Revolution. The painting foregrounds the patriots, rifles raised, and the deaths of the first to die in battle. This historical context made the display of my Uncle's rifle even more of an honor. The whole was larger than the sum of its parts, making the rifle's presence even more symbolic and just.

This experience really brought home the larger significance of my uncle's death in Normandy. The effects of his sacrifice, as strong as they had been, were not confined to our family. His death had been a part of a never-ending continuum—the ongoing fight for liberty. This realization blew me away.

Gradually coming back to myself, I turned to watching how everyone else was reacting. Liz was quietly reveling in the moment. Noreen looked like she could stare at Uncle Matty's historic rifle forever. Steven and Nicole were drinking everything in; I knew I would have a fascinating conversation with them later in the day. How long Monica and I had planned and dreamed of this moment! It was wonderful to watch it unfold in front of our eyes.

All too soon, it was time to say our goodbyes to Uncle Matty. Before we left the building, however, we had one more stop to make: the site where American Airlines Flight 77 crashed into the Pentagon on September 11, 2001. Randy led us to the place where the plane had impacted. It is now a corridor lined with plate-glass windows with ledges low and wide enough to serve as seats for anyone who wishes to stop to remember, reflect, or pray. We sat, bowed our heads, and observed a moment of silence in honor of the one-hundred, eighty-four people who had died on that hallowed site. It was a grave, but spiritual, moment for us all at the end of an emotional day.

Later, when I spoke with Steven and Nicole, they both felt moved and enthusiastic about all the things we had seen and learned. I expressed my hope that they would one day take over the responsibility of keeping Uncle Matty's legacy alive. Both eagerly accepted the challenge. They told me they felt honored and promised to write down some of their feelings about our Pentagon visit. It was extra special to me to hear them express how proud they were of their heroic great-uncle.

So it was that we concluded our mission and Liz's "I Just Won the Super Bowl" day by passing on Matty's legacy to the next generation. But Monica and I had no time to reflect on emotions—the next big event was less than forty-eight hours away! In just two days, we would all return to the old neighborhood in the Bronx to attend the first annual mass in Uncle Matty's honor at Saint Jerome's Church. Steven and Nicole, still full of energy at age twenty-four and twenty-nine, respectively, did indeed find time to write down some of their feelings about our visit to the Pentagon. Their thoughts are the best, most fitting close to a day our family will never forget and a chapter entitled "Mission Accomplished."

Steven: Seeing my great uncle's recently discovered M-1 World War II rifle inside the Chief of Staff's office in the Pentagon is a pinnacle moment I will remember for the rest of my life. If someone were to ask me to define the experience in one word, I would have to say, "euphoric." It was overwhelming, in the best way imaginable. To think that, out of the hundreds of thousands of men who died in combat for the United States in World War II, my great uncle, who was only a private in the military, is the one who is actually being honored individually inside the Pentagon! It's an unreal feeling, to say the least.

Personally speaking, I've always known that it was a privilege to be related to a man who made the ultimate sacrifice a person can ever make, but this past weekend at the Pentagon solidified that belief for me. My great uncle, who was just a pure, jocular teenager at heart, had the courage to serve and protect the country he loved. From now on, his legacy will always play an inspirational role in my life, and I am looking forward with the utmost pleasure to passing his captivating story down to younger generations of my future family. Seeing my great uncle's rifle displayed in honor is a moment I will always cherish, and I will honor him the best way I can by making sure that his story is never forgotten.

Nicole: For most of my life, I knew only one thing about my great Uncle Matty—that he fought in World War II and perished during the war. My grandmother, his youngest sister, hardly ever spoke of him, and no one in my immediate family was old enough to remember him significantly in any way. His life was essentially a mystery and was likely destined to remain one, until the discovery of his rifle. The culmination of this discovery and its meaning for our family have been truly incredible. It is both astonishing and mind-boggling to think about the journey we have been on since this rifle resurfaced in our lives. To travel to Washington, D.C., to witness the rifle on display at the Pentagon in the office of General Milley, the Chief of Staff of the US Army, was beyond thrilling.

Uncle Matty's rifle will eventually serve as an historical artifact for the rest of the world, but it symbolizes much more for our family. For us, it is as if we finally get to have a piece of our Uncle now. Because of this rifle, we have been introduced to the Uncle Matty we never knew, and we have learned about certain facets of his life in a way that we could never have imagined. We now know details about the time he spent in the Army, what he did in the war before he died, who his friends were, who his girlfriends were, what his hobbies were, and what he thought his future would bring. I know and think of Uncle Matty as a real person now, with a life that was lived, rather than as an ethereal figure of my family's past. When the rifle was returned, it was as if Uncle Matty had returned as well. I think that this was his way of letting us know that he had made his mark on the world, that he was here, and that he is home.

June 2016 Picauville. Monica and I with the current proprietor of the house that served as a makeshift hospital in the area where Uncle Matty landed on D-Day. General Collet took us for a tour, and gave us a wonderful history lesson on the very ground where the 508th PIR had fought. We remain uncertain as to the exact date of Uncle Matty's death, but know that his body was brought to this house. The typewritten date on his death certificate is "unknown," but "June 23, 1944" is handwritten beside it. This date, on Matty's cross in the American Cemetery, is probably when Graves Registration recovered his remains; another notice indicates these were in an "advanced state of decomposition." The current proprietor graciously permitted us to view the interior of her house. It was an emotionally overwhelming experience to stand in the place where my uncle's body last lay before burial.

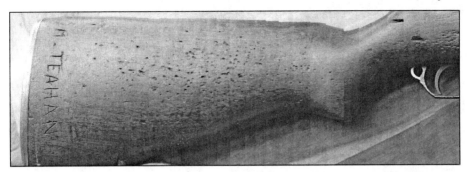

May 29, 2016 Paris. M. Teahan: This is how Uncle Matty engraved his name on his M-1 rifle. Notice the many small nicks in the wood as well: the M-1 was one of the first semi-automatic rifles, but sometimes the eight-round clip would jam. Paratroopers banged their clips on their rifle stocks to better secure the rounds so they would jam less often.

May 29, 2016 Paris. Kitty: Who was the mysterious girl whose name Uncle Matty engraved on the other side of his rifle stock? In December 2016, we traveled to Nottingham, England, in hopes of discovering her identity. There we met a lovely family whose mother, called "Kitty," had lived in the Nottingham area where Uncle Matty's unit trained for D-Day. We became friends and had great fun with the family, but there was no definitive proof that their Kitty was Uncle Matty's Kitty, too.

June 2016 Portbail, Normandy. Left to right: Valérie Gautier Cardin; World War II hero, Jack Hamlin; and Stephanie Pepin in front of the school where Valérie works. Jack and seven other World War II veterans were given heroes' welcomes at the school, where they helped to celebrate the anniversary of D-Day in a lively question-and-answer session with the students. Jack's smile is priceless!

June 2016 Normandy American Cemetery, Colleville-sur-Mer. 508th veteran George Shenkle (left) and Marine Iwo Jima survivor Bill Schott (right) with me at a Uncle Matty's grave. In a very touching moment, George and Bill came over in their wheelchairs to comfort me. They are both great exemplars of the Greatest Generation.

June 2016 Normandy American Cemetery. My wife, Monica, and I experience a very emotional and spiritual moment at Uncle Matty's grave. I believe that every American should visit the American Cemetery at least once in their lifetime to honor fellow Americans who gave their lives for the freedoms we enjoy today. The enormity of that sacrifice, the vast sweep of row after row of white crosses, has the power to change your outlook on life.

June 2016 Carentan, Normandy. One of several ceremonies we attended with World War II veterans to commemorate the anniversary of June 6. All of the veterans present were honored and received medals; several received the Legion of Honor, the highest award for outstanding service to the French nation that a non-citizen can receive.

Left to right, first row: Unknown veteran, Erwin Davis, Robert Essler, unknown woman with camera, Henry Poisson. Second row: Emery Horne (behind Henry), Vincent Hagg (behind Erwin) Cliff Goodall (behind woman with camera). Standing, upper left: Uncle Matty's French Angel, Valérie Gautier Cardin, tallking with veteran Bill Schott.

June 2016 Ste. Mère-Eglise, Normandy. World War II veterans pose with three (unidentified) active-duty 82nd Airborne troopers during the annual celebration of D-day in the first town liberated in France. World War II veterans, left to right: Erwin Davis, Bill Schott, Jack Hamlin, Cliff Goodall. Sitting: George Shenkle. Sigrid Van Eck stands behind George. Heads turn on the streets of Ste. Mère-Eglise as the veterans walk the streets. They were the rock stars of 1944, and remain the greatest rock stars of today!

June 2016 Picauville, Normandy. Monica and I with Colonel (now General) Collet at a ceremony for his good friend, World War II hero, Captain Chet Graham. Chet's last wish was that his ashes be spread over his D-Day dropzone. Colonel Collet performed a beautiful ceremony; Chet's granddaughter, Cyndi Robinson Mathews, was in attendance, and emotionally spread Chet's ashes over the dropzone.

June 2016 Picauville. Left to right: Lieutenant General Stephen Townsend (Commander, XVIII Airborne Corps), Susan Eisenhower (President Eisenhower's granddaughter), Lucien Hasley (proprietor of Lucien's Wall), Command Sergeant Major Benjamin Jones (82nd ABD), at a ceremony at Lucien's Wall, where Lucien has hand-sculpted more than a hundred names of American airborne soldiers who fought in Normandy. For 72 years, Lucien had searched for the identity of an unknown 508th PIR medic who had saved the life of his brother on D-Day; at the ceremony, Susan Eisenhower revealed the hero to be Private First Class Frank E. Mackey, Jr., from West Philadelphia. When the Germans invaded his aid station, PFC Mackey ensured the escape of his wounded and a young French woman acting as nurse, but he was bayonetted in the back. Tragically, he bled to death on the side of the road as his aid station went up in flames on June 7, 1944.

June 2016 Normandy American Cemetery. Chief of Staff of the Army General Milley and I saluting. I met General Milley at the cemetery to pay our respects to Uncle Matty. On our way to the gravesite, "Taps" started playing in honor of June 6, and everyone instinctually stopped, snapped to attention, and saluted. It was an outstanding and very spontaneous moment. *Photo credit SFC Charles Burden.*

June 2016 Normandy American Cemetery. Chief of Staff of the Army General Milley with Monica and me at Uncle Matty's grave. General Milley and his wife Holly went out of their way to make our trip special: Holly invited us to join them on their visit to the cemetery and their tour of Omaha Beach and Utah Beach. Barely visible, on the right side of Uncle Matty's cross, is the challenge coin that General Milley placed on Matty's grave. The coin will be passed down in our family to preserve Uncle Matty's memory. *Photo credit SFC Charles Burden.*

June 2016 Omaha Beach, Normandy. General Milley and I collect some sacred sand from the most fiercely defended Allied landing beach in Normandy. Despite the solemnity of the occasion, I could not help smiling during the entire time we spent with the General. *Photo credit SFC Charles Burden.*

Nov 2016 508th PIR Association Reunion, North Charleston, South Carolina. Middle, front row: Donna Palmer, President of the Family and Friends of the 508th PIR Association, smiles for the camera with Monica and me, surrounded by active-duty paratroopers from 2nd Battalion (2 Fury), 508th PIR.

Nov 2016 508th PIR Association Reunion. Lieutenant Colonel James Browning, Commander, 2nd Battalion, 508th PIR, signs a photograph of Uncle Matty's rifle, to be presented as a gift to General Patrick Collet. The 2nd Battalion was deployed to Iraq January 2017, but is scheduled to return home in September 2017, just in time for the 2017 Friends and Family of the 508th PIR Association reunion in October.

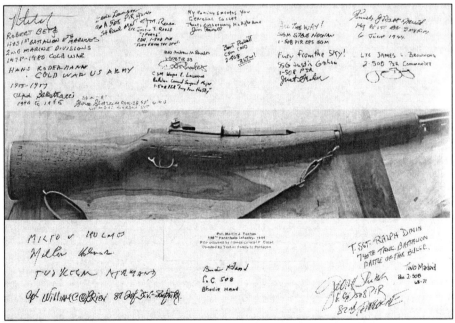

Nov 2016 508th PIR Association Reunion. A gift for my hero, French Army General Patrick Collet, Commander, 11th Parachute Brigade. General Collet volunteered an enormous amount of time and resources to acquire Uncle Matty's historic M-1 rifle, donate it to my family, and ensure its safe return to the United States. I will be forever grateful and felt proud to present him with this photograph. It is signed by 508th PIR World War II veterans Rock Merritt, Ernie Lamson, George Shenkle, and Brodie Hand; active-duty 508th Commanders Lieutenant Colonel James Browning (1st Battalion) and Lieutenant Colonel Justin Reese (2nd Battalion); other active-duty 508th members; and veterans from the New Jersey Battle of the Bulge Survivors' Group.

Dec 2016 General Milley's Quarters, Fort Meyer, Virginia. Left to right: I talk with Sergeant Major of the Army Dan Dailey; Army Chief of Staff General Milley; and the General's wife, Holly, who are absorbed in Uncle Matty's photo album. The album recounts our journey to France and the story of how Uncle Matty's rifle returned home.

Dec 2016 General Milley's Quarters. I happily pose with my uncle's rifle between Lieutenant Colonel James Shaw and Sergeant Major of the Army Dan Dailey. Colonel Shaw was instrumental in cutting through the red tape to bring Uncle Matty's historic M-1 home.

Dec 2016 General Milley's Quarters. I have the honor of being pinned by Sergeant Major of the Army Dan Dailey. When the Sergeant Major discovered I did not have an "Army Soldier for Life" pin, he removed his own from his jacket and pinned it on me! This photo captures both my feeling of pride and my speechless look. Meeting the Sergeant Major of the Army is an enlisted person's dream!

June 2017, General Milley's office at the Pentagon. My Mission Accomplished Moment! Oh, what a feeling! I sit at General Milley's desk, enjoying a peaceful and relaxing moment, as sister Liz gazes at Uncle Matty's rifle on display, cousin Noreen studies Eisenhower's globe, niece Nicole listens to our tour guide, and nephew Steven reads the handwritten note to General Milley from prior Chief of Staff of the Army General Raymond Odierno.

Dec 2016 General Milley's Quarters. Official group photo from the State Dinner hosted by General Milley and his wife, Holly. Left to right, front row: Sergeant Major of the Army Dan Dailey and his wife, French translator, French Army Chief of Staff General Bosser and his wife, Monica and I, Chief of Staff of the Army General Milley and Holly, Army Vice Chief of Staff of the Army General Dan Allen and his wife. Back row: General Joe Anderson (to the left, behind General Allen), Surgeon General of the Army General Nadja West (to the left, behind General Milley). *Photo credit SFC Charles Burden.*

June 2017, General Milley's office. On our first visit to General Milley, December 1, 2016, we presented him with a challenge coin on behalf of our friends, Bill and Christine Koch. The coin was in honor of their son, Steven Koch, who was killed in action in Afghanistan on March 3, 2008, during Operation Enduring Freedom. Steven served with 1st Battalion, 508th PIR, just as Uncle Matty had done. We were delighted to see the Kochs' coin displayed in the General's office when we visited the Pentagon six months after our first trip.

Dec 2016 Nottingham, England. Monica and I lift a glass with our new friends, Glyn Shipstone (left) and Graham Lawson, who operate Jump 44, a living history group. Glyn and Graham's knowledge of World War II prevailed as we toured all around Nottingham, tracing Uncle Matty's time there in 1944. We love those British Pubs!

December 2016 Nottingham. Monica and I meet Andrew Smart, a reporter for the *Nottingham Post*, who wrote two articles about our search for the mysterious Kitty. His articles spurred the interest of a family we met in Nottingham, whose mother had been named Kitty. The family was lovely, and our memories of our time together will last forever, but we left still wondering if their mother had been the Kitty whose name Uncle Matty had engraved on his rifle.

April 2017 Nottingham, grade school homework assignment. Uncle Matty's story touched the lives of four generations! This photograph was sent to us by Alice Pitt, Kitty's granddaughter, whose eight-year-old son Fred became so fascinated with the search for the Kitty Uncle Matty had known that he made it the subject of a history homework assignment. Uncle Matty's youngest fan combined photographs of Uncle Matty's M-1 rifle, a picture of his great grandmother, and one of himself, and wrote touching words about his understanding of how two people had comforted each other during horrible times. Just the possibility that his great grandmother Kitty had known Uncle Matty gave him a special connection to Matty's story. It is a great joy to me that four generations in Nottingham have connected in this British–American saga of World War II. *Photo courtesy of Alice Pitt.*

Dec 2016 Nottingham Council House. Monica and I proudly display the winning score of the annual Army–Navy football game, 21–17, standing with one of the famous stone lions at the city hall in downtown Nottingham. It was here that we learned that Army had beat Navy for the first time in fifteen years! Army had donned a snazzy new 82nd Airborne uniform, and like many other patriotic Army fans, we believed that paratroopers past and present had infused their team with the Airborne spirit. We had fun broadcasting the winning score from the spot where many 82nd troopers had been photographed in World War II.

June 4, 2017 Saint Jerome's Church, Bronx, New York. Monica and I posed with Peter and Ann Donahue and Monica's mother, Arline Spiro (seated), on the day of Uncle Matty's honorary mass. Peter is the son of Uncle Matty's best childhood friend, also named Peter Donahue. Our families lost touch after the war, but Uncle Matty has reunited us again.

June 4, 2017, Saint Jerome's Church. I speak at the first Annual Mass in honor of Uncle Matty. Father Correa kindly called me up to tell Matty's story. More than forty friends and family members and a hundred other parishioners attended. Uncle Matty got three standing ovations during the mass!

June 4, 2017 Bronx Brewery. Left to right: My brother, John (Jackie) Farrell, and I celebrate with our cousins Noreen Denett and Dee Farrell after Uncle Matty's mass in the manner he would have appreciated—with a cold beer at a friendly Bronx bar.

June 4, 2017 Bronx Brewery. Monica, my best friend and the love of my life, and I enjoy a beer to celebrate bringing the family together.

Dec 2016 Annual Army–Navy Football Game, Baltimore, Maryland. Legendary 82nd Airborne paratrooper, Command Sergeant Major Kenneth "Rock" Merritt with president-elect Trump after the Army–Navy game. Army won 21-17, beating Navy for the first time in fifteen years. Army fans believe their new 82nd Airborne uniform made the difference. Rock, who has met many presidents, served in World War II, Korea, and Vietnam, and made more than two hundred parachute drops. As a tribute to Rock and a thank you for his friendship, I close the photographs in our book with his picture. *Photo courtesy of Rock Merritt and the 508th PIR Friends and Family Association.*

PART FIVE

RECALLING TIMES PAST:
FRIENDS AND HEROES AT
HOME AND IN COMBAT

Chapter 18
UNCLE MATTY'S BEST FRIEND, JIM MCMAHON

Uncle Matty's best friend in the Army was Jim McMahon. The two were inseparable from the time they met at Camp Upton, Long Island, right up until the D-Day jump. Although I myself never had the chance to meet Jim, my sister Liz and he developed a friendship through correspondence and enjoyed each other's company at 508th PIR reunions. Jim was a great source of information on Uncle Matty and graciously shared everything he could remember. We later found out our mother had visited him after the war, and he had been able to answer many of her questions. No doubt about it: Jim was a very special person for our family.

The friendship between Jim and Uncle Matty is proof of the old saying "Opposites attract." Jim was as quiet as Uncle Matty was wild and outgoing. He served as Battalion Wire Chief, an extremely vital and dangerous function. Jim was in charge of maintaining the wire communications systems that connected the battalion headquarters with the front line rifle companies, a highly vulnerable network that required continual surveillance and was often disrupted by enemy patrols or artillery fire. Locating and repairing the frequent wire breaks required that "Mac" and his small crew operate day and night, in all weather, often exposed to enemy small-arms and artillery fire.

Jim completed his wartime service in the elite assignment to provide security for General Eisenhower at his headquarters in Frankfurt, Germany. He reached the rank of Sergeant and wore the stunning white scarf and gloves of General Eisenhower's honor guard. Among his many wartime honors, Jim was awarded the Bronze Star with Oak Leaf Cluster and two Combat Jump Stars. Above all, Jim's execution of his dangerous missions saved countless young American lives.

Left to right: Jim McMahon and Uncle Matty dancing like vaudeville pros. Both from the Bronx, the two of them met when they joined the army, and went through training, shipment overseas, and their unit's preparation for Normandy together. Jim last saw Matty when they shook hands before boarding separate planes on D-Day. Matty's old friend marveled as he recalled happy-go-lucky Matty, always the life of the party.

Although he was a very quiet, reserved person, Jim stepped out of his comfort zone in several letters he wrote to Liz. The letters show how close the two became, and Liz was both fascinated and touched by his words. He even told her she would make a great paratrooper!

The excerpts from Jim's letters below, provided with Liz's blessing, include anecdotes about his friendship with Matty. They are a good reflection of Jim's outstanding quality as a person and have been a precious resource in our attempt to find out more about our uncle.

Dear Elizabeth,

I received your very kind and informative letter today, and I must say that it is a pleasure to hear from the niece of my dear departed buddy Martin Teahan. I also see that you have met my good friend Mr. O.B. Hill. O.B. and I go back fifty-eight years, and if you met O.B., you met the best.

Yes, I knew your Uncle Marty. We were buddies from the very beginning of our Army tour of duty. Together, we went through basic training and paratroop training in this country and overseas. We first met in [...] Camp Upton out in Long Island, New York, where New York State sent all the new recruits. Marty and I were both from the Bronx, so this is where we were sent. At that time, we had been in the army about six or seven days, and we were together right up to D-Day, June 6.

On June 6, about 2:00 am, Marty was assigned to board one plane, and I was assigned to board another plane. Before boarding, we wished each other luck and shook hands. That was the last time I saw Marty alive. The rest of the story you know.

[...] Marty and I were [...] young (early twenties). We both liked a good time, and when you were with Marty, that's what you got—A GOOD TIME! We would meet girls and go to dances, bars, roller rinks, army canteens, etc. All these [...] were "fun places" during the war—there was nothing else.

He was a great dancer. He loved doing all those crazy "Jitterbug" steps that were so popular in those days. [...] The English girls loved to dance with him. More, they loved his New York Bronx accent, which was rare in England.

Sense of humor? He had a great sense of humor! For instance, there was this guy in basic training who never took a shower even after running and exercising all day. He smelled like a bear, so your Uncle Marty nicknamed this guy "Bathless Billy." Then there was another guy who had big, oversized, flat feet. Marty named this guy "Flounder Foot." There was another guy [...] who never shut his mouth. Marty would say in his Bronx accent, "Here comes Canyon Mouth!" Once we were waiting in a long movie line, and Marty said to me, "If I'd known how long this line was going be, I would have packed a lunch." That's the way he was—always with a little humorous remark.

Your Uncle Marty loved all the real old-time songs like "East Side, West Side," "Mary," "I'm a Yankee Doodle Dandy," "Down by the Old Mill Stream," and "Danny Boy." He knew all the songs word for word. If there was a piano [...], he would get the piano player to play some of his favorites, [and ...] get the guys in the room to sing the songs his way. [...]He became "The Mitch Miller of World War II." In time, he would have the whole room singing in harmony. He was a fun guy, [...] always talking about his old Bronx neighborhood (138th Street, St. Ann's Church, etc.). He loved his Irish heritage [and] Irish jokes. And stories! He had a million of them to tell.

In a more serious moment [...at] Fort Benning, Georgia, Marty, myself, and two other guys were lying in our bunks, making small talk about baseball, food, what's for dinner, etc. The question came up, "What are your plans after the war?" Most of the answers were, "Get married; Go to college; I don't know." Marty's answer: "I don't think I'll be around after the war, so I'm not thinking about it."

Take Care and God Bless,
Jim McMahon

Dear Elizabeth,

Just a note to let you know that I received your photos and copies of information [...] from the 508th website. (I did not know the 508th had a website.) Live and learn. [They] ... were very interesting to me and brought back a lot of fond memories of my youth. I want to thank you very much for doing all that work [...]. It must have been difficult and time-consuming for you. Thank you again.

As for the 508th reunion at Fort Mitchell, Kentucky, I am sorry to say [...] I am in poor health and not able to travel. You mention Robert Shields [as a] "Platoon Sergeant." Did you know that, later in the war, he received a "battlefield commission" and [...] became Lieutenant Robert Shields? Your uncle was very fond of him. They both played guitars. (See the photos you sent.)

If you attend the reunion, give my love to all.

Love,
Jim McMahon

Liz and Jim did, indeed, share a special bond. After all, as Matty's best friend, Jim would have known my uncle the best. Jim passed away on March 7, 2006. I greatly regret I never got to meet him. What a great guy he was! I hope he and Uncle Matty are having fun and enjoying themselves in Paratrooper Heaven. Rest in Peace, Jim McMahon, a wonderful friend and heroic 82nd Airborne paratrooper.

Chapter 19
UNCLE MATTY'S ARMY BUDDY, ART JACOBY

As of this writing, to my knowledge, Art Jacoby is the only 508th veteran still alive who was Matty's friend or had firsthand knowledge about his life. Uncle Matty was great friends with Art and was part of his crew, along with Jim Lutton, Garfield Wilkinson, Joe Atkins, and Frank Pesce, all hell-raisers. All were adept at skills like intelligence gathering, elusiveness, deception, and persuasion to get want they wanted, especially when it came to having fun and enjoying the moment. My sister Liz has told me many stories about Art, all of which convey him as a fearless paratrooper—smart, fit, often in trouble, but very skilled at talking his way out of it. Devoted to the 508th mission and all-out fighting the Germans, he would nevertheless have his fun, no matter what.

The official 508th PIR website lovingly describes Art as follows:

> *Arthur (Jake) Jacoby was an outstanding, courageous combat soldier, but a ne'er-do-well garrison soldier, always pursuing his own agenda and marching to a different drummer than his*

contemporaries. Jake was a magnificent patrol leader [who] habitually accomplished his missions and provided decision-makers with timely, accurate, and comprehensive information concerning the identification and capabilities of German forces in combat. Yes, Jacoby was admired, envied, and respected by his peers and, with reservations, by his superiors. Jake mastered the skills necessary to function effectively in the Intelligence section, e.g., develop sand tables, sketches, and maps, lead patrols, and [...] capture and interrogate prisoners.

Art Jacoby (right) and Uncle Matty (middle), on a break in training in Nottingham, England, shortly before D-Day. Art participated in every campaign of the 508th PIR in World War II.

Arthur Jacoby and his buddies Jim Lutton, Garfield Wilkinson, and Joe Atkins provided the core of the Battalion S2 Section [...], perform[ing] the most dangerous jobs in the battalion. However, at times, they acted as if World War II had been created just for them to have fun. When they were not leading an attack, patrolling behind the lines to determine the Germans' deployment or capturing Germans for interrogation, they were busy finding ways and means to improve their welfare or just to have fun. On or off the battlefield, nothing was sacred or exempt from their attention. If it was not under heavy guard, it was fair game, [and] often even some of the "guarded" refreshments and food were acquired. The four comrades were well trained [...]. Skilled in methods for infiltrating German lines and positions, and extremely adroit at capturing Germans and bringing them safely though friendly lines, they were irreplaceable, courageous, dependable, and successful in combat. If they did not exist, the 508th PIR would have had to create them! (www.508pir. org/pdf_files/bio_jacoby_arthur_b.pdf. Accessed: May 13, 2017.)

In May 2016, one of my major missions became to find and talk to Art to see what he remembered about my uncle. A Google search revealed only the obituary of his wife Betsy, his wife of sixty-nine years, who had passed away on January 22, 2013. The notice listed his phone number, but when I called it, I received an "out-of-service" message. As discouraging as this was, I knew I could not stop here. Might Art have passed away and joined his buddies in Paratrooper Heaven? If so, none of Uncle Matty's good friends were still alive to help tell the remarkable story of the return of his M-1 rifle. Given Art's special connection to Uncle Matty, I especially wanted to tell him the story of the rifle's repatriation—not only for personal reasons concerning our own family history, or even the history of the 508th, but because I knew the story would mean the world to Art.

The obituary notice mentioned the church that Art and Betsy attended, which, luckily for me, had a Facebook page. I liked it and left a voice message stating I would like to contact Art. The message was answered by the delightful Sara McDougald Poston, who was fascinated to hear that Matty Teahan's rifle had been found and that I wanted to talk to Art about it. Still bucking the odds, Art was alive and well and living in California. Sara graciously passed on my message. Near tears at the news, Art was deeply touched to hear about Uncle Matty and the discovery of his rifle, and was eager to talk to me. Wow! I was going to get my wish and talk to Art!

At 8:00 pm on May 18, 2016, I had the distinct pleasure of talking to Art Jacoby. He was indeed the special character I had heard so much about. The conversation was at first awkward, but after a few minutes we were talking to each other like long-lost Army buddies. Art said he got "real choked up" when he heard about the news. The paratroopers were brothers who truly loved each other. "It was sad for me losing so many guys on D-Day," is how he put it.

Here are a few of the stories Art recalled about Matty and his paratrooper buddies:

> *One day your uncle, Frank Pesce, a few others, and I were caught eating the officers' food in their quarters. We ate all the food and drank whatever booze we could find. The officers punished us and made us go outside and dig a 6x6 foxhole. We all were trained in demolitions for the D-Day Invasion of Normandy. One of the guys, I do not remember who, decided that we should just dig the outline of a foxhole and then place dynamite in the middle. So we did. Well, we blew stuff all over hell and caused such a scene that the officers ended up even more pissed off at us! We all got into trouble for blowing up the foxhole. As the ringleader, I was thrown in the brig. This was shortly before D-Day. On June 5th, they needed every available body, so I was let out. I made the jump into Normandy in my prison uniform!*

> *Your Uncle Marty was always having fun. He was just a fun-loving kid. All of the English and Irish girls loved his Bronx Irish accent and the way he sang and danced. Once he got on the dance floor, you could not get him off. They were crazy times. Marty told me the English and Irish girls believed that, if they had sex standing up, they could not get pregnant!*
> *Your uncle was wounded and captured, using his rifle as a crutch. He moved his hand, and a dirty Kraut shot him. That is how I was told he died.*

Art was ninety-two when I first contacted him. "Not one of our troopers chickened out on their jumps or missions," he was proud to tell me. "They all knew we would win—it was just a matter of when. I never lost a man on patrol. No detail was too small, and we were tuned in to everything surrounding us. We could all tell who the others were, even in the pitch-dark night. We kicked the shit out of the Germans."

Art participated in all of the 508th PIR campaigns and was awarded the Bronze Star and four battle star medals. He parachuted into Normandy and Holland, fought through the bitter cold, sunless days, and in the deep snows of the densely forested Ardennes, proceeded to the fortified Siegfried Line, and went all the way to the Roer River, the threshold to Germany. Art has now remarried and reluctantly agreed to his new wife's wish that he stop working. Amazingly, he says he's in great shape and still wants to work! What a fine example of the Greatest Generation's work ethic, so different from the attitude among so many in younger generations today.

I called Art after our return from our June 2016 visit to Normandy. I could sense he was almost crying when I told him about holding his buddy Marty's rifle, and how General Milley, the US Army Chief of Staff, met us at the gravesite to salute and say a prayer over his grave. He was deeply touched that his good buddy Marty was getting the honor and recognition he surely deserved. I told Art he would be invited to the Pentagon at the end of the year to attend a ceremony to officially donate Matty's rifle to the US Army. Stunned and silent for almost a minute, he was all choked up when he was finally able to speak. "Yes," he said. "I will certainly go to the Pentagon—if I am still alive."

Chapter 20
A FAMILY FRIENDSHIP WITH THE DONAHUES

My journey to bring Uncle Matty back home has been an exercise in connecting a series of improbable dots. One experience led to another; the first connection introduced me to the next. Every time I thought the chain would break, something new would emerge. Eventually, the chain led back all the way to Peter Donahue, my uncle's very best childhood friend. Peter and Uncle Matty used to hang out on 138th Street together. They played all the typical Irish South Bronx street games, and when it got hot, they would cool off in the Harlem River by jumping off the Willis Avenue Bridge. How do I know these things? My sister told me, based on conversations with our mother and grandmother. "Oh," mom reminisced, "Peter Donahue—he was that skinny kid who ate hotdogs in my mom's apartment."

Looking back now, it's fascinating to me to see how the dots to Peter Donahue got connected. Soon after Uncle Matty's rifle had been found in France, I wrote an article about it for the press and submitted it to fifteen publications. To my surprise, eleven of them published it! Bill McWeeney, who graduated from Saint Jerome's

School in 1940, and who'd also grown up on 138th Street, read the article and posted it on The Bronx Board, an on-line forum that I had no idea existed. The forum is a great way for people who grew up in the Bronx decades ago to share stories and pictures and find old friends. That's where Peter Donahue's son, Peter Jr., read the story and responded that his father and Uncle Matty were best friends.

Pete Donahue, the son of Uncle Matty's best friend, Peter, and I marvel at the incredible story of Uncle Matty's rifle and reminisce about how close our families used to be back in the 1940s. Thanks to Uncle Matty, our families have now reconnected, and Pete and I have become great friends.

Bill McWeeney responded to Peter Jr.'s post, saying he would like to speak with him. Then he hunted down my telephone number and gave me a call. Bill and I quickly became great friends, and began a frantic search for the mysterious Peter Jr. This went on for more than a month, but we never gave up and even asked the Bronx Board to reach out to us. Bill and I were determined to find our man, no matter what we had to do. Finally, one day Peter Jr. personally responded with the following email. It turned out that he checked the Bronx Board only every six weeks or so.

Hello Jim,

I just noticed your email from the Bronx Board and wanted to contact you. My father often spoke of your uncle and what good friends they were on 138th St before the war. My dad died early at forty-seven in 1970 and my recollections are fifty-five-plus years old, but if I can be of help to you, please let me know.

Regards,
Pete Donahue Jr, formerly from 430 E. 138th St.

Pete Jr. and I quickly arranged to speak on the phone. Of course, we hit it off. Our first conversation lasted for an hour and a half! We shared stories about his dad, my uncle, and our own experiences growing up in the Bronx. Just like Bill McWeeney, Pete has a great memory. His stories and recollections are priceless. Before we spoke, I had sent him some pictures of Uncle Matty and the old neighborhood, and Pete was able to identify some of the people I didn't recognize. These were old photos, classic black-and-whites and sepia-toned snapshots dating from before and just after the war, where the guys were hanging out on 138th Street, for example, or clowning around on at Rockaway beach. This had always been one of Uncle Matty's favorite spots, and now I knew that he'd shared some of the happiest moments of his brief life with his best buddy, Peter.

Pete Jr. also identified two of Uncle Matty's other very good friends, Billy Burke and Mike Noonan. Billy had been the best man at Peter's wedding, and Mike Noonan had served as an usher. Pete Jr. told me if Uncle Matty had survived, he would surely have been a part of Billy's and Mike's weddings, and I know they would have been at Matty's wedding, too. Peter Donahue would probably have been his best man.

By the time Pete and I finally got off the phone, he'd invited Monica and me to his house. We arrived at Pete Jr.'s on Saturday, October 29, 2016, along with my mother-in-law, Arline. We were all very excited to meet Pete and his wife, Ann, and reminisce about our families. Having Monica's mother with us made me very happy. Her husband Phil, my father-in-law, had passed away in August 2014. Phil had been like a father to me. He was a veteran of the Korean War, and I know he would have loved Uncle Matty's story. Arline was so excited that her eyes were almost popping out of her head. Her step had a little extra skip in it as we entered Pete's house.

Pete Jr. and Ann graciously received us and seemed as excited as we were to explore our mutual family connections. Pete volunteers for the EMS squad in Toms River, New Jersey, and he recounted a conversation he'd had with a buddy on his squad about Uncle Matty's Facebook page. No sooner had he said a few words than his friend stopped him in his tracks. "Are you kidding?" he excitedly asked. "I've been following that story on Facebook for months now! It's fascinating!" It is, indeed, a small world. I've been amazed to watch how interest in my uncle's story has exploded. It was wonderful to hear how Pete Jr. and his buddy realized they, too, had a connection to it.

Soon we were all looking through their family photo albums, starting with pictures of Pete's father during the war. Matty's old friend Peter had served with the Army Air Corps in the Pacific. His had been a crucial job: he operated a switchboard in Tinian, the launching point for B-29s that dropped the atomic bombs on Hiroshima and Nagasaki. Peter had told his son about his time in the Pacific, including the horrific sight of Japanese parents murdering their babies by dropping them off a cliff, and then committing suicide by jumping off themselves, because they were so terrified by propaganda that portrayed Americans as beastly monsters. We were deeply touched when Pete described how his dad had mourned the death of Uncle Matty. After the war, his dad had worked for Con Edison in New York City. Matty's old friend, the skinny kid who'd devoured so many hotdogs at our home, often visited my mother and grandmother after Matty's death, and I'm certain his visits were a comfort to them.

After the photos of his father in the war, Pete's family album turned to pictures of the old neighborhood on 138th Street. The photographs were very similar to those I'd shared with Pete Jr. Turning the pages and reminiscing, we suddenly came across a photograph that stunned me beyond words. *Oh, my God! That's my mother, right smack in the middle of Pete's family album!* When I finally exclaimed, "That's mom!" Arline instantly stopped drinking coffee and eating cake and sprang up like a sixteen-year-old kid. "Let me see! Let me see!" she demanded. Arline would not be denied—she took control of the moment! She grabbed the album and stared at the picture. "How were Peter and my mom connected? Why is her picture in this album?" she asked, and a flurry other questions.

Actually, the story was very simple. Because mom and Uncle Matty were so close, they would often hang out with each other's friends, hence her portrait in Pete Jr.'s album. The portrait, which none of us in the family had ever seen, was obviously a high school graduation picture. I do have her diploma, dated January 1941. Yes, our mom was beautiful, and she was smiling in the picture. It was taken when she was only eighteen, before Uncle Matty was killed in the war, before she had met my father.

Seeing her picture as a beautiful, young woman, still full of innocence and possibility, just on the verge of the hard realities of war and personal fate that would later rule her life, I felt overwhelmed by emotion. It also pumped up my adrenaline. This was true for everyone else in the room as well, and especially for Arline, who enjoyed the surprise discovery even more than the rest of us. The dots had again been connected, and this time they ended with an exclamation point!

Pete Jr. told me he'd moved up to the North Bronx, just as I had as a teenager. We shared memories of playing Stickball, Off the Point, Johnnie on a Pony, and many other street games. Of course, we'd also frequented the same Irish bars. He gleefully reminisced about the bars on Kingsbridge Road, one of which was called "The Lodge."

It was a bar I, too, had frequented—perhaps a little too often. Pete and I now wonder if we were ever there at the same time. It seems very likely to us both.

I next showed Pete and Ann our photo album devoted to Uncle Matty. It was a lot of fun. In the official photograph of Matty's 1938 graduating class from St. Jerome's School, we could now identify Peter Donahue and Billy Burke. Pete Jr. was amazed at the photographs from Normandy, especially those of General Milley at Uncle Matty's grave. He marveled at the pictures of Uncle Matty's rifle, and agreed that General Collet is a hero. Pete, too, holds him in the highest respect for what he has done for me and my family.

After our meeting with Pete Jr., I set up a phone call between him and Bill McWeeney. Bill was excited to see Pete Jr.'s address from the old neighborhood. He remembers it as the only apartment building to have a self-serving elevator in the South Bronx! Bill called it a "luxury building" and said he often snuck into it just to ride the elevator!

Bill and Pete Jr. both wrote to me after their phone chat:

Bill: I had a long & satisfying talk with Pete this morning. I knew all the Dwyers, John, Tommy, Danny & Eddie. They lived across the street from us on 137 St. Eddie is the only one still alive. I located him in upstate NY about a year ago, and called him. Pete did live at that address I recognized at the LIDO GARDENS on 138 where we kids would ride the self-service elevators.

Peter Jr.: I had a delightful conversation with "Williemac" this morning. I had to tell him that he lost his South Bronx accent and acquired a Texas drawl. He laughed and blamed it on his wife. He is a well-traveled man, and I will keep in touch with him going forward. He sounds much younger than his ninety years, and I really enjoyed his retirement story about how at sixty-two he enrolled as a freshman in an Irish college in Ireland for a year.

Add another footnote to this being a small world. Bill was friends with my deceased uncle, John Dwyer. They lived across the street from each other on 137th Street and Bill knew the entire Dwyer family.

Connecting the dots leading to Peter Donahue turned out to be a very special and rewarding process. Together, Pete Jr., Bill McWeeney, and I were able to fill a lot of gaps in the stories of all of our families and help bring back to life the old Irish South Bronx, just as it had been in Uncle Matty's heyday. Bill has become a great friend, and Pete Jr. and I have renewed the old friendship between our families. Monica and I look forward to future visits with him and his lovely wife. Maybe best of all, our connections to Uncle Matty have allowed us to write a new chapter in the story that all of our families share and pass this down to younger generations.

Uncle Matty, thank you! I can see you now in Paratrooper Heaven, smiling down upon us as you lift up your glass and toast a job well done! *To connecting the dots! To the future!*

Chapter 21
A FAMILY FRIENDSHIP
WITH O.B. HILL

The story of Uncle Matty and the return of his rifle would not be complete without his good friend, O.B. Hill, the Headquarters Company, 1st Battalion Message Center Chief, and a legendary 508th PIR soldier who earned the Bronze Star and Purple Heart with Oak Leaf Cluster. On his many visits to Normandy after the war, O.B. would always offer up a prayer at the gravesites of his friend Matty and their Commanding Officer, Captain Gerard Ruddy, in the American Cemetery at Collville-Sur-Mer. "The guys in the graves are the real heroes," he always said.

Jumping in first position at the head of his stick, Captain Ruddy was killed by machine-gun fire on D-Day. Lt. McElligott, who had directed O.B. to switch places with him, jumped as second man out, was wounded in the stomach and captured by the Germans. O.B. paid special honor to Captain Ruddy for the rest of his life—of all the men in his plane, only the last four jumpers, himself included, had escaped being killed, wounded, or captured.

On June 6, 1974, while honoring Captain Ruddy at his gravesite some thirty years after that fatal day, O.B. believed he heard a message

O.B. Hill and my sister Liz met each other in June 2000, on the 508th Association's trip to Normandy. They struck up a correspondence and developed a special relationship. In one amazing letter, O.B. recited the entire song "Phil the Fluter" word-for-word. This was one of Uncle Matty's favorites, and O.B. said he performed it with gusto to the great entertainment his buddies. *Photo courtesy of Joe Hill, son of O.B. Hill*

from the good Captain: "Do something to get the men together," he said. O.B. took this as a calling from his fallen CO, and thus it was he founded The 508th Parachute Infantry Regiment Association.

O.B. recalls this experience in his unpublished *Executive Summary of the 508th PIR*:

> *The original idea for the 508th Association came to me while I was visiting the grave of my Company Commander at St. Laurent Cemetery, located at Omaha Beach in Normandy, France. Bill Goudy and I were standing at his grave, reflecting on some of the experiences of our time with this great man. We both agreed that he was truly a wonderful man and that any of his men would have followed him through the fires of Hell. I have said many times, with complete honesty, that Captain Gerard A. Ruddy was the finest man that I have ever met. I am now seventy-nine years old, and that statement is still completely true. Many have said that I must have gone through too many artillery barrages or that I landed on my head one time too many, but I still say that the idea to start a reunion came to me from Captain Ruddy during our visit to his grave that day.*

As the Founder and Permanent Chairman of the 508th Association, O.B. Hill worked tirelessly on behalf of his fellow veterans and had the pleasure of seeing interest in the Association grow and its membership greatly expand. Veterans of World War II famously bottled up their emotions and refused to talk about the war. He knew from experience just how important it was for his fellow troopers to have an outlet and a place to talk to members of their own units who had lived through the same experiences. The creation of the 508th Association also allowed family members and friends of the regiment to learn about their loved ones' experiences and meet their brothers-in-arms. As the veterans themselves aged and passed away, the Association became an increasingly important way of keeping the unit's special history alive, as younger generations picked up the torch and became more involved in Association activities and in archiving, transcribing, recording, and otherwise discovering and preserving the experiences of their parents and grandparents during the war.

This was certainly the case for my sister Liz Farrell, who became fascinated by our Uncle Matty early in life, perhaps from listening to our mother's and grandmother's stories and frequent references to their lively, funny, rapscallion of a brother and beloved youngest son. Liz joined the Association early on. "Meeting O.B.," she told me, "was one of the most important things that ever happened to me." An enthusiastic participant from the start, Liz soon found a sense of community with the veterans and their families, and participating in reunions, learning about Uncle Matty, his buddies, and the regimental history, and helping to document and preserve the 508th's proud past became nothing short of a calling. As she wrote in the Fall 2002 edition of the *508th PIR Association Newsletter*:

> *My uncle, Martin Teahan, was in 508th Headquarters Company, 1st Battalion. He was KIA on June 6, 1944, in Picauville. In 1990, I was put in touch with O.B. Hill. He sent me a wonderful letter. He had been very good friends with my Uncle Martin. What a treat and an honor it was for me to speak to someone from the 508th who knew my uncle so long ago!*
>
> *In June 2000, I met O.B. in Normandy for the first time. Meeting O.B. and other 508ers and visiting my uncle's grave will remain as one of the highlights of my life. I learned of the intense bond of friendship that was forged among the men of the 508. Getting a message from O.B. was always good fun. I simply adored him like everyone else did. I'm glad I have this opportunity to thank all of you for what you did so long ago. Please rest assured it will never be forgotten and neither will O.B.*
>
>

Thanks for your kindness,
Liz Farrell

O.B. and my sister Liz had begun communicating on August 23, 1990, and had since become the best of friends. He was a treasure trove of information about the heroic missions in which he had participated and greatly helped Liz on her lifelong mission to find out anything she could about Uncle Matty. O.B and Liz considered themselves family, as the following sample from his many letters to Liz show. Equally valued by them both, this emotional bond and special friendship answered many of Liz's questions about what Uncle Matty must have been like.

23 August 1990
Dear Ms Farrell,

I just received a copy of your letter [...] regarding Martie [Matty] Teahan. Martie was in my Company, Headquarters Company First Battalion, of the 508th Parachute Infantry. He was a very good friend and I have visited his grave in Normandy on numerous occasions.

In my opinion, Martie was above the average Paratrooper. He had a wonderful sense of humor, was a great conversationalist, was well liked by everyone who knew him, and could sing Irish songs like no other. I have no idea why, but I can still remember the words to one that he sang regularly. It was about a character known as Phil the Fluter. Martie could sing it with the proper Irish brogue, and it was most entertaining.

During many of the events that I attend, we are given a few moments for a silent prayer [...]. Since the invasion of Normandy, I have always used that silent prayer time to remember Martie along with Earl Wilson and some others. I mention Earl because he and Martie were very close.

I do not [...] have any of the details concerning how, where, or when Martie was killed. At our reunion this year [...], I will be asking for the details, and I feel certain that someone there will have the facts. If I learn anything at all, I will notify you when we return home. [...]We are scheduled to return about September 13. My wife and I are celebrating our 50th wedding anniversary [...] and have planned a trip to Massachusetts, New Hampshire, Vermont, and Maine for after the reunion.

Martie [...] could always be counted on for full support in whatever our assignment happened to be. He was never one to cause any trouble. As I said, Martie was just one of those men everyone liked. As you said in your letter, "He was a special person."

I would very much like to have some of the photos that you mention. I have searched through what I have and cannot locate anything that Martie is in. I will be sending you a copy of a book written by one of our British friends regarding our time in Nottingham, England, before the invasion of Normandy on June 6, 1944. (David J. Pike, Airborne in Nottingham, 1991). The photo at the bottom of page 28 shows part of our Company in line for coffee and doughnuts just before the invasion. Martie is not in that photo, but he most certainly was in the line. Perhaps I will be able to locate something more appropriate while at the reunion. Many of our men still have articles from that time [...].

Sincere Airborne Wishes,

O.B. Hill

September 27, 1990

Dear Elizabeth,

Forgive my informality, but as a niece of Marty, you are practically considered to be one of the family. During our time in the service, all of us seemed to be like brothers. Some were closer than others, but all of us had the deepest respect for each other. I was an only child, so maybe it seemed more like a big family to me than it did to some of the others. I know that I thoroughly enjoyed having so many that I could call close friends.

I mailed your letter to another from our company. Marty and Jim McMahon were good friends also. I am certain that Jim will be happy to read your letters, and you most likely will hear from him. I am sure Jim remembers the song "Phil the Fluter." As well as I can remember, the words were:

> *Have you heard of Phil the Fluter*
> *From the town of Ballymuck*
> *Sure the times were going hard with him*
> *In fact the man was bruck*
> *So he sent out invitations*
> *To his neighbors one and all*
> *Of how he would like their gaiety*
> *This evening at the ball*
> *But before going out*
> *He was careful to suggest to them*
> *That if they found a hat*
> *That was convenient to the door*
> *The more that they put into it*
> *The better would the music be*
> *The better would the music be*
> *The battering on the floor*
> *With a root and a toot*
> *And a diddle on the fiddly*
> *Walking down the middle*
> *Like a herring on the griddle*
> *Walking all around and over to the wall*
> *Sure and hadn't we the gaiety at Phil the Fluter's Ball*

I couldn't type in the Irish brogue, but perhaps [...] someone in your family [...] can remember this same song. [...] Following the reunion, my wife and I flew to Boston, got a car, and drove through parts of New England, Massachusetts, Maine, New Hampshire,

Vermont, and up into Canada. It was the first time in that area for my wife and the first time that I had the opportunity to see any of the scenery. I was always there on business. Rush trips.

I was in Normandy again this January, and each time, I [...] visit the graves of all those from my company. There are far too many of them there: Our Battalion Commander, our Company Commander, our First Sergeant and others. All of them were good men. They were all brave, loyal to their country, and proved that they would give their all in the effort to keep our way of life safe from those who were out to destroy it. I am proud to have been a part of that effort, and I will always remember those who were with me. They remain in my memory as the finest men that I have ever known.

I look forward to hearing from you again. During our reunion, I will read your letter to those from HQ, Co. 1st Bn. who were with us in Normandy. I feel sure that someone there will be able to furnish us with some of the details.

Faithful people such as you are not common in our day and age. I commend you highly for what you are doing. You can be sure that during my next visit to Ste. Laurent Cemetery in Normandy, I will spend some extra time with Martie.

Thank you very much for giving me the opportunity to express my opinion of a Great Trooper. Your uncle was truly one of the finest.

Sincerely,
O.B. Hill

8 October 1990
Dear Elizabeth,

Got the photos, and they are terrific. I was able to recognize several. [....]One of them in several shots is John Sivetz. He was the best buddy that I had. His family consisted of a younger brother and an older sister. His brother was in school, and his sister was in the Coast Guard. John would go on furlough for one day with them and then go to my house in Indiana. He was just like one of the family. He passed away three years ago. [....]

Another who is in several of the photos is Jim McMahon. [....] Jim is the other one in the photo of the two in their underwear shorts. He and Marty were pretty close also. [....] The [...] two in Class A uniform kicking up their heels and holding their hats in their hands are Marty and McMahon. The guy in the jeep is me. Like many of the others, I never did learn that we were supposed to be serious. If I remember correctly, I think that I was acting as if I were going to steal the jeep.

In past meetings and in print, I have said that I have never met a finer bunch of men than those that I served with in the 508th. It is still a true statement. They were great then, and they are great today. Many other units say that we now have the finest association in existence, and I think it is true. If it is true, it is due to the men who are in it. They were one of the best fighting teams in the U.S. Army in WWII, and they are still among the best today. I am very proud to be one of them.

Thanks again for the photos, Elizabeth. I will continue to try and find someone who might have some information on how Marty was killed. It is possible that someone is still around who was with him. I'll keep looking.

Take good care.
O.B. Hill

18 December 1991
Dear Elizabeth,

Thank you so very much for the Christmas card and for [your] note. [....]Christmas has always been extra special with me.

This past year has been one with a lot of events [...] for the 508th Association. Our reunion was great, and we had a mini-reunion also of just my company, [where] I told the others of our letters back and forth. I can assure you that I am not the only one who remembers Martie with many pleasant things. He was quite a guy and was well liked by everyone in the company.

I also got to visit Normandy in November and will be going back in June. We are preparing the schedule for the 50th anniversary of D-Day, and there will be three-hundred, fifty of us in the group. It will be the first trip back for many of them and will no doubt be the last for some also. We are losing them far too quickly.

If any of us can ever help you in any way, please do not hesitate to ask. You will find that all of our crew are anxious to do what they can for the families of those that were with us so many years ago. Please keep in touch.

Sincere Airborne Wishes,
O.B. Hill

4 July 1994
Dear Elizabeth,

Sorry to be so late with this reply. [...]My family and I went back to Normandy for the D-Day ceremonies and from there [...] through all of the countries where the 508th fought during the war. There were three-hundred, fifty of us in the group, and it was a beautiful trip. Every possible emotion was shown along the way. I have been back many times, and every trip is different. I am convinced that no one will ever forget any of the experiences of being in the war. Like most [veterans] I have spoken with, [my] memories come back just as if they had happened yesterday.

Thank you so much for the papers regarding D-Day. I have quite a collection from most of the states, and my son made six videocassette tapes of the TV coverage. I read for a while, watch tapes for a while, and then I realize that I am not getting caught up with my letter writing, so I write for a while. I will have a very complete file of D-Day materials when I get all of them put together.

I have not been in New York for quite a long time. Did go through Kennedy Airport one time on the way to Europe but had no time. You can bet that if I do get there, you will get a call. It would be a real pleasure to meet you.

Sincere Airborne Wishes,
O.B. Hill

The French consider O.B. Hill to be a hero, and he developed a particularly close relationship to the people of Normandy, who even named a street in his honor, Chemin O.B. Hill, in Beuzeville-la-Bastille. It was here that O.B. was blown off the bridge by German artillery fire on D-Day, as he recounts in *My Normandy Invasion Experience*. Over the years, O.B. spent so much time in Normandy, he considered it his second home. As far as the people of Normandy were concerned, O.B. was family.

O.B. passed away in June 2002. Rest in peace, O.B. You are a hero, loved by my sister Liz and by so many others. Although I never had the pleasure of meeting you, after reading the many letters between you and Liz, I, too, consider you family.

Chapter 22

ROCK MERRITT AND THE BATTLE THAT STARTED IT ALL*

by Eve Meinhardt

For most Sergeants Major, becoming the Command Sergeant Major of a corps is the culmination of their careers. Retired Command Sgt. Maj. Kenneth "Rock" Merritt not only helped create the job of the XVIII Airborne Corps Command Sergeant Major, but he also held the position twice.

Shortly after the Japanese bombed Pearl Harbor in December 1941, then eighteen-year-old Merritt sought his discharge from the Civilian Conservation Corps, which was created to help unemployed young men find work as part of Franklin D. Roosevelt's New Deal. From there he went to work helping build Camp Gruber, Oklahoma, and Camp Hale, Colorado. He then went to work in a naval shipyard in California. In October 1942, Merritt decided to join the military.

"I told my cousin, 'They're going to draft us anyway, and then they'll send us wherever they want. I'm going to beat them to it and volunteer, so I can pick what I do,'" Merritt said.

Command Sgt. Maj. (Ret.) Kenneth "Rock" Merritt stands in front of a wall filled with some of his military awards. Merritt served for thirty-five years and jumped with the 508th PIR on D-Day and in Operation Market Garden. He received the Silver Star for disabling a machine-gun nest. Photo credit Eve Meinhardt/Paraglide

His original plan was to join the Marines because he liked their uniforms. While waiting to talk with a Marine recruiter, he looked up and saw a poster on the wall depicting a paratrooper.

"I was standing there in that recruiting station and saw that picture of a paratrooper under the canopy with a Thompson sub-machine gun resting on top of his reserve. At the bottom of the poster, it said, 'Are you man enough to fill these boots?' Well, between that and the $50-a-month in jump pay, I told the recruiter to sign me up," he said.

Merritt said he weighed only one-hundred, twenty pounds at the time, and the recruiter told him he wasn't going to make it. He did and was sent to Camp Blanding, Florida, on Oct. 19, 1942. The next day, he and the other recruits sent to Camp Blanding were marched down to headquarters.

"Nobody really knew how to march yet, except me, because I'd learned it when I worked with the CCC. They came out and read the orders from the War Department saying that we were now part of the newly activated 508th Parachute Infantry Regiment," recalled Merritt.

The Warner, Oklahoma, native spent the next three years fighting along with his brothers in the 508th. He jumped as part of Operation Market Garden and fought in the Battle of the Bulge. As he sat in his Fayetteville home, Merritt, now eighty-seven years old, said he knew the battle that people wanted to hear most about.

"Want me to tell you a little bit about Normandy?" Merritt asked, as he looked up with a smile.

"The 508th PIR had been training for an airborne operation since their arrival in theater. For about seventeen weeks, the paratroopers conducted exercises and night jumps while temporarily residing in Ireland and near Nottingham, England. On June 5, 1944, the 2,056 officers and soldiers of the 508th PIR loaded up and prepared to jump into France. From midnight to 3:00 AM, the paratroopers descended on Normandy.

"It must have been an awful sight to see that many planes coming in," said Merritt. "It took one-hundred, twenty C-47s to drop our regiment that night. Today it could be done by 13 C-17s."

Few of the paratroopers actually landed at their objective, and units were scattered. Merritt said that, five days later, he learned devastating news about his chain of command.

"The most important thing I recall about Normandy is that my entire chain of command was wiped out. I remember every single one of their names—Lieutenant Colonel Batcheller, our battalion commander; Captain Ruddy, the company commander; Lieutenant Snee, the assistant platoon leader, First Sergeant "Snuffy" Smith; and my platoon sergeant, Alva Carpenter," he said. "That's not a very good morale booster for a twenty-year-old corporal who's a squad leader."

The objectives, Merritt said, blended together—"one hill, one river, one bridge." On July 3, the 1st Battalion, 508th PIR was ordered to hold base Hill 131 until "the last man fell." He was now a buck sergeant and said he was determined to keep as many of his men alive as possible. He went to the Company C first sergeant, 1st Sergeant Leonard Funk, who later received the Medal of Honor, and got a box of grenades. Funk's company had suffered heavy losses, with only 37 men left from the original 198.

"I'll never forget that day," said Merritt. "It was raining, and there was a loudspeaker nearby blaring German propaganda. There was a machine gun firing at us all the time. I told the Alpha Company platoon leader, 'I'm going out there to knock out that damn machine gun.' I went up there and knocked that gun out. Later, General Ridgway awarded me the Silver Star for that."

On July 13, Merritt and his fellow paratroopers returned to England. Of the 2,056 who went in, only 900 came out after just six weeks of fighting.

"We didn't get any replacements while we were in Normandy. When we came out, they gave us seven days of leave in-country, and then we started training again for Operation Market Garden."

When the war ended, the men of the 508th took over the task of guarding General Dwight D. Eisenhower's headquarters. Merritt and ninety other men reenlisted. He said his wife was not thrilled with his decision.

"My reenlistment didn't go over too good with my wife, Sally. She didn't like that at all," he said. He and Sally had married in 1943, shortly after he joined the service. That reenlistment was the first of many, as Merritt continued to serve for thirty-five years. Of those thirty-five years, he spent thirty-one on jump status.

He served in many capacities during his career, spending the majority of his time stateside at Fort Bragg with various units in the 82nd Airborne Division and the XVIII Airborne Corps. Merritt hit all the "hot spots" overseas, including Korea, Vietnam, and the

Dominican Republic. During his two stints as the XVIII Airborne Corps Sergeant Major, he served under seven corps commanders. At his change of command, XVIII Airborne Division Corps commander Lieutenant General Hank "Two-Gun" Emerson presented one of his "two guns," .357 Magnum pistols, to Merritt, whom he called "his right hand."

Merritt said he is now proud to call Fayetteville his home. He remains active in the Fort Bragg community and will tell anyone who asks that the 508th PIR is the best unit in the Army.

*Originally published as "Operation Market Garden, Battle of the Bulge, Korea, Vietnam, and the Battle that Started It All for Paratroopers Around the World," *Paraglide On-Line*, November 11, 2010. Reprinted by permission. Many thanks to Eve Meinhardt for her excellent article and photograph of Command Sergeant Major (Ret.) "Rock" Merritt and to the editors of *Paraglide On-Line*.

PART SIX

**TORCH BEARERS: YOUNGER
GENERATIONS PRESERVING HISTORY**

Chapter 23
LIZ'S SPECIAL CONNECTION TO UNCLE MATTY

Liz's fascination with Uncle Matty started at the young age of five. Our mother noticed some particular gesture Liz made with her hands and said, "Oh, my God—this is exactly what Matty did!" This was the start of a special relationship between Liz and our mother that bonded them as best friends for life. Mom started sharing pictures, letters, and documents about Uncle Matty with Liz; Liz immediately fell in love with the handsome young Matty and hoped to marry a soldier just like him some day.

Liz has always had a special connection to Uncle Matty and in many ways feels obligated to keep his memory alive. She has researched his life, read everything there is to read on the 508th Parachute Infantry Regiment, and viewed every video she could find. Wondering about what Matty must have gone through, Liz was both haunted and fascinated. What was he thinking? Did he suffer? Did he know he was going to die? These and many other questions fueled a passion that kept her up late at night. Liz would leave no stone unturned: if there was anything more to find out about Matty, she was going to find it.

Mom often talked about taking a trip to Normandy with Liz. She dreamed of laying flowers and praying at his grave, but lung cancer made this an unfulfilled dream. In 2000, Liz fulfilled our mother's wish when she traveled to Normandy with the Family and Friends of the 508th Parachute Infantry Regiment Association. It was a bittersweet experience for her to take that trip without our mother. On the other hand, Liz has formed real and special relationships with people who knew Matty, become a member of the 508th PIR Association, and created a profile page for Uncle Matty on the Association website.

Liz writing Uncle Matty's name on a café wall in Normandy on her June 2000 trip to France with the 508th PIR Association. Liz was one of the earliest members of the Association and has devoted decades to learning about the regiment's history and honoring her heroic uncle.

Thanks to 508th veterans James McMahon and O.B. Hill, Liz was even able to get a firsthand account of what Uncle Matty was like. As she herself explains the evolution of her growing involvement:

> *My communication with Matty's unit and the fellow paratroopers he knew began in 1989. The* Daily News *published an article for readers who wanted to connect with World War II*

friends or family members in the hopes of finding information. It included an address and a form for inquiries. I knew Matty's unit, battalion, and such, so I filled it out and mailed it in. A while later, I heard back: they had sent my information to an organization called the 508th PIR Association, headed by a man named O.B. Hill. Mr. Hill had started this group as a way to get all the guys reconnected again and have reunions every year to keep in touch. He had already been back to visit France several times after the war and always visited the graves, especially Matty's. He told me he felt survivors' guilt. He was very emotional on these visits. When I took the trip to France with the 508th Association and at all the reunions I attended as well, Mr. Hill and the other veterans impressed me with how honorable they were. All of them said they were just doing their job. The real heroes were in the graves.

For future generations of our family to come, Liz recorded the statement below about her conversations with our mother and grandmother to preserve their memories and feelings about Uncle Matty. She also conveys her own experience as a "daughter of D-Day" who is trying, like so many others of her generation, to understand the experiences of her older loved ones, fill in the many silences in the family's history, and help to bridge the gap between the generations.

I dedicate this record to past, present, and future generations of our family. My uncle Marty (Matty) Teahan was only twenty years old when he died in World War II. He was attached to the 508th Parachute Infantry Regiment, 82nd Airborne Division. He was only seventeen when he enlisted, and my grandmother, Nora Teahan (Mamie), did not want him to go. He trained at Camp Mackall in North Carolina to become a paratrooper. He chose that because paratroopers were considered elite and therefore received more money. He wanted my grandmother to have the money to help her out. One of the people he met was a Mr. O.B. Hill. (Remember this name). After their training, they were sent to Nottingham, England, to wait for orders on when the invasion would take place in Normandy. They kept training there and waited for months to receive their orders. It was a very tense situation to say the least, but they all tried to keep their sense of humor.

Finally, on the morning of June 6, 1944 (D-Day), they left England and boarded their planes. I can't imagine what must have been going through their minds; I can only wonder. From what my mother (Ann Teahan Farrell) found out, he made his jump safely and met up with his troop. They asked if anyone wanted to volunteer as a scout and go on ahead to see if it was safe. He volunteered because most of the men in the unit were married, and since he was single, he felt he should go instead of them. That was the type of person he was. As he was walking, he was shot in the leg, captured by Germans, and brought back to their headquarters for questioning. As he was sitting there, one of the Germans thought he was going for a gun and killed him. My grandmother was sent a telegram, and I don't think she was ever again the same. This is the story my mother found out from a friend in Matty's unit when he visited her after the war.

My mother loved her brother very much. Before he left home for the last time in December 1943, he gave her a gold bracelet to remember him by, which she treasured her whole life. Over the years, she always remembered and talked to me about Matty. She also showed me pictures that he had taken right before the war with his buddies in the Bronx and pictures from his time in the Army. I came to be very interested in him. My mother sent flowers to be placed on his grave every year on Memorial Day. It is a tradition that I continue to this day and hope will be carried on.

I also came across an article about an organization that finds reunions for war veterans and their units. I don't know why, but I felt I had to find out about Matty's unit. I felt like Matty was telling me to do this. I knew Matty's unit number from pictures

that he had taken, and I sent that information to this organiza-
tion. I didn't hear back for a long time and forgot about it.

Then I received the first letter you will see after you read this.
Little did I know that I would find someone who knew Matty
well. His name is O.B. Hill (previously mentioned above), and
the letters that follow are from him. Mr. Hill's letters show how
honorable these men were. [...] Following the letters is a copy of a
book he sent me describing life in the 508th Parachute Infantry
*[*The 508th Connection *by Zig Boroughs].*

Also, I have attached an article the Daily News *had in their*
50th Anniversary of D-Day special edition. It mentions Matty as
one of the soldiers who died who was from New York (Manhattan).
I also have other information and pictures attached.

I'm doing this so you will remember who he was and what
he did for you.

Elizabeth Farrell

Liz's correspondence with O.B. Hill is included in Chapter 21,
"A Family Friendship with O.B. Hill." Fittingly, the 508th Parachute
Infantry Association asked her to write the "Last Jump" article on
Uncle Matty for their newsletter. Here is Liz's very touching tribute,
written in 2005.

We can never forget what the World War II veterans did for
us. Much too often, it is taken for granted. There was a place and
time when it wouldn't have been taken so lightly. I am writing
this in the hope that more people will show up for Memorial Day
parades, ceremonies, etc., and more children will study the history
of the war in school and realize what sacrifices were made for them.

I had the honor and privilege to go back with World War II
veterans of the 508th Parachute Infantry Regiment Association to
the places they had landed so long ago. This was the unit my uncle
Matty belonged to in Headquarters Co., 1st Battalion. Fifty-six

years ago, my Uncle Matty joined other paratroopers landing in Normandy and was killed the first day, on June 6, 1944, near a church in a town called Picauville. He was just twenty years old. He stays forever young there and will be forever remembered in the Normandy American Cemetery.

Born Martin J. Teahan on December 3, 1923, with blue eyes and dark, curly hair, he would be called "Matty" because of an Irish inflection in his mother's voice. The middle child, he had one brother and two sisters, one of whom was my mother. They grew up in the South Bronx in New York City, like many other immigrant families during the Depression. Enduring this would serve them well for the adversity that was to come. Matty grew up a very likable person; friends seemed to flock to him. Genuinely nice and funny, he was a person [... who would make you] feel good, especially when he sang. My mother was very close to him, and when I was growing up would always talk about him. She would show us pictures of him and his friends in Rockaway Beach in the summer of 1939. When I read his school yearbook from grammar school in 1936, a friend had written that Matty was the knight who loved to help damsels in distress—a message that meant something at the time but is now long forgotten. It could bring a smile to your face to know its meaning.

Later on in the Army, he would take pictures of himself and his buddies in the 508th and show how they tried to keep their sense of humor through it all. The surviving veterans that I met have the same camaraderie and humor now that they did back then. They were a generation that accepted the cards that were dealt them. If they hadn't been who they were, we wouldn't be who we are now. They served their country, were called to right an unspeakable horror, and did so honorably with unfaltering and undaunted determination.

My mother always wanted to go to Normandy to visit where my uncle was buried—to reclaim him, not in body but in spirit.

As fate often does, it interrupts your plans, and my mother passed away before ever getting a chance to go there. I told her I would go for her someday, and this promise I kept on my recent trip. Even though I never knew my uncle, I feel a bond with him that is so strong. If there is such a thing as a past life, I'm sure I would have known him then. Now, fifty-six years later, I came back to learn something I was destined to know. You can, indeed, learn something from people who jumped out of planes in the dark hours of the morning with enemy fire directed at them and being far from their drop zone. I don't think the veterans realized how much I treasure the moments I spent with them.

In Normandy, early in the morning, I woke up and heard the bells from the church and the birds singing along with the rooster crowing. It sounds so peaceful now. I wonder what it sounded like fifty-six years ago. What was my uncle thinking and listening to? As I walk down the narrow streets in Normandy, I can't imagine the fear of the soldiers walking down the same streets back then, and at the end of each corner waiting to see if something would happen. Ste-Mère-Eglise Church is in the town. It is a thousand years old and hauntingly beautiful. They have a replica of the paratrooper who was caught in the steeple on the morning of D-Day. It hangs as he did. The town is very appreciative of American involvement in World War II. The little children come up to veterans ask for their autographs and say "Thank you."

During the numerous ceremonies and gravesite visits, there is a feeling that time has stood still. All the pain and sense of loss is as evident now as it was back then. Now that the veterans are older, they have the time to reflect back on things. There is no mistaking they are the guardians of their fallen comrades, and they take this task very seriously. They don't have to be this caring, but they are, and their loyalty is truly inspiring. They can teach us something about the survival of the heart. I have much to learn from them. As I visit my uncle's grave, I feel like his spirit lives on.

They gave so much of their youth and saw things way beyond what anyone has the capacity to comprehend. They walk now as older men walk, but once they were young and had the dreams of young men. Their dreams were forever changed and forever altered. And dreams and nightmares bring them back to a far-distant place—a time that should never have been, but, once unleashed, would be forever in the memory of all generations to come.

Their mixture of courage, heroism, and humility is inspiring to say the least. Their generation is the blueprint that all succeeding generations should copy. They don't call themselves heroes, but I will do it for them. They are much more than that. They made it so that I could laugh and play as a child without care, grow and think for myself as an adult, and challenge as well as respect other people's thoughts. This gift they gave is priceless, and I can never repay it. All I can do, as a recent movie said, is to "earn it."

As for my uncle, once upon a time, he helped damsels in distress, but in the end, he did much more than that: He helped the world get its smile back. Having been around these veterans on this trip, it is such a comfort to know that my uncle was with the very best. Matty, if he could say something now, would lift a glass to all his buddies and smile and say about their lives, "You've made me proud, a job well done." And in return, we can hold a glass to him and say, "Here's to you, Matty! I'll be looking at the moon, but I'll be seeing you."

Chapter 24

WALKING WITH GHOSTS: A TALK
WITH GLYN SHIPSTONE

*G*lyn Shipstone and Graham Lawson, who operate Jump 44, a living
history group devoted to World War II in Nottingham, England,
were early followers of Uncle Matty's story on the Facebook page I set up,
www.facebook.com/unclemattycomeshome. Our mutual interest in the 508th
Parachute Infantry Regiment led us to become great Facebook friends,
and when Graham found out Monica and I were coming to Nottingham
in December 2016 to visit the sites where Uncle Matty had trained with
the 508th for the Normandy Campaign, he immediately offered to pick
us up at the airport and help us trace Uncle Matty's time in Nottingham.
Wow, this is so generous! I thought. Little did I imagine the extent to
which Glyn and Graham would go to make our trip extraordinary.

The dynamic duo took us to visit all the 508th PIR sites in Nottingham
and gave us a history lesson greater than any top history professor ever
could deliver. We also met members of their Jump 44 World War II
Living History Group, all of whom were devoted to making our trip the
best ever and to sharing the history of Uncle Matty and the 508th in
Nottingham. We were so impressed with Glyn and Graham's knowledge
and devotion to the American soldier in 1944 that I asked Glyn to record
his thoughts about his passion for living history and what it means to

him. He graciously agreed, and the resulting "talk" below is based on the transcription of his recording. Thank you, Glyn and Graham, for all you've done for Monica and me, and for honoring our Uncle Matty. We will never forget your kindness!

Our living history group, Jump 44, represents members of the 508th Parachute Infantry Regiment (PIR) and 307th Engineers, which were both attached to the 82nd Airborne in World War II. We also take American and British veterans and their families and

Left to right: Graham Lawson, me, and Glyn Shipstone. Glyn and Graham are World War II reenactors with a true passion for keeping history alive. They were extremely instrumental in helping Monica and me retrace our uncle's steps and learn about his time in Nottingham, where the 508th PIR trained for the Normandy Invasion. I'll never forget that fantastic ride at Folkingham Airstrip, where Glyn drove us down the very runway where Uncle Matty took off for Normandy!

friends to various battlegrounds and other sites in the UK and France. Most often, these visits are tailored to the individual itineraries and wishes of people seeking information about their relatives or hoping to trace the wartime footsteps of a specific veteran.

It all started in 2000, when my good friend Graham Lawson took a World War II battleground trip to Normandy. His interest in the Allied D-Day invasion had been sparked by a split dollar bill that had been ripped into three by paratroopers at the Admiral Rodney Pub near Nottingham. Graham and I both come from the area, and the 508th trained here at Wollaton Park before the Normandy jump. The idea was that, when the three paratroopers came back from France, they would join the dollar bill back together again. Well, two of them came back, and one of them didn't. So that's how Graham got started, by learning things like this.

At that time, I wasn't yet into the 508 PIR or, more generally, a student of military history. I was, however, very much involved in doing my family tree. It took me about eight years, but it later stood me in good stead, because when you do a family tree, you have to learn about individuals. To thoroughly research each one, you have to learn as much as you can about that person. You look at pictures and read stories and letters so you can transport yourself into that person to know what he or she was thinking. To find out how people were feeling, to understand what they were thinking at a certain time, is invaluable for research.

As I was saying, Graham was the catalyst for the establishment of Jump 44, our living history group. He and I have been buddies since about 1999. He is really a good mate, and we think a lot alike as well. Long before we started reenacting, Graham met veterans and their families here in the UK. For example, he took Jimmy Wynne from the 508th around to Folkingham, where Jimmy took off for Normandy, and Saltby Airfield, where he took off for Market Garden. Graham took him to Wollaton Park, and, of course, they visited the Jerusalem pub, where the 508th would go whenever they were in Nottingham Town Center. Visits like these usually took place at the end of May, because veterans would come to the UK first and then go over the Channel to France for the Normandy, June 6 celebrations. Graham always tried to go with them or would meet them over there later on.

Graham's involvement with the 508th PIR also took him to reunions in America, where he met more veterans and their families. When he came back, he always had a lot of stories to tell. I would sit there literally open-mouthed, listening to him talk about battles and the veterans he'd met. These firsthand accounts sowed the seeds for me to learn about the 508th in Nottingham. I could have asked Graham to share more of his knowledge with me, but this would not have been right. I started from scratch, the same way he had done. Then, once I'd picked up enough knowledge of the 508th myself, I started to ask Graham to fill in the gaps.

Around 2012, Graham and I were chatting, lamenting that not many veterans were returning to the UK because time was marching on, or they were in ill health. So we decided to start Jump 44. Initially, it was intended to be just the two of us attending events at Wollaton Park with the aim of keeping the memory of the 508th alive. But, my—how things have progressed.

Sadly, not many veterans are still alive, but Graham and I personally take veterans' families around when they come over to the UK, and we include other members of Jump 44 whenever we can. Like Graham and myself, they are all keen to meet veterans and the families of these brave troopers and pay them their respects.

I started to get involved in research on the 508th PIR around 2011. Knowing all the stories that Graham had told me gave me a good head start. Researching on my own was just a natural progression from being mates with Graham. It rubs off on you, doesn't it? If your mate's involved in something, you get involved in it as well. And, for me, it's been a life-changer. It does—it changes your life. First of all, you sit down and start reading. You never stop reading, actually—you're always learning. You read books, debriefing accounts, war diaries, as much information as you can get—not the kind of information that's in the mainstream. American archives are a brilliant resource for material. You can access quite a lot, and some of the diaries and debriefing accounts there are invaluable.

You read one book and then another book, and they overlap each other. But when you start reading debriefing accounts, you can put all the battles and other stories in as well, so it makes a massive picture. You can see how things evolved from day to day—from hour to hour, really. You have to have some switch-off time, because it can jellify your brain. You have to have some down time, a week or two away from it. I had three months away from it once. It takes that much out of you just to learn everything. Apart from that, it's all fantastic. We've got some great memories—some real good laughs and magical moments with British and American veterans alike.

Doing living history events also came about as a natural progression from Graham's earlier activities with the veterans. We set up a camp that has everything on it, just like the 508th would have had at a front-line command post. Of course, we don't kick civilians out of their homes! We set up tents and display ammunition, a wide range of weapons, engineering, demolition and communications equipment, a first-aid tent, and other things that we use to try to explain to the public what it was like for the troopers during the war. We answer questions and tell certain stories to interest the public in learning about what we do and why we do it. There are hundreds of 1940s events all up and down the UK, at Wollaton Park, Nottingham Castle, and Woodhall Spa, for example. There are so many, in fact, that we have to be very choosy as to which ones we attend. The public loves them.

We've always been highly thought of for what we teach. Actually, we don't really "teach" people—we just give them information and try to kindle a spark. If you can set that spark in people, then you're halfway there. You're getting them to want to know more. And that way, the memory of the veterans will carry on, won't it? We don't just attend events; everyone in our group participates and is knowledgeable enough to answer all the questions from the public.

All the living history groups are like this, but we are a bit different because we also take the veterans and their families out when they come from America. To be able to do that, you have to know your audience. You have to relate to them. It's inevitable that things do get emotional, and you've got to pick your time and know when to carry on with things or not, when, emotionally, things start ticking into place.

Why we do this is an odd question to answer. It's giving something back, and it's wanting, needing, to learn, because we have to learn—a hell of a lot. It's our way of saying "Thank you." To have the honor of showing veterans around Nottingham and taking them back to their old haunts like Wollaton Park and whatever—there's nothing like it, is there? To take a veteran back to his last place of safety in the UK right before he boarded that C-47 to fly out into the lion's mouth, so to speak, is invaluable.

Taking the veterans around is different from taking their families around. With the veterans, you listen mostly and make mental notes. Each word they say is a glimpse into past events. And you can learn from these past events firsthand. It's such an honor to take a veteran around and listen to his words. You stand there open-mouthed at some of the things they come out with. I mean, let's face it: They made a tremendous sacrifice. Even those who survived made a sacrifice—they sacrificed their whole youth to fight for our freedom. Their families had to give up their loved ones for years, not even knowing them sometimes when they came back. They were a different person when they came back. How could you go through the war, see all of those atrocities, and come back the same person? They went off to war a boy and came back a man. Every war is an atrocity. War is a horrible thing. They'd never be the same, so even their families had to get to know them again. That's why I say their families made sacrifices, even if their loved one did return. It's really something you've got to be passionate about to understand.

You listen to the veterans' stories, and it's like a scholar listening to his master. Sometimes a veteran will go quiet if he's talking about the war, and that's because he's reliving a mental image. You leave the mental image for a moment, because he's got to relive it; then you bring up another point, and you don't dwell on that fact again. You've got to know your subject, know the person you're talking to. You get used to it. It's very odd to be able to take a veteran around and make him happy. Some of them are naturally happy, and some of them aren't. Each individual is different. Nobody's the same. We all read accounts of what happened out there, but to get it firsthand is something else. If you don't hear these stories, and they're not written down, they're going to be lost forever. So it's really precious for us.

Taking the relatives of veterans around requires a different approach altogether. It can be quite difficult in its own way. The families are relying on you to be able to tell them things and to show them things like the places that their loved ones visited while they were in the UK or France. I try to go a bit further and try to help the family feel what the veteran was feeling or experiencing at a certain time and place. Because of all the research I've done, when I go to places like Wollaton Park, Folkingham, or North Witham, where the 82nd Pathfinders went, or whenever I go to Sainte-Mère-Eglise, I don't see what everybody else sees. What I see is mental images—I see battles, events that went off. It's like walking with ghosts.

To give you an example: Folkingham Airfield now is an empty, cracked runway with bits of farm machinery at the side, all overgrown around the edges. There are bales of straw halfway up the runway— the runway's been cut in half. But when I stand at Folkingham, I don't see just an empty runway. I don't see any of that—I see planes turning in circles, planes at the edges of the runway, tents on the infield. I hear shouting; I can hear paratroopers over at the far end playing volleyball. I see engineers on the wings—one of them has a radio, and I can hear that radio playing. And in the distance, I can hear a plane choking itself up. It's just been fixed; it's breathing itself into life for the first time in a couple of days because it's been out of action. I see and hear all these things, mixed with a bit of Glen Miller in the background. If my words can convey these feelings to the veterans' relatives, it gives them the feeling of what their loved one was seeing and feeling at the time. It all comes from just doing your research. Anyone can do it.

When Jim Farrell and his wife Monica came here, the main thing I wanted to make them feel at Folkingham and at Wollaton was the feeling of Jim's Uncle Matty. I wanted them to feel that he was here. We took them on a ride in the car up the runway at Folkingham. I don't know if I saw it right, but from Jim's face on that runway, I think he felt it then. That was the same place Matty had been. His plane, Chalk #4, flew off from that very place, that very runway. It's got to have been special to him. It was special to me, anyway! And I know it was special to Jim.

When we went to Wollaton Park, I showed Jim and Monica photographs so they could picture the tents. I showed them where the USO show was, and we stood more or less back of where Councillor Frederick Mitchell, the Lord Mayor of Nottingham, had watched the show. I told them where the troops had been, watching from the sides. You could actually *feel* it. And I could hear it—I could hear the singing on the stage. The stage looked like a boxing ring. I don't know why, actually—probably need a bit more research there! But I could hear that lady singer. Like I say, I seem to walk with ghosts. It's sometimes a bit sad. It's just the way I am from all the research I've done.

A good friend of mine, Thomas Stumpner, lives up in Wisconsin, and I've done a good bit of research into his uncle, Private John Daum, who was killed on D-Day. I took Thomas's sister Rita, her husband Milt, and her daughter Betsy around the airfield, but the thing that sticks in my mind is when I took them to Wollaton Park. They were here obviously to learn and get the feeling of what John Daum was like and what he went through. John Daum's been a quest. It's his main picture that gets you to want to know him. He looks so young. I became friends with Thomas just by asking about pictures of John.

Thomas and I became great mates. He sent me countless letters from John to his parents, pictures of John, pictures of his mother—I've even got pictures of his great grandmother. I've done John's basic family tree and know where they came from in Germany. I've got pictures of John when he must have been three or four years old and stories about how he used to ride to his cousin's farm on this balloon-tired bike over five miles of potholed roads. They weren't tarmacked—they were just dirt roads at the time. So I have mental images of John right away, starting from when he was a baby. I know all about his parents, what he did when he grew up, where he worked, right up through joining the Army, training, and dying in Normandy.

But to return to why Wollaton Park was so special when I took John's niece Rita and her family around: I drove in through the gates and turned right. I stopped the car, turned it off, and read a letter out. The letter was written on May 10, 1944, and it was John's last letter home. He said things like, "Thank you for the sweets. No more need for any cigarettes—there're plenty of them knocking about." It was just the basic stuff—what everybody missing his family would write. The date of May 10, when John wrote the letter, was quite important in context, because it was actually May 10 that day I was showing Rita, Milt, and Betsy around. It was exactly seventy-two years later to the day.

I knew the area where John's company, Company B, was tented, so after reading the letter, I pointed out the window and said, "Just over there—that's where he wrote this letter." I had the feeling that, to be able to do that, to show a family exactly where a person's last letter home was written, is invaluable. How can you put that into words? I can't, anyway. The feeling it gives me when I'm able to do that is priceless. It's beyond all the vocabulary I've got, anyway. I'm not that clever.

To sum up, it brings me great, great pleasure to take the families of veterans around. It's a way of giving something back. Graham feels exactly the same, so what I've said goes for the both of us. I bat off Graham quite a bit, and he bats off me quite a bit. Graham knows a lot more stories and a lot more about events than I do, and he's been involved with the veterans and their families a lot longer than I have. But we think alike and, when we're out at places like Wollaton Park or the Jerusalem pub, he'll drop me a line. It's more like dropping a hint—bring this up, or bring that up—because I do most of the speaking. Graham always says he's not a talker, but he is. He can really put on the spiel when he wants to.

We've got great people in our living history group. They're all like us in trying to convey ideas and experiences and events to younger generations so that they can carry on in the same spirit. I know I'm not going to be able to do it forever, and Graham isn't, either, so we're going to have to get someone else to carry on. I don't think they teach history enough at school—not the right history, anyway. Things like World War I and War World II should not be forgotten. They *cannot* be forgotten, because if we forget, we're going to make the same mistakes. It's inevitable. We're doing it now. Humans are just killing themselves for no reason.

Graham and I love what we do, and I hope I've been able to give people some insight about why we do it. The only sad thing, really, is that other work to earn a living always seems to get in the way. We just wish we could do more to say "Thank you" to the veterans and their families for the sacrifices they made for our freedom. If we can get one person, one young child, to visit a grave, or wear a poppy for Remembrance Day or Memorial Day, or even hang a flag out of the bedroom window, it's all worth it.

Chapter 25

UNCLE MATTY'S FRENCH ANGEL, VALÉRIE GAUTIER CARDIN

At least four times every year, Uncle Matty's French Angel Valérie Gautier Cardin places flowers on his grave and the graves of twenty-four other heroes at the American Cemetery in Normandy. For the families of veterans killed in action in France, it is both emotionally and logistically difficult to visit their loved ones' graves. Valérie considers her visits a sacred act that must be accomplished at all cost, regardless of bad weather, whatever else is going on in her life, or any other obstacle. Valérie did not ask to be crowned as an Angel; it was an honor bestowed upon her by adoring World War II veterans and their families. Who is Valérie, and how did she become Uncle Matty's French Angel?

Valérie grew up in the town of Creances, Normandy. Her parents and grandparents taught her at a very early age to honor and respect the American soldiers who gave their lives to liberate France. This was personally important to Valérie and her family because the horrors of the German occupation had been visited upon them. Her grandfather had been obliged to leave his home in Normandy and

Uncle Matty's French Angel, Valérie Gautier Cardin, visiting Uncle Matty's grave in June 2017. Valérie pays tribute to Uncle Matty and more than two dozen other World War II veterans by decorating their graves four times a year. She was immensely helpful with the arrangements for our 2016 trip to Normandy, and is a Farrell family friend forever! *Photo courtesy of Valérie Gautier Cardin.*

forcefully transported to Germany to work for the Nazi war effort. Valérie thus grew up with a special connection to American veterans, and her mission to help and honor them seemed to be preordained. If she lived by a credo, it would be: *We can never forget what the American Veteran did to liberate France.*

In 1992, when Valérie was just fourteen, her parents told her to see if she could help an American veteran who was standing outside of the town post office, looking lost. In a foreign country where he did not speak the language, 505th Parachute Infantry veteran Bill Sullivan was, in fact, very confused, but he had a serious, somewhat spiritual look on his face. Unbeknownst to Valérie, Bill was on a new Normandy mission he felt he had been called to carry out. He had taken part in the D-Day Invasion with the 82nd Airborne, and he had now returned to France determined to find the family who had helped and hosted him on those dangerous days in June 1944.

Valérie tried her best to discover what Bill wanted, and he did his best to express why he was there, but the language barrier was too great. Bill would say something, and Valérie would look confused; Valérie would say something, and Bill would look confused. Bill remarked with enthusiasm, "I drank a lot of Calvados here!" Finally, Valérie took Bill into the post office to see if anyone could understand what he was looking for. Again, she had no luck. She then decided to take him home to her parents to see if they could find someone who could help him. A trooper from the legendary 82nd Airborne, Bill was not about to leave without accomplishing his mission!

Meanwhile, back at Valérie's house, the confusion continued. Her parents turned to their townspeople to ask for more help. Finally, someone recognized Bill as the American paratrooper who had spent time with his family in June 1944, and Bill was reunited with his special French friends. It turned out to be a long and lasting friendship: Bill returned to Normandy every year for twenty-four years straight to visit Valérie, "adopting" her family and the town. As I write this now in June 2017, Bill is still living but no longer able to undertake the journey to France.

Bill was only the first of many American veterans whom Valérie took under her wing. Some, like Bill, were survivors; others, like Uncle Matty, were not. Being their Angel meant Valérie looked after them, assisting the living on visits to Normandy, and honoring the dead by tending their final resting places. Returning to Normandy can be very difficult for veterans of the war: they experienced so much death and destruction, anguish, wounds, and trauma that retracing their own footsteps and those of the buddies they lost often overwhelmed them with emotion. And yet the need to return is always there—the need to remember, the hope to reconnect with strangers who had helped them, often at the risk of their own lives, the desire to visit the graves of good friends fallen, the search for some sort of closure, or coming to terms with the past. Valérie, now their liaison, helps make these returns as easy, happy, and memorable as possible. For her, each veteran, each grave, each family, each story is different and distinct, and all are special and unique.

Valérie and Bill struck up a correspondence by phone and letter, and kept it up as the year rolled around and it came time again for him to visit France. Word spread. Every year, Valérie took on more veterans. As time wore on, family members, too, found shelter under her wing. This family-like feeling was an emotion often felt between Valérie and the veterans who were lucky enough to be under her wing. But Bill was the first, and their special relationship grew so close they became like brother and sister.

Anyone under Valérie's wing is protected. She visits graves at the American Cemetery at least four times a year to place flowers and say a prayer. Over time, she has extended her reach by enlisting the middle-school children at the school where she works to visit the gravesites as well. She often accompanies family members to graves and cries and prays with them. This can be a wrenching experience, and sometimes the crying can be nonstop, but no matter the circumstances, Valérie never says "No" to a veteran or their family. Her actions and commitment have been so inspiring that several other French citizens have stepped up to help her honor the veterans. Monica and I were amazed at the cemetery by what we witnessed of her ministry in 2016. She and her fellow "Angels," Stephanie Pepin and Jocelyne Paris, showed unmatched kindness in making themselves and their vehicles available to transport veterans wherever they needed to go. At many events, the veterans were guests of honor at well-attended ceremonies in which they received awards, and transporting eight World War II veterans all aged ninety or older can be quite complicated, to say the least. But nothing stopped these Angels: Wherever they needed to go, they went, and whatever they needed to do got done. The sweetest sight ever is to see these Angels give their heroes a kiss. The smiles on the faces of Angels and veterans both could solve any world conflict.

As years went by and the Greatest Generation began to pass away, the ranks of the veterans dwindled. Throughout this period, Valérie continued to befriend them and their families. Valérie has answered hundreds of phone calls, helped to plan numerous returns to France, and answered countless questions. Despite a very busy life of her own, which included working and raising a daughter, she responded to every letter, call, and eventually e-mail and text from those she took under her wing. To stay up late to respond to a veteran during waking hours in a U.S. time zone was small sacrifice, given all these men had gone through for her and her country on those fateful days in June. Over the last few years, Valérie has spread her wings and begun to attend reunions of the 508th PIR and other veterans' associations. As you can imagine, she's a big star at the ceremonies.

All too soon, Valérie began to realize that the clock was ticking away for the heroes she loved so well. Each year, each month, and then seemingly each day, someone special was lost. In 2012, most surviving veterans were in their late eighties or older, and the realization that some would never return to Normandy began to haunt her. Angels like Valérie cannot see this happen without taking action. Many people who grow up in Normandy know the history of World War II, but the stories Valérie heard firsthand from surviving veterans made a huge impact on her life. She became so driven by her involvement, I can only call it divine devotion.

Valérie heard many stories of young soldiers who had died or suffered horrific wounds, stories of men who were haunted by nightmares or wracked with the guilt of survival. She wanted to enable as many veterans as possible to come to France so the country they had liberated could honor them and thank them for its freedom. Valérie took this goal as a critical mission she'd been called upon to accomplish. The sad truth was that many veterans who wanted to return could not afford to do so, but she was determined to take them under her wing.

In 2012, Valérie established a non-profit organization, Veterans Back to Normandie, with the objective of funding the trip of every single living World War II veteran who fought in France and wished to return. The organization raises funds in France, the United States, and elsewhere to purchase airline tickets, and arranges housing and meals with French families who host the veterans during their stay. Gratitude runs high, and there is no shortage of host families in Normandy. And there are no expenses whatsoever for the veterans. Valérie makes it a point of honor to bring them back so they can personally see and feel the gratitude of people in France today, and know that their bravery and sacrifice in 1944 will never be forgotten.

"Please come back before it is too late," I often heard Valérie say. No matter how many veterans she is caring for, she always has room for one more under her wing. As of 2016, her organization has completely funded the return of nearly thirty veterans. All were awarded medals and honors, and many received the French Legion of Honor, the highest award that can be given to a non-French citizen.

In June 2016, Monica and I also had the pleasure of visiting Valérie's school in Portbail, Normandy. As committed to teaching the young as she is to helping those who fought the war, Valérie has helped her school to develop a curriculum including World War II history. As part of their classes, each June students meet American veterans and get the opportunity to ask them questions. I was astounded by the exchange. The look on the children's faces was priceless, and their hunger to know what had happened in the war and what it had felt like for the Americans was inspiring. Their questions were well thought out, and their eyes were glued on the French interpreter relaying the veterans' responses. To witness such a transmission of history was a very gratifying experience. Valérie, in essence, was passing down to children the history her parents and grandparents had transmitted to her as a girl. As the expression goes, *History repeats itself.* This is what makes learning it so critical. The end of the question-and-answer session at Valérie's school is sometimes just the beginning of a greater education. Many of the veterans and students become friends and correspond for years, continuing to learn about and from each other.

Valérie and I have been friends on Facebook for a few years now. I at first was well aware that she was Matty's French Angel. But I also learned she knew many personal things about him too, including his happy-go-lucky attitude, his superior singing and dancing ability, and, of course, that he was a lady's man. In April 2016, I created a Facebook page about Uncle Matty and the discovery of his rifle. Valérie read it, was elated for my uncle and my family, and phoned to personally congratulate me. At that point, we developed into great friends, and she took me, too, under her wing.

My wife and I had the trip of a lifetime in Normandy. Our decision to go happened in a flash. Colonel Collet invited us over to see the rifle which was then in his possession, and to meet the Chief of Staff of the US Army, General Milley. How could we possibly say "No"? The invitation came in April, leaving us little time to plan. I had no idea how to go about it: Monica and I had never been to Europe. Not to worry, Valérie told me! She would make sure that everything went smoothly. Where should we stay in Normandy? No problem! Valérie scheduled everything at the hotel—and it's a good thing she did, as they spoke little English. What should we do in Normandy? A needless worry! Valérie had us busy every moment. Our French Angel got us invitations to wonderful events in Carentan, Ste-Mère-Eglise, and many other ceremonies in honor of the veterans. Amidst all this, she made sure we could have time to spend at Uncle Matty's graveside. The presence of about two dozen of the students from Valérie's school made this visit extra special for us. The students laid flowers on Uncle Matty's grave, and at Valérie's request, I spoke about Uncle Matty at the gravesite. What a wonderful and unexpected opportunity to witness the lively interest of young people in Normandy today in learning firsthand the history of the times of their great-grandfathers, and what a pleasure it was to relate Matty's story, and hence play a part, no matter how small, of transmitting that history!

On the lighter side, Valérie also got the veterans tickets to see a burlesque show in Paris. Yes, we, too, were invited! I will never forget that night out on the town in *gay Paris* with the veterans. The smiles on their faces will be forever engrained in my memory.

Monica and I have been home from France for quite some time, but Valérie and I still communicate almost every week. I don't know how on earth she manages to do it all, but I'm happy that Valérie is Uncle Matty's French Angel and that she has now become our Angel, too.

Chapter 26
LUCIEN'S WALL, *LE MUR DU SOUVENIR*

L ucien Hasley began to build Lucien's Wall on the side of his house in 1982, and the site has become a hallowed monument. Located at the edge of the small Norman village of Le Port Filiolet near Picauville, Lucien's *Mur du Souvenir* (the "Wall of Remembrance") stands as a shrine to the men who fought in the area on D-Day, including approximately two hundred 82nd Airborne Division troopers. Lucien has literally engraved in stone the names of the units that battled in the vicinity and the names of approximately one hundred of the men who fought there. He intimately knows the story of every man whose name appears. Monica and I were mesmerized as we read the names of the soldiers, some killed in action, some critically wounded, others survivors. The names of some of Matty's buddies were engraved there as well, including 508th veterans O.B. Hill and Captain Chet Graham.

We first learned about Lucien's Wall and were invited to attend a special ceremony there, thanks to General (then Colonel) Patrick Collet, who introduced us to Cyndi Robinson, the granddaughter of Captain Chet Graham, who passed away in 2015. Captain Graham wanted his ashes to be spread over the Picauville drop zone, where he had landed on D-Day, and we were invited to the ceremony. Driving there through the scenic French countryside, we first stopped at the legendary Lucien's Wall, where Susan Eisenhower, Ike's granddaughter, had come to present the findings of extensive research she had conducted on Lucien's behalf and to reveal the name of an heroic, but heretofore unidentified, medic who had saved the life of Lucien's younger brother on D-Day. General Collet had kindly arranged for us to be present at this spiritual ceremony as well.

The 508th Brick on the memorial wall built by Lucien Hasley in Le Port Filiolet near Chef-du-Pont, Normandy, where he has sculpted the names of many of the American paratroopers who fought to liberate his village. This is truly a spiritual place. On June 4, 2016, we here had the pleasure of meeting General Eisenhower's granddaughter Susan as she presided over a ceremony at Lucien's Wall.

When you get close to Lucien's Wall, your emotions take over. The history of the brutal fight for freedom that took place on this sacred ground is apparent. Here occurred acts of tremendous bravery, the horrible torture and killing of many human beings, and everything in between. The names of so many soldiers are engraved all over the wall that it is impossible not to get lost in thought about the men who fought and all too often died here. Gazing at it, running our fingers over the surface, Monica and I were lost in emotion for all the young soldiers and French inhabitants who endured the brutal reality of D-Day. I can only imagine that, for Lucien Hasley and Susan Eisenhower, the successful culmination of a seventy-two-year quest to find the name of the heroic medic who had saved the life of Lucien's brother was one of the most powerful experiences that anyone could ever have.

Personally, I felt that day as if I were receiving messages from spirits. Perhaps these feelings were Uncle Matty's way of sending me a message so strong that it overpowered all my other thoughts. The message was telling me I must write the story of Private Martin Teahan and the return of his rifle seventy-two years after D-Day. What did the return of his rifle mean to me? My conversations with Susan Eisenhower; Lieutenant General Townsend, the Commanding General of the XVIII Airborne Corps; and General Collet validated my desire to write Uncle Matty's story, fueled my motivation to do so, and stoked my devotion to the task. Never in my life did I think I would write a book, but that day at Lucien's Wall removed any possible doubt I could ever have that this was indeed what I needed and wanted to do.

Lieutenant General Townsend, present with his delegation, gave a powerful but emotional speech, stating that all Americans should come to Normandy and learn what happened there. I agree with the General one hundred percent; as he so eloquently put it, our history cannot be lost. The ceremony was extremely touching; at one point, Monica and I silently looked at each other, and each of us saw that the other was about to tear up. We and all the other English speakers in attendance were glued to our interpreter's every word. This was Ben Trumble of D-Day Tour Company, who proved to be a wonderful interpreter. There was one funny moment when the height of the heroic medic was given in meters, and no one seemed able to get the conversion right. It elicited a needed moment of relief, and everyone enjoyed the laugh.

Ben did a terrific job, and I was so moved by the ceremony that it set a light bulb off in my head. I needed a chapter on Lucien's Wall in the book! Ben kindly agreed to participate, and wrote the following account of what happened to Lucien's village on D-Day, condensing and translating Lucien's French presentation. It is a riveting story of the survival skills of the French, the heroism of the paratroopers, and how luck sometimes decides whether you live or die.

LUCIEN HASLEY ON D-DAY

Translated and adapted by Ben Trumble

After four long years of war they came, suddenly, out of the night sky. Just after midnight on the 6th of June, Lucien Hasley's parents sat at their kitchen table. Flashes from exploding antiaircraft shells lit up their home as waves of American C-47 aircraft passed just five hundred feet above them. Over the next two hours, almost thirteen thousand U.S. paratroopers would fall from the sky, the vanguard of the greatest invasion in history. The liberation of Europe had begun.

Lucien was ten years old on that memorable night, the oldest of four boys who lived in a small rustic cottage in a hamlet of just twelve houses—and to add to the drama unfolding about them, his mother was eight months pregnant! As the house shook to the sound of the huge Pratt and Whitney engines roaring overhead, the windowpanes and his mother's ornamental wall plates vibrated and rattled in sympathy.

His father realized something extraordinary was happening. Waking his four young children, he dressed them and then put his sleepy charges back to bed. He no doubt realized that the decisions he made over the next few hours could mean the difference between life and death for him and his family.

Lucien's was a very "ordinary" family. His father worked on the land, and his mother had started work at age eleven (!) cleaning for the Château de Bernaville a few miles away, before marrying at age sixteen. Their life, as seen through modern eyes, must seem incredibly harsh, yet, in fact, it was the norm; it was very much a harshness shared. From June 1940 to June 1944, life had continued pretty much as normal in their part of the world—or as normal as life in a defeated and occupied country could be. Lucien vividly remembers the arrival of the first German occupation forces in late June 1940. Six years old, he was at the village school in Amfreville when the children heard the sounds of motorcycles, many motorcycles, approaching on the dusty road.

To children of that era, any motor vehicle was interesting, as they were so rare. They excitedly ran to the windows to watch the long column of German motorcycles with machine-gun-mounted sidecars roaring by. The children all chattered in excitement, pressing their faces to the glass to better see. Their teacher, who knew exactly what this meant, stood with tears flowing down her cheeks.

Asked today, Lucien will tell you that the Germans in occupation were very "correct." There were rules to be followed and curfews to remember, but in this rural setting, life generally continued its course, with the usual wartime privations—food being the main one—always on their mind. Commodities were rationed, but they survived—again, a problem commonly shared.

The years of German rule rolled on, and rural life did its best to carry on as normal. Harvest festivals, spring sowing, marriages, births, and deaths continued, and the war was little heard of. Censorship and the lack of radios in poor communities meant that actual news of the war was very limited, though it was generally accepted by 1944 that liberation might not be too far away. To small children such as Lucien, the Germans were just like gendarmes in different uniforms. This was not a plunder occupation as was the war in the east: here the Germans were told to "get on" with the civilians, and to some degree this was not that difficult. If they wanted something from a shop, they'd pay for it, though Lucien remembers they'd walk straight to the front of the queue. These were the victors, after all!

He remembers being sent as a seven-year-old to carry a jar of cream to his aunt's house in Ste. Mère-Eglise. This was a round-trip walk of maybe ten miles. After dropping off the jar, he wended his way home via the top road just outside of Ste. Mère. I wonder what the view of such a thing would be today, or whether in some "civilized" parts of the world a child alone on such an errand would ever be seen again. It was a late July afternoon, hot and dusty, and Lucien had a five-mile walk ahead of him. Approaching from behind he could hear a clanking noise that was slowly growing louder, and eventually, a German sergeant on a bicycle passed him by. The clanking was his bayonet tapping on his metal gas mask canister as he pedaled along.

After a few yards the German stopped, and turning to watch Lucien approach, he asked, "Who are you?"

"Lucien," he replied.

"And where are you going on this hot day?"

Lucien said he lived in Port Filiolet and pointed in the general direction. The German looked down the dusty road, smiled, and pointed to the crossbar of the bicycle. Lifting Lucien onto the crossbar, the German pedaled him home the full five miles, right to his door. As the little boy dismounted, the German merely smiled, waved, and then pedaled off. Lucien never saw him again.

His memory of that day is as fresh as if it had happened last week: the smell of the soldier's leather ammunition webbing and belts, the "aroma" of the wool uniform, sweat-soaked on a hot day. Lucien often wonders, since the German was not a young man, if perhaps he had a son his age back in Germany somewhere. Maybe he, too, was a country lad, and since the Germans rarely got leave, this was his way of making some contact with the life and the little boy the war had taken from him.

Lucien's mother had tragically lost two babies since the start of the German occupation. Most probably, these infant deaths were due to an illness brought on by the measures the Germans had taken to hinder any local Allied landings. Besides the concrete-and-steel fortifications of the Atlantic Wall, the occupiers had resorted to many simpler and less costly measures to impede the Allies. One measure was to keep the low-lying fields flooded in order to provide a barrier to Allied troop and armored movement in the area.

Since the time of the Romans, every year the fields around Lucien's home for several miles in any direction had flooded to a depth of up to six feet between the months of December and March. This still occurs today; it is a natural inundation caused by heavy annual winter rains. Over the centuries, all property and roads had been built ten feet higher than the surrounding fields in order to cope with these winter floods, which are similar to the inundation of the Nile.

In the 1700s, a canal had been dug near Carentan, and lock gates now controlled the flow of water, stopping sea water from coming in twice a day and allowing the river water to egress. However, in winter, with the high seasonal rains, the fields still flooded, as they had always done. This was a seasonal event lasting just three months. By March, the horses and cattle were brought down from high ground, and the fields once again were a tranquil scene of rural life until the following January, when the cycle would start again.

This natural cycle was interrupted in 1942, when the Germans locked closed the estuary gates near Carentan, and the annual flood, with no means of escape, remained. The winter of 1943 added to the water and made matters worse. The unexpected result of this flooding was that the water ceased to flow. In the hot summer months of 1943–44, it became stagnant, and with stagnant water came mosquitoes. These were the cause of many deaths. Tragically, it seems they took two of Lucien's siblings.

In the early hours of that historic night of June 6, Lucien's parents sat at their kitchen table, knowing something momentous was happening. His mother went to the window. Looking west, she exclaimed, "An aircraft in flames has just crashed in Founcroup!" This was Lucien's grandmother's village, and today the Manor of Founcroup is Lucien's home. Missing the houses by just a few yards, the aircraft exploded on impact, and his mother saw the flash from the explosion. As this happened just half a mile from their home, everyone heard the blast.

The wreckage of the aircraft indeed fell in Founcroup. One of their neighbors, Adrienne Bueuckly, let curiosity get the better of her and went into the garden to see what was happening. Looking into the night sky, she exclaimed that so many parachutes were coming down that they "looked like grapes on the vine."

As dawn broke on that day of days, Lucien's father stepped from his small cottage. There, just feet from his door, was a soaking-wet United States 82nd Airborne paratrooper. By the early dawn light, his father noted the "stars and stripes" patch on the paratrooper's arm and saw several other paratroopers as they silently moved into the tiny village and started to dig in. Some were injured, and several had no weapons, having lost them on the jump.

Later that day, Lucien's father called the villagers together and they weighed their options. There were twenty-three persons in total, thirteen children and ten adults. The battles raging within earshot meant that they were likely to become casualties whether they tried to move away from the fighting or stayed where they were. Sensing that staying put and together was the better option, the villagers abandoned all their houses and moved into the central house in the middle of the village. If fighting broke out, it was likely to hit the edges of the village first.

Lucien's little brother Albert, aged seven, had been ill since the previous day. Lucien is pretty sure this was his fault, caused by some foolery on a garden swing the preceding afternoon. Becoming bored with just pushing his brother back and forth, he'd wound the seat around several times and then let it go. Albert had fallen off and banged his head, and had now been vomiting almost continuously for several hours. They transferred the boy the fifty yards to the "safe" house and placed him on a mattress on the ground floor, still looking very ill. Later that morning, an American medic arrived in the village with two injured paratroopers and took over the house at the end of the village, owned by Monsieur and Madame Laisney. This he converted to a first-aid post, prominently placing a Red Cross flag outside.

Knowing little Albert was very sick, the Laisney's eighteen-year-old daughter Yvette thought that the medic might be able to help him. Given that neither could speak the other's language, Yvette explained as best she could that a seven-year-old boy in a nearby house was seriously ill and asked if he could help. She seems to have got her point across; the medic left his post, and they dodged together from building to building until they reached the house where the villagers had taken refuge. Seeing the boy on the mattress and noting how small he was, the medic took off his helmet and jacket so as not to frighten him. Kneeling down to examine the boy, he fairly soon concluded that an inner-ear problem was probably causing the vomiting.

Airborne medics always carried the perfect solution for airsickness in their jacket: Dramamine. He stood and, taking a tablet from his pocket, slowly said to Lucien's father, "Give him this, and I'll come back and see him tomorrow," just as a family doctor might have done! Given the state of confusion, exploding ordnance, and general uncertainty of the first forty hours of D-Day, this was a very human response to the plight of one small boy. He then put his helmet and jacket back on and returned to his first-aid post at the edge of the village.

Albert recovered fully within a few hours, and Lucien's father decided that the villagers should move to another place of safety. From the top-floor window, he observed that the Germans were within sight of the village and feared they might believe that

American soldiers were at the property. Suddenly feeling that the safe house might not be as safe as he had thought, he herded everyone into a small barn some eighty yards away. It proved a fortuitous move. Within the hour a single, heavy mortar shell, most likely German, fell on the village, hitting the safe house and collapsing the walls and part of the roof. The villagers had had a lucky escape—and it was not to be their last.

Yvette had returned to the first-aid post with the medic to help tend the wounded. Later the following day, she was still there helping when a German truck drove into the village. Seeing the Red Cross flag flying at the house, the driver slammed to a stop. Five German soldiers jumped out and moved to enter the building. The medic, seeing the truck arrive, told Yvette to get the wounded out the rear door while he held the front door closed. The Germans tried to smash their way in, but the medic held the door long enough for Yvette and the two wounded to evacuate from the rear of the building. Tragically, as the medic himself tried to exit, the Germans broke in and bayoneted him in the back. Dragging him from the house, they tossed an incendiary grenade into the building, which very quickly set the entire house ablaze.

Alerted by the noise, other American paratroopers arrived on the scene, and the fighting that ensued left two paratroopers dead along with five of the Germans. Some of the Germans managed to remount their truck, and the survivors took off, heading west, followed by a fusillade of American bullets. However, even with the arrival of his comrades, it was too late for the medic. He could not be saved. He died some little while later from loss of blood, lying by the roadside in this small French village.

A second paratrooper, possibly also a medic, came up and knelt by his side, gave him a cigarette, and talked to him, providing what comfort he could as the life of this young, big-hearted American slowly ebbed away. Opposite, the fire raging in the house was all-consuming. It devoured the much-needed medical supplies that the medic had carefully stored there. Lucien's pregnant mother ran to fetch her young son as he stood transfixed by the flames and told him to quickly run to the barn, the new safe house. He remembers standing, awestruck, in the road just fifty feet away, seeing the house blazing from end to end, and hearing the crack of exploding roof tiles as flames from the windows and rooftop leapt high into the air.

One mile away, the fierce battle for Hill 30 had begun as Colonel Thomas J.B. Shanley and more than two hundred 82nd Airborne paratroopers undertook their assigned mission—the capture of the hill. The Germans well knew the strategic value of this small piece of high ground and were equally determined to stop them. The U.S. paratroopers, dug in around Lucien's village since early on the 6th, moved out on June 7 to join in the fighting at Hill 30.

Shortly after, a convoy of German trucks drove into the village, and some one-hundred, fifty German soldiers dismounted. They fanned out rapidly and professionally through the village, looking for Americans as their officer had the villagers—men, women and children—dragged from their cover. The villagers had taken refuge in the ditches and foxholes dug by the American paratroopers in order to avoid collapsing buildings in case fighting broke out in the town. As the Germans rounded them up, the officer himself, pistol in hand, reached into the foxhole where Lucien was taking cover. Grabbing him by the collar, he yanked him bodily out of the hole and threw him in with the rest of the villagers. They then were stood, hands over their heads, by the wall of the barn. The soldiers rapidly formed a semi-circle around them, their weapons leveled.

The German officer in charge, enraged, paced back and forth behind his men, shouting for several minutes in unintelligible German. Lucien often says that he felt at any second the officer would snap his fingers and the shooting would begin. Matters, and in particular, the officer's agitation, were not helped by the spent bullets from the battle for Hill 30 more than a mile away that were repeatedly heard striking the roof of the barn.

Gaining control of himself, the officer finally calmed down and ordered the villagers into the barn. They were confined there for the next thirty hours. They had no food, just a little milk, and a bucket for obvious purposes. On the late evening of June 8, as the Germans on Hill 30 were retreating, the Germans in Lucien's village also made ready to move out. Before the German column got clear of the village, it was ambushed by 82nd Airborne troopers.

For the next five hours, the villagers cowered in a corner of the barn as the air was filled with the noise of battle. Rifle and machine gun fire, screams, and exploding grenades rent the night air, but just before dawn, all became silent.

Even when things had been quiet for quite some time, the villagers remained in a huddled group, crouched up against the gable wall of the barn. Suddenly, the barn door burst open. Standing there in the morning light was a soldier. He surveyed the crouching villagers with his Thompson machine gun before slowly lowering the barrel and pushing his helmet back on his head. "Don't be afraid," he said in a French they could actually understand. "I'm Canadian. I've come from Utah Beach. What are you all doing in here?" The villagers had no way of knowing that "Utah Beach" was the Allied code name for "La Plage de La Madeleine," the beach at the nearby hamlet of La Madeleine. The stranger was a Canadian trooper working with U.S. forces who spoke what Lucien describes as "old French."

Lucien's father got to his feet and explained they had thought they were safest in the barn because of all the fighting. Taking a bundle of wires and detonators from his pocket, the paratrooper replied that the wall they had been hiding behind had been primed with explosives by the Germans! He had just pulled the detonators, defusing the device. The Germans had intended to blow up the barn as they left the village, collapsing the rubble onto the road to form a roadblock in order to slow down the advancing Americans. The paratroopers had ambushed the retreating column before they could hit the firing switch, and the enemy had abandoned the firing mechanism in the confusion. But the circuit and explosives had remained "live" all through the fighting! Another lucky escape—although this time, Lucien's father was rather left lost for words.

Going outside, the villagers saw that the road was now a hive of activity, full of passing columns of American soldiers, tanks, and vehicles. It was at that very moment, Lucien says, that the villagers "now knew the long-awaited liberation had finally arrived." With the arrival of more Americans, the immediate threat receded, and his family returned to their cottage on June 10. Fifty-five Germans had been killed in the hundred yards of ground that make up the footprint of the tiny village.

Every building showed the signs of battle, some worse than others. Their own little cottage was a scene of devastation. All the windows had been blown out; machine-gun bullets had raked the interior walls. The armoire had been ransacked for the little it contained, and the contents of their drawers and all the family linen lay strewn across the floor. Lucien's mother responded by setting to work with a brush; all the children joined in, and within a short while, they had cleared up the mess as best as they possibly could.

An amusing event also took place in the village on June 10, breaking the series of tragedies that had occurred in the course of the previous days. Tom Porcella, a private in the 508th Parachute Infantry Regiment, 82nd Airborne, walked up to Lucien's hamlet, having spent the last four days living on nothing but his wits and K-rations. As he approached the village, he smelled the odor of cooking wafting on the breeze, coming from one of the old courtyards. Private Porcella followed the smell. Crouched in a rubble-strewn yard was Madame Lagueste, whose kitchen and house had been badly damaged. She had formed a circle of stones in her courtyard, lit a fire, and was now busily cooking crêpes. Tom walked up, deeply inhaling the smell of cooking, and stood there, staring at the pan. After a bit of staring, Madame took the hint and offered him a crêpe. Tom didn't need asking twice. The crêpe disappeared, quickly followed by another and a third. Tom decided to leave before he overstayed his welcome.

Walking into the main road by what is now Lucien's home, he came up to a fellow trooper who sat there, cleaning his gun.

"Where'd you get that?" he asked, seeing Tom munching on a crêpe.

"'Round the back," Tom replied. "There's some woman cooking them."

Needing no second invitation, the solder stood and was about head off to get a crêpe himself, when he turned and asked, "Hey, what's she called?"

Tom came up with the first name that came to mind. "Crêpe Suzette!" he replied.

The word spread—as did the name—and over the next several days, "Suzette" cooked many a crêpe for hungry soldiers passing by on their way to battle. The name also had a long life, with even the local French referring to Madame Lagueste as "Crêpe Suzette." And so the name followed her long after the war, until her death in the 1980s.

As an outpouring of the gratitude he felt to the liberating forces, in 1982, Lucien Hasley built a memorial wall with his own hands at the side of his house. Lucien's Wall proudly displays the names of many of those brave men who fought and many who died there during the traumatic days of June 6–10, 1944. There has, however, always been one sad exception to this honor roll—the medic who saved his brother's life. For more than seventy years Lucien tried, without result, to find the name of the kindly medic who went out of his way to help his brother and had died so tragically and so young himself.

In March 2016, Susan Eisenhower visited Le Port Filiolet with a group of her students. She was much moved by the story of the young medic. On return to the States, she put substantial effort and resources into tracing the man—and found him. On June 4, 2016, at a ceremony held at the commemorative wall, she presented her findings to Lucien, thus closing the circle for an eighty-two-year-old French "boy" who still remembers fondly the sacrifice of the brave and kindly young American who helped his brother.

The medic was Private First Class Frank E. Mackey, Jr. of the 508th PIR, 82nd ABD

Enlisted: August 1942

Hometown: West Philadelphia

Frank was married to Loretta and had a son, John Mackey. John was just eighteen months old when his father died. After graduating high school, Frank became a plumber and pipe fitter and supported his mother and siblings. He joined the airborne mainly for the additional pay of $54.00 a month as he continued to support them along with his wife and child.

His high school yearbook entry read:

Ambition: To find seats for the standing army of the unemployed

Activities: A Patrol; Senior dancing club; Alternate Senator

Susan Eisenhower paid her respects and laid a wreath at Frank Mackey's grave in the Normandy American Cemetery at Colleville-sur-Mère. It is a truly fitting end to this story.

Our special thanks to Lucien Hasley and to Ben Trumble, the translator of Lucien's story, who helped make our trip to Normandy so memorable and contributed so much to this chapter.

Ben Trumble, D-Day Tour Company, "Standing in the Footsteps of Heroes," may be contacted at:

www.dday1944tours.com
The Manor, Picauville, 50360, France
Tel: 0033 964119107
In France: 0964119107
SKYPE: ddayguy

Epilogue

SAINT JEROME'S CHURCH: UNCLE MATTY BRINGS THE FAMILY TOGETHER

Was there any way to bring the family together in honor of Uncle Matty? This was the question my brother Jackie and I sat pondering one day in March 2017. Was it possible? Where could we do it? And how? We mutually concluded that it was possible, that we could definitely do it, and that there was only one place even to consider: Saint Jerome's Church at 230 Alexander Avenue, in the South Bronx, New York City.

Saint Jerome's parish is where Uncle Matty grew up, and he attended Saint Jerome's School. The church is where my mother and father met, and the place that they got married. My brothers, sisters, and I grew up there, too: It was where we were christened, where we took our first communion. In short, St. Jerome's was the center of our family universe. It was here, too, inside this beautiful church, that my dream of bringing Uncle Matty's rifle back home originated. And seeing Matty's name on the plaque at St. Jerome's honoring the parish war dead triggered me to write this book. Yes, St. Jerome's was just the place to bring the family together again, and Uncle Matty was just the person to accomplish this near-impossible mission.

Many families have feuds, fights, and splits—divisions so deep and wide that they often tear families apart for decades, sometimes all the way to the grave. My family, too, has had its share of feuds. But miraculously, every now and then, a life-changing event helps to heal the old wounds and reunites the family. I was betting that the near-miraculous return of Uncle Matty's rifle, which had brought back our beloved, long-lost uncle in spirit, was such an event.

June 4, 2017: The first Annual Mass at Saint Jerome's Church in Uncle Matty's honor. Four generations of the family came together to honor Uncle Matty's symbolic homecoming in the guise of his rifle. A new family tradition is born! As Bill McWeeney, who grew up in Saint Jerome's Parish in the thirties and forties, commented, "I have not seen that many Irish folks gathered in front of St. Jerome's in more than fifty years!"

And so I called Saint Jerome's Church and arranged a mass to be held in Uncle Matty's honor. The mass was to be held on Pentecost Sunday, June 4, 2017, at 10:30 a.m. Shortly after scheduling it, I learned from my cousin Danny that Uncle Matty's godchild, Rose Flynn Lofaro, was still alive. Now aged 82, Rose, whom I had never met, lived in North Jersey, just an hour's drive from our home. We first spoke on April 10, 2017. To describe that first phone call as "emotional" would be an understatement. Rose remembered Uncle Matty as a happy-go-lucky kid who loved to entertain his family and friends, and always cheered them up with his million-dollar smile. When I told her the whole story about finding Matty's rifle, our journey to Europe, and how the rifle was now hanging in the Pentagon, she at first was stunned, then thrilled, on top of the world to hear it. For me, talking to Rose that day for the very first time was a greater feeling than winning the biggest lottery in history. We quickly felt like old friends, and she immediately said she would attend the mass on June 4th.

Talking with Rose had felt so special that she was one of the few correspondents to whom I sent some early chapters of this book. I also sent her all the articles published to date (she especially liked the one from the *Irish Echo*) and pictures of Uncle Matty, dating from his days on 138th Street and his time in the Army. Rose loved it all, and we spoke on the phone several more times before the mass. She was so proud of her godfather Matty that she quickly spread the news to all her family and friends, who were equally amazed and happy to hear the story. Before too long, in my eyes, Rose Flynn Lofaro was a rock star!

I had never before scheduled or promoted a mass in anyone's honor. My brother Jackie, however, attends mass every Sunday, leads Bible-study groups, and is generally active in his church, so I leaned on him for advice and guidance. Jackie had attended other honorary masses. "The parish priest mentions the person honored at the beginning and then performs a regular mass. That will be the extent of honoring Uncle Matty, at least to judge from the honorary masses I've attended," he informed me.

I knew Jackie was right, but somehow I had to do something for my family and Uncle Matty's memory to make his mass on June 4th special. This may sound funny, but I viewed this like a paratrooper mission, like the time I'd prayed to Uncle Matty to help me drive my father's broken-down car in reverse for two whole miles on the busy Bronx Streets, and actually managed to make it to his mechanic. Thinking about that story ("I Owe You Big Time, Uncle Matty"), I decided that the parish priest, Father Correa, should know something about Martin Teahan before he celebrated a mass in his honor. Surely, Martin Teahan, and all of the other sixty-four men whose names were on that plaque in St. Jerome's, deserved something more than a mere mention! Suddenly, I was struck by a vision of how to accomplish my mission: I would show Father Correa the same chapters from my book and the same articles and pictures that I'd sent to Rose. *Yes!* I thanked Uncle Matty for the inspiration. And then I prayed to him that Father Correa would read them!

The months of April and May kept Jackie and me busy informing all of our family and friends about the mass, setting up an events page on Facebook, and inviting everyone to attend. *Uncle Matty, you are one cool dude! Dozens of people have said yes, they'll attend!* Positive responses came from not only our immediate family but also from about fifteen family members whom we'd never known even existed!

One particular positive response meant the world to my sister Liz and me: When Uncle Matty was a kid, his best friend was a boy from the neighborhood named Peter Donahue. The two were inseparable and did everything together. Peter Donahue was no longer alive, but his son, Pete, would represent his father at the mass, which he, moreover, would attend with his wife, his son, and his brother Brian. To say Liz was excited to meet Pete for the first time is the understatement of the century. *Thank you, Uncle Matty! Not only are you bringing the family together, you're rekindling friendships that are decades old!*

As the news of Uncle Matty's mass kept spreading, more and more people responded that they would attend. To my great surprise and pleasure, a Gold Star Mom from the Bronx signed up on the Facebook event page I had set up. Her name was Emily Toro, and her son, Isaac Cortes, had served with the elite 10th Mountain Divison. Isaac was killed in action on November 27, 2007, when his vehicle hit an IED in Amerli, Iraq, during Operation Iraqi Freedom. In the years since his death, Emily has devoted herself to the memory of her son and to promoting causes for veterans. She is the Vice President of Rolling Thunder Chapter 1 New York, for example, which provides tremendous support on veterans' behalf on a wide range of issues. I was thrilled that Emily would be attending and very much looked forward to meeting her. I vowed to myself that I'd do something special for her, but at the moment, I didn't yet know what that might be.

Do you believe that things happen for a reason? I ask, because Emily had recently been honored for her devotion to veterans' causes by a certain four-star General. Take a guess who that General is? Those of you who said, "Army Chief of Staff General Mark Milley," give yourselves a pat on the back! You are correct! Remarkably, General Milley, who had been so instrumental in bringing Uncle Matty's historic rifle back home, had recently sent a letter to Emily, thanking her for her work. I imagine him signing her letter at his desk, with Uncle Matty's rifle hanging on the wall. Emily was proud of that letter, and we felt a special bond because of our shared connection with one of the most powerful and gracious military leaders in the world today.

Another very special person I hoped could attend the mass was my mother-in-law, Arline Spiro. Arline is the best mother-in-law in the world. Her husband Phil treated me like a son, and she treats me now like a best friend. Phil, a veteran of the Korean War, passed away in August 2014, and I so wish he could have had the pleasure of seeing Uncle Matty's story unfold. Arline, now eighty-seven, would need to attend in a wheelchair. When I invited her, she replied, to my great surprise, "I would not miss it for the world."

Finally, June 4, 2017, arrived. I'd been waiting for this day for months now! I was up early, so excited about the mass that I'd hardly slept. *Good morning, Uncle Matty! Today's your big day! Today you're bringing the family together!* Monica, Arline, and I arrived at Saint Jerome's at 9:15 a.m. We figured that we'd be the first to arrive: We were wrong. We weren't the only ones excited about the mass! Rose's husband, Bob Lofaro, and their daughters were already there, and so was another second cousin, Anne Dolan Cunningham, who had also brought her children. Jackie was there, too. All the relatives we had never seen before thought that he was me, and everyone was asking him all sorts of questions. Need I tell you that Jackie was reveling in the attention?

Uncle Matty's godchild, Rose, had taken a recent fall and very unfortunately would not be able to attend. We all felt very bad for Rose, as we knew how much attending the mass had meant to her. In addition to her husband, Bob, attending for Rose were daughters Cindy and Diane; Diane's husband, Ben; and Rose's grandson, Christian.

I'm happy to report that just as Bob and I were introducing ourselves, Rose called Bob's cell phone and asked to talk to me. Talking to Rose on the phone, right outside of Saint Jerome's Church, with Bob and the rest of her family all there next to me, gave me a wonderful feeling that I'll never forget. Next, Peter Donahue and his family showed up. By the time the ceremony was ready to begin, a total of about forty family members and friends had gathered to celebrate Uncle Matty's mass.

It was Pentecost Sunday. Three children were taking their first communion, and Saint Jerome's was packed. With all this going on, Maria, the church administrator, had gone out of her way to reserve ten rows for us at the front, right-hand side of the church. This was very fitting, because this was where the plaque bearing Matty's name and those of all the other parishioners killed in World War II was located. At the moment we filed into the pews, my thought was that Uncle Matty, Uncle Jimmy, Aunt Francie, mom, and grandmother Maime must be looking down on us with pride and joy to see the reunion of their big Irish-American family on this special occasion.

Of all places to get together! How perfect it was that it happened at Saint Jerome's.

Minutes before the mass, I spoke with Father Correa, who told me he had read everything I'd sent him. He, too, was thrilled by the mass in Uncle Matty's honor and personally delighted to celebrate it. Father Correa also told me he would call on me at the mass to speak about Uncle Matty. *Wow! What an unexpected honor!* Although I hadn't prepared a speech, in a way, I'd been preparing for this very moment for fifteen months, researching and writing my book. I knew the whole of Matty's story best, and I felt confident I could execute this new twist to my mission. I even thought it would be fun!

Father Correa started the mass promptly at 10:30 a.m. Right off the bat, he said that the mass was in honor of Martin Teahan, a kid from the parish who had died in World War II. He then eloquently spoke of how he now feels differently whenever he passes the plaque honoring St. Jerome parishioners killed in World War II. Learning about Matty had made seeing the plaque a more meaningful experience every time he looked at it.

Father Correa's opening remarks brought everyone in the church to a standing ovation. This indeed, was no ordinary mass, and it would continue to become more special and emotional yet. About fifteen to twenty minutes into the mass, Father Correa returned to the subject of Uncle Matty, which once again elicited clapping and a standing ovation. *Wow! This is incredible!* I thought. Looking around to see how everyone was reacting, it looked to me like they all were feeling the same elation and energy that I was.

After communion, near the end of the mass, Father Correa called me up to speak. I was on cloud nine and wanted to tell everyone everything I knew about Uncle Matty. *Calm down, Jim,* I told myself. *You have only a few minutes.* I talked about my first two goals when I began writing this book. Number one: To bring Uncle Matty's rifle back home to the States. Number two: To bring the family together at Saint Jerome's Church. I proudly told everyone that, thanks to their attendance, together we'd all accomplished these near-impossible goals.

At this exact moment, I was struck with an inspiration: *Wow! This is the perfect time to recognize Emily Toro and do that something special for her that I've been wanting to do ever since we met!* Unscripted, I asked her to stand up and thanked her for her devotion to her son's memory, and for all her work in promoting veterans' issues. It had suddenly dawned on me that young men from the Bronx like Uncle Matty and Emily's son Isaac have made the ultimate sacrifice for *generations* so we in St. Jerome's could have the freedoms we enjoy today, like celebrating this mass on June 4th. I went on to mention how the top military leaders from the United States and France had marveled over Uncle Matty's rifle and that I was sure our highest leaders, like General Milley today, also honor her son's ultimate sacrifice for our freedoms. Even from where I stood, up in the pulpit, I could see how strongly this message resonated with Emily.

Before my concluding remarks, I had one more person to recognize. Do you know who that was? If you answered "Liz," you get five stars. Liz has devoted nearly her whole life to documenting and honoring Uncle Matty. I can only begin to imagine the emotions she was feeling as I asked her to stand up. I could see that she was crying, but I also knew that these were tears of joy, pride, and accomplishment. This book, the mass, the display of the rifle at General Milley's office in the Pentagon—none of it would have happened without Liz's early devotion to Uncle Matty and her passionate interest in preserving our family history.

It gave me great pride to tell everyone congregated in Saint Jerome's Church about the efforts and sacrifice Liz had made to make this great day possible. With this tribute, I concluded my remarks. And yes! It was only five minutes long! The final, and longest, standing ovation in honor of our heroic Uncle Matty immediately erupted. Afterwards, everyone in attendance passed by the plaque to read Matty's name and the names of fellow parishioners killed in World War II.

Outside the church, Arline and I thanked Father Correa for all he'd done for us and discussed establishing an annual mass on Pentecost Sunday in Uncle Matty's honor. "Jim," he said, "it gave me great joy to meet your family. I would love for us to do this annually." Thus, the annual mass in Uncle Matty's honor at Saint Jerome's Church was born.

Following an honorary mass for a relative, what do you think forty or so mostly Irish Americans do? C'mon, this is an easy question! Of course, we all went out to drink and eat! Off we went to the Bronx Brewery on 136th Street, located about one mile from St. Jerome's Church.

Most of us there wanted to talk about the mass. For many, it was the first chance to catch up in a good, long while; for others, it presented an opportunity to get to know members of the family they'd never before met. Looking around, I saw that everyone had a smile and were chatting away, just as I'd imagined they'd done back in the day in the old Irish South Bronx. One thought was clearly on everyone's mind: We absolutely must get together again, so everyone can meet the new family rock star, Rose Flynn Lofaro! I'm happy to say that all of us left with this mutual goal in mind. Rose is Uncle Matty's godchild: Trust me: This is serious, and we will accomplish it!

Jackie and I are already planning the second annual mass in Uncle Matty's honor. It will take place on Pentecost Sunday, May 20, 2018, at Saint Jerome's Church in the Bronx. I hereby invite all readers of this book to this and all future "Uncle Matty" masses! Jackie and I have set the goal of contacting the families of the other sixty-four other men listed on St. Jerome's plaque, to invite them, too, to the annual mass in Matty's honor. These sixty-five heroes from the Greatest Generation should never be forgotten, and Jackie, my family, and I all will do our very best to make sure they are not! *Uncle Matty! You did it, pal! The family got together, we had a great time, and we are set to do it every year! RIP.*

ACKNOWLEDGMENTS

The last fifteen months of my life have been magical. I am lucky to have my wife, Monica, by my side, keeping me focused. Thank you, Monica, for taking many of the photographs in this book. I would not have been able to write the book without you. I love you, Monica, now and forever!

Army Chief of Staff General Mark Milley was instrumental in bringing Uncle Matty's rifle back home and arranging for its current display in his office. Many thanks, General Milley, to you and your outstanding staff for inviting us to the State Dinner on December 1, 2016, where French Army Chief of Staff General Jean-Pierre Bosser presented the rifle to me as the representative of the Teahan family. It is a moment I will never forget. General Milley: Monica, my family, and I all look forward to joining you in 2019 for the permanent donation of Uncle Matty's rifle to the new National Museum of the United States Army.

One of the most remarkable people I had the pleasure to meet while writing this book was Bill McWeeney. Now living in Houston, Texas, Bill was born just two years later than Uncle Matty and grew up in the same Irish South Bronx Streets. Bill generously shared his vivid recollections of our old neighborhood and was the cornerstone to the chapter on "Uncle Matty's Irish South Bronx." We've spoken dozens of times since his first phone call, and it always feels as if I'm speaking to my best friend. Thank you, Bill, for your time and friendship: Monica and I greatly look forward to meeting you in person this December!

Monica and I with Piper, our Golden Retriever. Monica greatly supported me throughout our entire journey and took most of the photographs in this book. Piper nobly sacrificed her favorite activity—swimming—to lie at my feet and help me with my writing.

Many wonderful people from France have helped me along this journey. General Patrick Collet, you are my hero. Uncle Matty's story began when you located his historic rifle. You are a Farrell Family Friend for Life! Valérie Gautier Cardin, you are Uncle Matty's Angel and have become a dear friend. Thank you and our American friend, Manny Vider, for setting up our trip to Normandy in June 2016. I will always fondly remember the June 6 ceremonies we attended in honor of the World War II veterans you sponsored. Your "Veterans Back to Normandie" Foundation has provided so many deeply significant experiences for returning veterans that it's no wonder you are near and dear to their hearts!

The board members of the Friends and Family of the 508th PIR Association could not have been more helpful in our research on this project. Thank you, Dick O'Donnell, Donna Palmer, Troy Palmer, Ellen Peters, and Chris Helms! To Uncle Matty's buddy and 508th World War II hero (retired) Command Sergeant Major Rock Merritt: Our meeting and phone conversations are among the greatest honors of my life. I also thank the U.S. Army, editors of *Paraglide On-Line*, and reporter Eve Meinhardt for the permission to republish the fine article on CSM Rock Merritt in this book.

The fine website of the 508th Family and Friends Association (www.508pir.org) enabled me to locate two important contacts from Uncle Matty's Army days. Art Jacoby, Matty's great friend from 1st Battalion HQ Company, remembered a great deal about his buddy Martin Teahan, and I am very pleased to include a chapter on Art in this book. Another of Uncle Matty's great friends was the legendary O.B. Hill, 1st Battalion Message Center Chief in Headquarters Company and Founder of the 508th Association. O.B. passed away in June 2002, but thanks to the 508th Association website, I was able to contact his son, Joe Hill, who graciously gave permission to publish his father's personal remembrance, "My Normandy Experience," here in book form for the first time.

Our excellent maps were quickly provided thanks to the talents of Carl Mauro II at Carl Mauro Design. Carl's uncle, Steve Mauro, jumped into Normandy with the 2/508th and fought at Hill 30, and his father, Carl Mauro I, fought with the 504th PIR. Thank you, Carl! Unless otherwise indicated, all photographs are from the Farrell Family Collection, U.S. Army sources, or public domain. Warm thanks to all friends and colleagues whose contributions have enriched our story.

Research on Uncle Matty in Nottingham, England, was made possible by Nottingham residents Glyn Shipstone and Graham Lawson. Your devotion to American veterans is touching and contagious, and your way of communicating the "living history" of World War II is positively inspiring! Your hospitality and in-depth knowledge made our trip to Nottingham unforgettable—especially that drive down the run way at Folkingham! We will always be mates! Till we meet again!

Many thanks, too, to Andy Smart, who published two articles in the *Nottingham Post* about our search for "Kitty," Uncle Matty's mysterious girlfriend, and to Joan Wallace, who provided photos for the articles, documenting our trip. These articles caused readers John Straw, Ric and Lyn Straw, Frank and Teena Straw, and Greg and Sally Antcliff to reach out to us: Many thanks to you all for your warmth and generosity as our Nottingham hosts as we explored the possible links between our families. We look forward with pleasure to meeting again.

I never thought I would write a book, but this was a calling from Uncle Matty—saying "No" was not an option! I could not have completed this project without my editor and dear friend, Gayle Wurst, at Princeton International Agency for the Arts. Gayle and I were introduced by a mutual friend, Jim Hockenberry, author of the historical thriller, *Over Here*. Gayle has helped to publish a great many books on the 82nd Airborne Division, including co-authoring *Descending from the Clouds*, a memoir of the 505th PIR in World War II. Our meeting was meant to happen!

On June 4, 2017, we held the first honorary mass for Uncle Matty at Saint Jerome's Church in the South Bronx. To Father Correa and the dedicated staff at Saint Jerome's: On behalf of the extended Farrell family and all our friends who attended, thank you for Uncle Matty's beautiful, very special mass. We are delighted that an honorary mass in Uncle Matty's name will now be an annual event! Peter Donahue, your father and Uncle Matty were best friends. Thank you for reliving memories with us, showing us your photo albums, and attending the mass with your family. It is amazing how our family friendship has been renewed after seventy-two years! Gold Star Mom Emily Toro: Your attendance at Saint Jerome's deeply touched our hearts. Your son, Isaac Cortes, is a hero, and I was honored to recognize his service at the mass: He and Uncle Matty, two young men born in the Bronx in different eras, both gave their lives for our freedom.

My immediate family has been a wonderful support during the writing of this book. To my brothers, Martin and Jackie, and sisters, Pat Regina and Liz Farrell: Thank you for your contributions to the cause. Jackie, I forgive you for telling my stories so often! You remember some of them better than I do, and I needed your help to write them down! Liz, this book and the amazing adventures we've had while writing it would never have taken place had you not devoted yourself for decades to researching and documenting Uncle Matty and his unit. Thank you! We are partners in this story! Be proud of your Uncle Matty!

Special thanks to Noreen Denett, Danny Werner, Rose Flynn-Lofaro, and to all my other family members who shared their stories and helped to celebrate Uncle Matty's mass. And finally, to one last very close and loyal Farrell family member: Thank you, Piper, for your patience and silent support, and for sacrificing some of your swim dates so I could have time to write this book! You are the World's Best Golden Retriever!

God bless all the World War II veterans for the sacrifices they made for our freedoms. RIP Uncle Matty: Your legacy will live on forever!

CPSIA information can be obtained
at www.ICGtesting.com
Printed in the USA
FSOW02n0234011117
40437FS